Modeling, Evaluating, and Predicting IT Human Resources Performance

Modeling, Evaluating, and Predicting IT Human Resources Performance

Konstantina Richter
University of Magdeburg, Germany

Reiner R. Dumke
University of Magdeburg, Germany

CRC Press
Taylor & Francis Group
Boca Raton   London   New York

CRC Press is an imprint of the
Taylor & Francis Group, an **informa** business
AN AUERBACH BOOK

CRC Press
Taylor & Francis Group
6000 Broken Sound Parkway NW, Suite 300
Boca Raton, FL 33487-2742

© 2015 by Taylor & Francis Group, LLC
CRC Press is an imprint of Taylor & Francis Group, an Informa business

No claim to original U.S. Government works

Printed on acid-free paper
Version Date: 20141217

International Standard Book Number-13: 978-1-4822-9992-2 (Hardback)

Visit the Taylor & Francis Web site at
http://www.taylorandfrancis.com

and the CRC Press Web site at
http://www.crcpress.com

Contents

List of Acronyms

A
AAII: Australian AI Institute agent development
agr: agreeableness
ANN: Artificial Neural Networks
AOSE: Agent-Oriented Software Engineering
AUML: Agent-oriented UML

B
BA: Business Analyst
BBN: Bayesian Belief Network
B-COTS: Building COTS Software Systems

C
CAME: Computer-Assisted Measurement Evaluation
CARE: Computer-Aided Re-Engineering
CASE: Computer-Aided Software Engineering
CBSE: Component-Based Software Engineering
CMMI: Capability Maturity Model Integration
co: conscientiousness
COCOMO: Constructive Cost Model
COTS: Commercial Off The Shelf
CURE: COTS Usage Risks Evaluation

D
D: Detection
DCOM: Distributed Component Object Model
DoE: Design of Experiments

E
EJB: Enterprise Java Beans

F
FFM: Five Factor Model
FMEA: Failure Mode and Effect Analysis

G
GA: Genetic Algorithm
GUI: Graphic User Interface

H
HF: Human Factors
HIPO: Hierarchical Input Process Output
HOOD: Hierarchical Object Oriented Design
HRF: Human Risk Factors

I
iCASE: integrated Computer-Aided Software Engineering
ID: Identifier
IMPACT: Imperative Maryland Platform for Agents Collaborating Together
int: intelligence
IS: Information Systems
ISBSG: International Software Benchmark Standards Group

M
MAS: Multi-Agent System
MaSE: Multiagent Systems Engineering
MASSIVE: Multi-Agent Systems Interactive View Engineering
MIPS: Million Instructions Per Second

N
NN: Neural Networks

O
O: Occurrence
OCEAN: Openness, Conscientiousness, Extroversion, Agreeableness, Neuroticism
OMT: Object Modeling Technique

OOD: Object-Oriented Design
OOSA: Object-Oriented Software Analysis
OOSE: Object-Oriented Software Engineering

P

PCA: Principal Component Analysis
PCMM: People Capability Maturity Model
PM: Project Manager
pr: performance
PSP: Personal Software Process

Q

QE: Quality Engineer
QSM: Quality Software Management

R

RA: Risk Assessment
RC: Risk Controlling
RDD: Responsibility-Driven Design
RED: Risk in Early Design
RM: Risk Management
RPN: Risk Priority Number

S

S: Severity
SA/SD: Structured Analysis/Structured Design
SA: Software Application or Software Architect
SAM: Structured Analysis Methods
SD: Software Development or Software Developer
SE: Software Engineering
SEI: Software Engineering Institute
SFMEA: Software Failure Mode and Effect Analysis
SHF–FMEA: Software Human Factor FMEA
SLIM: Software-Lifecycle-Management
SM: Software Measurement
SOA: Service-Oriented Architecture
SODA: Societies in Open and Distributed Agent spaces
SOSE: Service-Oriented System Engineering
SP: Software Product
SPP: Software Production Process

SR: Supporting Resources
SRE: Software Risk Evaluation
SS: Software System
ST: Software Tester
SWOT: Strengths, Weaknesses, Opportunities, and Threats
S/W: Software

T

TL: Team Leader
TSP: Team Software Process

U

UPS: Uninterruptible Power Supply
UML: Unified Modeling Language

V

V&V: Verification and Validation

Preface

IT human resources evaluation is one of the current key themes in the IT area worldwide. Successful management of human resources can have a strong influence on the position of an IT company in the market. Numerous IT methods exist to model and analyze the different roles, responsibilities, and process levels of IT personnel. Some of these techniques are embedded in the corresponding software process evaluation, often in the form of rules or suggestions such as PSP* or TSP†. However, these descriptions neglect to take into account reasons for the rigorous application and evaluation of human errors and the associated risks. In addition, IT human resources evaluation suffers from a scarcity of investigation of personal characteristics such as motivation, cooperation, achievement, concentration, and the like that would facilitate human performance evaluations in a careful manner.

This book is based on our experience and addresses this specific research area. For a successful investigation into this area, the basics of IT human performance must be identified, analyzed, and evaluated. Furthermore, in order to achieve a desired quality of human performance prediction, a detailed investigation of IT human factors and their relationships is necessary.

This book comprises eight chapters. The first chapter gives the motives and short overview of the essential research goal of the described new approach. The second chapter provides an overview of the state of the art of existing methods of human risk evaluation. The third chapter addresses human factors in software engineering in general. In the fourth chapter we describe the application of a modified version of the failure mode and effect analysis (FMEA) method that leads to the role-oriented characterization of the different IT personnel responsibilities. The fifth chapter provides a detailed analysis of these IT role-based human factors using the well-known Big Five method. In the sixth chapter we apply our newly developed approach of IT human factor evaluation using the design-of-experiment (DoE) method. The seventh chapter describes an implementation of the approach as a web portal and validation in a number of industrial environments. Finally,

---

* PSP—Personal Software Process.
† TSP—Team Software Process.

the eighth chapter summarizes any conclusions and future directions in order to qualify IT personnel performance.

The major significance of this book consists of the developed IT human factor evaluation approach that is rooted in existing research and then enhances existing approaches through a strict use of software measurement and statistical principles and criteria. The essential results are

- The discussion of the IT human factors from a risk assessment point of view. This includes the essential aspects of the human errors, failures, and mistakes, and core aspects of software process resources themselves.
- The rigorous investigation and adaptation of the existing human factor evaluation methods such as IT expertise and Big Five in combination with powerful statistical methods such as FMEA and DoE.
- The profound analysis of human resources within the different software processes such as development, maintenance, and application under consideration of CMMI* process level five.
- The derivation and validation of the approach in essential industrial settings worldwide.

Konstantina Richter
Reiner Dumke
Magdeburg, Germany

---

* CMMI—Compatibility Maturity Model Integration.

Acknowledgments

We wish to express our gratitude to our partners and colleagues who supported us during the past decade in our research in human factors and risk analysis. Special thanks go to Professors Georgiev and Petar Antonov, TU Varna, Bulgaria, who have helped us in many common works in their laboratories in order to execute our prediction models.

The basics of IT personnel analysis and evaluation were discussed and developed with the help of our research partners Prof. Alain Abran, Quebec University of Montreal, Canada; Prof. Andreas Schmietendorf, HWR, Berlin, Germany; Prof. Juan Cuadrado-Gallego, Alcala University, Madrid, Spain; Dr. Luigi Buglione, SEMQ, Rome, Italy; Prof. Pierre Bouquet, ETS, Montreal, Canada; Prof. Ken-ichi Matsumoto, Nara University, Nara, Japan; Prof. Cornelius Wille, FH, Bingen, Germany; Prof. Mitsuhiro Takahashi, SE Center in Tokyo, Japan; and Prof. Olga Ormandjieva, Concordia University, Montreal, Canada.

Furthermore, we express our thanks to our industrial partners Dr. Christof Ebert, Vector Consulting, Stuttgart, Germany; Dr. Mathias Lother, Bosch, Stuttgart, Germany; Harry Sneed, Anecon, Vienna, Austria; Francis Paulish, Siemens, Munich, Germany; Detlef Guenther, VW, Wolfsburg, Germany; Dr. Stefan Frohnhoff, sd&m, Frankfurt, Germany; and Heike Hegewald, CSC, Wiesbaden, Germany, for providing a valuable background and application area for our research and investigations.

About the Authors

Konstantina Richter (née Georgieva) earned her master's degree at the University of Magdeburg after receiving her bachelor's degree at the Technical University of Varna (Bulgaria). Her master's thesis investigated the testing of aspect-oriented programs and was finished in 2007. She earned the award for best student in her year. From 2008 to 2012 she was a PhD student in the software engineering research group at the University of Magdeburg. She has participated in several international conferences on software processes, software testing, software measurement, and software quality in Rome, Nara, and Las Vegas, among others. Her PhD thesis on human resources performance is the basis of this book and involved validation in worldwide IT companies including Siemens, Bosch, German Telekom, VW, Alcatel, and IBM. Currently she works in the IT department of the financial government center of Sachsen-Anhalt in Magdeburg.

Reiner R. Dumke is a retired professor at the Otto-von-Guericke-University of Magdeburg with software engineering as his research field. He is one of the founders of the Software Measurement Laboratory (SML@b) of the computer science department at the University of Magdeburg and coeditor of the *Software Measurement News Journal*. He is the leader of the German Interest Group on software metrics and works as a member of the COSMIC, DASMA, MAIN, IEEE, and ACM communities. He earned a diploma degree (MS) in mathematics in 1970 followed in 1980 by a PhD dissertation in computer science on efficiency of database projects. He is the author and editor of more than 30 books about programming techniques, software metrics, metrics tools, software engineering foundations, component-based software development, and web engineering.

Chapter 1

Introduction

1.1 Motivation

In the present era of globalization, based especially on computer media and applications, organizations of all industrial sectors have to face various problems in order to be successful in the marketplace. Competitors have to respond to demands for low prices and high quality, along with bright service capabilities and a short development life cycle. It is obvious that these demands are almost impossible to meet, and because of this the requirements for employees in software development are continuously expanding. Employers are demanding more and more, but very often they choose the inappropriate person for a particular job or expect results that are beyond the capabilities of the particular employee.

Subject matter expert Capers Jones (2001) characterizes the sad state of software production efforts today and summarizes: "In general, software is a troubled technology plagued by project failures, cost overruns, schedule overruns and poor quality levels. Even companies as Microsoft have trouble meeting published commitments or shipping trouble-free software."

So, the question arises as to how we can help the software industry. How can we support the software development process? An innumerable variety of methods are meant to be used in the development process, but the main resource for every company—the people—seems to be overlooked as a point of optimization.

Presently development importance is concentrated on hardware and software. Money, time, and ideas are invested in new software and hardware achievements, but no one focuses on the third component that is vital for successful software engineering, the people. Employees are left to manage on their own in the new situation. Methods evaluating the influence of individuals over the software process do not exist, and in this way everything is left to happen by itself.

Because of this the objective of this book is to present a model that is able to evaluate employees' performance. This method will assist in the process of personnel acquisition and in this manner introduce better quality in the software engineering process. The right people chosen in the right manner and also their motivation are the most important software resources, crucial for the achievement of better results.

The work quality in today's software companies is extremely important. It is the basis for everything else, and as we have already explained, as the goal is to develop fast and cheap, the people and the way that they work are becoming an inseparable part of a good software development process. Practical applications can be seen in widely accepted methods for optimization such as process maturity (CMMI, 2002) and personal and team processes (PSP/TSP). "Adopting PSP and TSP can be a very effective method for accelerating an organization's progress to higher CMMI maturity levels." This idea, proposed by the Software Engineering Institute (SEI), shows how important the process of personnel elaboration is and also shows where our model is meant to be applied. Another point that motivated our research and that is also very important for the application of our model is Agile development. This new type of software development organization, extremely dependent on communication and personality types, shows once again the importance of human traits in the software process.

There is one more point that strengthens our motivation: the well-known list of risks from Peter Neumann (1985).

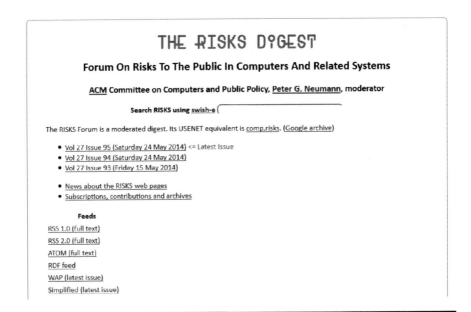

Figure 1.1   The Risks Digest website by Neumann.

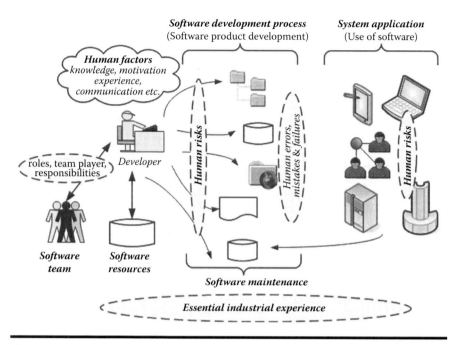

Figure 1.2 Aspects of the performance-related human factors approach.

In Volume 27 from 03.06.2014 (Figure 1.1) we can see shocking news: "Air France 447: Smart planes still vulnerable to human error—On flight 447, the handoff from computer to pilots proved fatal for the 228 aboard" (Neumann, 1985). This human mistake motivates our statement precisely: choosing personnel with a defined psychological profile can be crucial for performance in a particular software firm and even life-deciding as in this accident.

Led by these ideas our research went through many different stages: from looking for existing similar methods in other fields to adopting engineering solutions in order to find the most important human characteristics in software development, and to that end, the development of a method able to prognosticate an individual's performance based on his or her special traits. The background of our approach is shown in Figure 1.2.

In order to fulfill this complex task we went through the following steps:

1. Investigation of existing software risk assessment methods in order to find out if they cover human factors, Chapter 2.
2. Summarizing all different methods for investigation of human slips, mistakes, and errors and looking for existing methods that evaluate the human influence in the software process, Chapter 2.
3. Investigating software engineering basics in order to find where the personnel take a critical part, Chapter 3.

4. Summarizing the basic software team roles and examining their responsibilities, Chapter 3.
5. Adopting the FMEA method for software engineering needs in order to find the failure modes conducted from software personnel and in this way the influencing human factors, Chapter 4.
6. Finding a method that could be adopted for the evaluation of the human factors specified in Chapters 2 through 4. By adoption of the Big Five theory for software personnel we were able to measure the most important human traits and to observe their influence over software performance, Chapter 5.
7. Evaluating human traits and choosing a specific method for estimation of their influence over IT human resources performance. We used them as input factors for design of experiment, used to develop a predictive mathematical model for human productiveness, Chapter 6.
8. Validating the gained method for prediction of IT human performance based on the individual's characteristics and evaluating its effectiveness and correctness in real conditions, Chapter 7.

1.2 Structure of the Book

Although the introductory chapter of the book is concerned with the problem's motivation, subsequent chapters focus on the development steps of the proposed method and its validation.

The remainder of the book is structured in the following way: Chapter 2 examines and investigates the history of the risk management field and then focuses on analysis of risk assessment methods, to reveal their inadequacies. In the second part of this chapter the human factors in software engineering are discussed. An overview is given of different types of characterizations for human errors, mistakes, and failures and the influencing factors are brought to light. This chapter is the basis for the research that follows, as it reveals the problem of ignoring the critical influence of IT human factors in software development. It concludes with the observation that an adequate method or model that can be used for IT human performance evaluation does not exist.

Chapter 3 is concerned with the software engineering background on which the book is built. After explaining the different aspects of the software engineering field the chapter delves deeper into software organizations. In this way we were able to find the most common organizational structure in the software field with its roles and corresponding responsibilities. The analysis of the IT roles with their competencies and responsibilities is used as the basis for specifying the important human factors in the process of software engineering, which are input for the next chapter.

Chapter 4 examines a well-known method for failure analysis—the FMEA (failure mode and effect analysis)—and adopts it for the needs of software engineering. With the adoption of the method and with the discovered competencies (specified in the previous two chapters) we were able to analyze the roles in the software development process and to find the failure modes for every role and the standing behind specific human factors. The IT human features discovered will be utilized in further evaluation of human performance.

Chapter 5 explores and adopts a special theory that can evaluate the discovered human traits (from Chapters 2 through 4) and can also estimate employee performance in connection with them. These already specified human factors are estimated, using the possibilities of the Big Five theory. It gives us the opportunity to match the known human factors to special psychological traits and to visualize the dependence between them and the individual's productivity.

Chapter 6 reflects the development of the specific model for IT human performance evaluation. The discovered (in Chapter 5) dependence between personal factors and productivity had to be modeled in an experimental way. For this goal we have chosen a specific experimental design, design of experiments (DoE), as it gives the possibility of finding the connection between different factors with a limited number of trials. The result of the chapter is the obtaining of an adequate model that describes employee performance in a predictive way.

Chapter 7 is the validation of the developed prognostic models for prediction of the IT human's performance. There are real case studies and a specific web application that was developed as an implementation of the new model. They all prove once again the accuracy and adequacy of the developed method and show its extreme importance for improving the quality of the software engineering process.

Chapter 8 summarizes the results and main contributions of the book and gives proposals for further development and application of the model.

References

CMMI (2002). *CMMI for Systems Engineering/Software Engineering/Integrated Product and Process Development.* CMU/SEI-2002-TR-004, Software Engineering Institute. Pittsburgh, PA: Carnegie Mellon University Press.

Jones, C. (2001). Software measurement programs and industry leadership. *STSC CrossTalk*, 14(2): 4–7.

Neumann, P. (1985). *The Risks Digest.* viewed May 1, 2014, http://catless.ncl.ac.uk/Risks/26.54.html

Chapter 2

Software Risk Management and Human Factors

In this chapter we focus first on risk management in general and then on special risk assessment methods. We investigated their mechanisms and the data that they use and discovered where they are lacking in the sense that they don't consider personnel as a crucial part of the risk management process. Based on that observation our research continues on existing methods, taxonomies, and types of human factors that play the role of risks in software development. We end with summarizing the influencing factors for employees' mistakes and failures and we use these data as the foundation for our further research (see Figure 2.1).

2.1 Overview of Risk Management Development

Trying to encompass the complete history of software engineering risk management we have to start from the first attempts made in this field by Nolan (1973, 1979) and McFarlan (1974) who proposed models for managing risks in information systems. In the late 1970s Alter and Ginzberg (1978) stated that risk factor analysis can increase the success rate in software development. In 1982 Davis (1982) announced a new method based on requirements determination for selecting the most suitable development approach.

Despite these attempts, risks in their real scope were not addressed until the late 1980s, when the pioneer in software risk management, Barry Boehm, published his first and most fundamental approach, "A Spiral Model of Software Development and Enhancement" (Boehm, 1988). Later on his work was complemented by

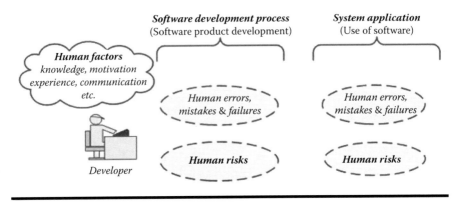

Figure 2.1 Human factors and risks.

Charette and others (Charette, 1989, 1990; Boehm and Ross, 1989; Ould, 1990; Boehm, 1991). These fundamental works were subsequently used by the Software Engineering Institute (SEI; Van Scoy, 1992; Carr et al., 1993; Higuera et al., 1994; Higuera and Haimes, 1996; Sisti and Joseph, 1994; Dorofee et al., 1996) for developing a new methodology for risk management based on risk taxonomies.

Other approaches for software risk management were devised by Karolak (1996), Michaels (1996), Pandelios, Rumsey, and Dorofee (1996), and Hefner (1994). There also were several risk categories and taxonomies proposed in the fundamental methods of Boehm and SEI. In our paper (Georgieva, Farooq, and Dumke 2009a) we summarizd existing software development risks and proposed a new risk taxonomy for the software testing process. Other quantitative approaches appeared in the middle of the 1990s from Bowers (1994), Fairley (1994), and Berny and Townsend (1993). Kontio (1997, 2001) proposed a new method for risk management where he theorized risk scenarios that were built over six elements (risk factor, risk event, risk outcome, reaction, risk effect set, and utility loss).

In the late 1990s and afterward, several approaches for software risk analysis were developed separately from the famous ones, and they are summarized in our paper (Georgieva, Farooq, and Dumke, 2009b). Because they are used for risk analysis, which is part of risk management, we devote special attention to them, and they are the milestones for our scientific motivation.

A small number of industrial reports have been published, so we give just few examples: Boehm (1991), Chittister, Kirkpatrick, and Van Scoy (1992), Eslinger et al. (1993), Meyers and Trbovich (1993), Morin (1993), Fairley (1994), Gemmer and Koch (1994), Hefner (1994), Williamson (1994), and Conrow and Shishido (1997).

Many different risk assessment frameworks were proposed over the years. For example, McComb and Smith's (1991) framework identifies system failure factors covering 15 key risk areas from project planning and execution to technical and human factors. Barki, Rivard, and Talbot (1993), composed a list of 35 features connected with software development risk, based on a literature survey of more than 120 projects.

Thomsett (1992) invented a risk assessment questionnaire model and proposed a new project management paradigm that recognized people-oriented values as very important in the traditional organization structure and with this he was one of the first to put an accent on people in the process of risk management.

SEI risk taxonomy, already mentioned, was an important contribution in the field of risk management because it pioneered a very comprehensive questionnaire and software risk evaluation method (Carr et al., 1993; Sisti and Joseph, 1994). Another risk assessment framework was proposed by Lyytinen, Mathiassen, and Ropponen (1996) and was later expanded upon by Keil et al. (1998).

Applegate, McFarlan, and McKenney (1996) published a book about information systems management, where a project risk assessment questionnaire was the tool to evaluate the risk degree in different IT applications. Another method was developed by Moynihan (1997, 2002), who collected a list of risks and planned their mitigation after interviewing particular project managers. Project failure because of unmanaged risk is a widely recognized theme in the project management community. The general process and principles of project risk management are applicable to all kinds of software projects. There is quite extensive literature on generic project risk management and we name only the most comprehensive works such as Wideman (1998), Chong and Brown (2000), Pritchard (2001), Chapman and Ward (2002, 2003), Kendrick (2003), Mulcahy (2003), and Smith and Merritt (2002). The latest trends are to extend risk management over safety, environmental, and business risk (Waring and Glendon 1998; Cooper et al. 2004) or to address the so-called "positive risk" (Hillson, 2004).

If we have to make an observation about the evolution of software risk lists in the past two decades, we have to start with McComb's 50 issues (McComb and Smith, 1991; Barki, Rivard, and Talbot, 1993). After that Thomsett (1992) created a more extensive questionnaire; the most famous questionnaire for software project risk came from the Software Engineering Institute (SEI; Carr et al., 1993). McConnell (1993, 1996) created another risk identification questionnaire but focused on the software code and schedule. In the well-known book of Capers Jones is a list of 60 software project risks (Jones, 1994). Lyytinen (2000) also created a questionnaire covering the main software development risks. Cockburn (1997) summarized some of the current knowledge on effective risk management strategies into reusable risk resolution patterns.

The Software Engineering Institute stresses their research on the importance of teamwork in risk management and as a result they have united their ideas into a team risk management method (Higuera et al., 1994). Another work in this direction is by Kontio, who examines the effectiveness of group work in his *Riskit* method.

In the dynamic world that we are living in, risk management is recognized to be a major part of successful software engineering and because of this it is covered by all the "bibles" of software engineering and project management such as CMMI

(2002), Thayer and Dorfman (2002), Pressman (2004), Sommerville (2004), McConnell (2004), Abran and Moore (2004), and *PMBOK® Guide* (2004).

These important milestones in software risk management give us a solid basis to motivate our research work. We have seen the lack of methods for the evaluation of human productivity in the software development process and at the same time we were able to recognize the major importance of human factors as a crucial risk element. So for us the idea to develop a method for evaluation of human performance was a logical conclusion.

2.2 Incompleteness of Risk Assessment Methods

Risk assessment methods are one of the most important elements in the process of risk management. These methods consider numerous aspects while assessing and estimating the risks. Because software development is a human-intensive activity, diverse factors related to human behavior also play a key role in this situation. Software risk assessment methods should take into account all these factors in combination with each other. Hence, we next give a short overview of the current applied risk assessment methods and their consideration of human factors.

Observing the principles of risk management given by the International Organization for Standardization, described in ISO/FDIS 31000 (ISO, 2009) it is clear to see the following statement: "Risk management should take into account human factors. The organization's risk management should recognize the capabilities, perceptions and intentions of external and internal people that may facilitate or hinder attainment of the organization's objectives" (p. 42).

This statement gives a strong motivation to our thesis that human factors are at the center of the risk management process and that they should be a part of the risk assessment methods. Other evidence emphasizing the role of human factors in software engineering and the software development process include the people capability maturity model (PCMM) and the pair programming development technique.

Based on Boehm's classification of risk management we focus on methods for risk analysis and the lack of consideration of the human factors in them. The methods for risk assessment are very important in the risk management process because they may predict the success of a particular project. Realizing their crucial role in the process of risk management we have to realize also that the main actors in every process are human, and their actions may cause different issues or problem situations. Here is a simple example: in medicine, the safety of different machines is maintained by people. Thus it is clear to see how important the people are in this case. Any mistake can lead to the death of a patient. It is the same in the software development process: any risk brought by a human can be crucial for the whole system.

Risk assessment since 1995 has been briefly summarized below to see the mechanism of work. The risk assessment methods are very different by their nature: they explore different structures in the software development process, use different techniques, and are applied over different phases in the development process. So, we are able to see a great variety of techniques. The methods are investigated particularly for their consideration of human factors while assessing and estimating risks. Our goal is to stress the importance of humans in the development process inasmuch as people stay at the source level and they should not be underestimated. It is not possible to achieve a complete risk assessment or risk management of a system if we do not also include the human factors in it.

There are a variety of human factors studies: human error analysis, human factors engineering, and human reliability analysis (Baybutt, 1996). The errors that people commit can be seen in different perspectives, for example, in the work process of people with other people, people with equipment or with procedures, tasks, and others. A basic classification of the human errors (Baybutt, 1996) distinguishes between slips, mistakes, violations, sociotechnical, and coming from management. We describe all different types of problems caused by employees later in this chapter.

The following methods for risk assessment are grouped according to the basic technique used. Every method is described briefly and is analyzed for its emphasis on human factors in addition to other risk factors.

2.2.1 Neural Networks–Based Risk Analysis Methods

Artificial neural networks (ANN, or just neural networks, NN) are modeled after the biological neurons in brain structures. The individual neuron models may be combined into various networks made up of many individual nodes, each with its own set of variables. These networks have an input layer, an output layer, and one or more hidden layers. The hidden layers provide connectivity between the inputs and outputs. The network may also have feedback, which will take result variables and use them as input to prior processing nodes. With the help of NN, modeling of various different directions in the software development process is possible and in this manner finding the potential risks.

2.2.1.1 Influence Diagrams for Software Risk Analysis (Chee, Vij, and Ramamoorthy, 1995)

Input: Software metrics data collected at various stages of software development.

Technology: Influence diagrams, kinds of NN, used for probabilistic and decision analysis models.

How it works: The method uses the conditional independence implied in the influence diagrams in order to determine the information needed for solving a problem. Influence diagrams are used to provide quantitative advice for software risk management, improving upon traditional ad hoc software management techniques.

2.2.1.2 Enhanced Neural Network Technique for Software Risk Analysis (Neumann, 2002)

Input: Software metric data.

Technology: Principal component analysis and artificial neural networks (PCA-ANN). Uses pattern recognition, multivariate statistics, and NN.

How it works: This is a technique for risk categorization in which principal component analysis is used for normalizing and orthogonalizing the input data. A neural network is used for risk determination/classification. The special feature in the approach, namely cross-normalization, is used to discriminate datasets containing disproportionately large numbers of high-risk software modules.

2.2.1.3 Neural Networks Approach for Software Risk Analysis (Young et al., 2006)

Input: Software risk factors, obtained through interviews/questionnaires.

Technology: Combination of principal component analysis, genetic algorithms, and neural networks.

How it works: Based on the SEI and interviews with professionals in the field, taxonomy and factors for software risk are created. After processing these data are used as input for the NN analysis. The method is divided in the following steps:

1. Predict the risks with standard NN.
2. Predict with the combination of NN and PCA.
3. Predict with the combination of generic algorithm (GA), and NN.
4. Combine the three steps and make an overall prediction.

2.2.1.4 Software System Quality Risk Analysis Using Bayesian Belief Network (Young et al., 2007)

Input: Project risk factors selected through a Delphi method based on historical project data.

Technology: Bayesian belief network (BBN), Delphi method.

How it works: The method is based on BBN and predicts and analyzes the changing risks of software development based on facts such as project characteristics and two-sided (contractors and clients) cooperation capability at the beginning of the project. BBNs are used for the analysis of uncertain consequences or risks and the Delphi method is used for the network structure needed for the BBN. The method is used to evaluate the software development risks in organizations.

In the system for risk assessment, proposed in the method are considered problems connected with lack of experience among the employees. Anyway we cannot say that the method considers all different human factors, because of the complex nature of the human being.

2.2.2 Qualitative-Based Risk Analysis Methods

Qualitative methods are methods that take into consideration different qualities. They collect information with the help of different questionnaires. In this way they analyze not numerical but qualitative data and based on it give the possibility for risk analysis.

2.2.2.1 SEI Risk Management Paradigm Software Risk Evaluation (SRE) (Williams, Pandelios, and Behrens, 1999)

Input: Software risk information, obtained through interviews/questionnaires.

Technology: Questionnaires.

How it works: The SRE addresses the identification, analysis, planning, and communication elements of the SEI risk paradigm. The method implies the following:

Trains teams to conduct systematic risk identification, analysis, and mitigation planning

Focuses upon risks that can affect the delivery and quality of software and system products

Provides project manager and personnel with multiple perspectives on identified risks

Creates foundation for continuous and team (customer/supplier) risk management

2.2.2.2 Quality Risk Analysis for Whole Software System (Young et al., 2007)

Input: Project risk factors based on historical project data selected through a Delphi method.

Technology: Causal network, Delphi method.

How it works: The method is based on causal networks and predicts and analyzes the changing risks of software development based on facts. These facts are project characteristics and two-sided (contractors and clients) cooperation capability at the beginning of the project. The causal networks are used for the analysis of uncertain consequences or risks and the basic network structuring was performed by the Delphi method. This method helps organizations to evaluate the software development risks.

2.2.3 Software Metrics–Based Risk Analysis Methods

A software metric is a measure of some software property and it is important to know that the metrics give quantitative information about different software characteristics that could be used for risk analysis.

2.2.3.1 Software Risk Assessment and Estimation Model (Gupta and Sadiq, 2008)

Input: Measurement error, model error, assumption error in function point estimation.

Technology: Risk exposure and mission-critical requirements stability risk metrics.

How it works: The risk is estimated using risk exposure and software metrics of risk management, which are used when there are changes in requirements. Initially the model estimates the sources of uncertainty using measurement error, model error, and assumption error.

2.2.3.2 Risk Assessment Model for Software Prototyping Projects (Nogueira, Luqi, and Bhattacharya, 2000)

Input: Requirement, personnel, and complexity metrics.

Technology: Different software metrics.

How it works: The method introduces metrics and a model that can be integrated with prototyping development processes. It claims to address to some extent the issue of human dependency in risk assessment but it is not clear how exactly, because there are no mentioned metrics for that.

2.2.3.3 Source-Based Software Risk Assessment (Deursen and Kuipers, 2003)

Input: Source code information.

Technology: Code metrics, questionnaires.

How it works: The method focuses on primary and secondary facts. *Primary facts* are obtained through automatically analyzing the source code of a system with code metrics, and *secondary facts* are obtained from people through different questionnaires, who are working with or on the system. Both kinds of facts are of different type information, so there is a need for bridging between them. Then the information obtained is used to form a plan to minimize potential risk.

2.2.4 Early Risk Estimation–Based Risk Analysis Methods

Analysis in the early stages of software development is one of the focuses in the process of risk estimation and mitigation. It is much cheaper if we can encounter and overcome the problems in the early stages than if we do this at a late stage of the software development process.

2.2.4.1 Methodology for Architecture-Level Reliability Risk Analysis (Yacoub and Ammar, 2002)

Input: Severity of complexity and coupling metrics derived from software architecture.

Technology: Dynamic metrics, architecture elements.

How it works: This is a heuristic risk assessment methodology for reliability risk assessment, based on dynamic complexity and dynamic coupling metrics that are used to define complexity factors for the architecture elements. Severity analysis is executed with failure mode and effect analysis applied over the architectural models. A combination between severity and complexity factors is used in order to identify the heuristic risk factors for the architecture components and connectors.

2.2.4.2 Software Risk in Early Design Method (Vucovich et al., 2007)

Input: Software functionality, historical function-failures, historical failure severities.

Technology: Function-failure design method.

How it works: This method identifies and analyzes the risk presented by potential software failures. The software function-failure design method demonstrates the corresponding risk in early design (RED) method for the software domain, to provide a software risk assessment based on functionality, which is often the only available information in the early stages of design. RED allows the early assessment of risk, which can guide more detailed risk assessment, provide a test-case development guide, and help in deciding whether a software product has been tested enough.

2.3 Risk Management Summary and Further Research Motivation

Let us summarize the risk management methods as the gallery of software risks:

Crisis management: Nolan (1973, 1979) and McFarlan (1974) proposed models and a project portfolio for managing the crisis in information technology and the risks in the information systems. Alter and Ginzberg (1978) proposed that risk factor analysis can increase the success rate in software development. Davis (1982) created a new method based on requirements determination for selecting the most suitable development approach.

Risk management: The pioneer in software risk management, Barry Boehm, published his first and most fundamental approach "A Spiral Model of Software Development and Enhancement" (Boehm, 1988) about risk management. His work was later complemented by Charette and others (Charette, 1989; Boehm and Ross, 1989; Charette, 1990; Ould, 1990; Boehm, 1991).

Risk taxonomies: Several risk categories or taxonomies were proposed in the fundamental methods of Boehm, SEI, and a few others. The paper by Georgieva, Farooq, and Dumke (2009a) showed a summary over existing software development risks and proposed a new risk taxonomy for the software testing process. Other quantitative approaches were developed by Bowers (1994), Fairley (1994), and Berny and Townsend (1993).

Risk scenarios: Kontio (1997, 2001) devised a new method for risk management where he proposed risk scenarios that are built over six elements (risk factor, risk event, risk outcome, reaction, risk effect set, and utility loss).

Risk analysis: In the late 1990s and since, several approaches for software risk analysis were developed separately from the famous ones; although they are used for risk analysis they are very specific and cannot be taken as generalized methods for risk management.

Risk experience: Risk experience as industrial reports have been published by Boehm (1991), Chittister, Kirkpatrick, and Van Scoy (1992), Eslinger et al. (1993), Meyers and Trbovich (1993), Morin (1993), Fairley (1994), Gemmer and Koch (1994), Hefner (1994), Williamson (1994), and Conrow and Shishido (1997).

Risk frameworks: Many different risk assessment frameworks were proposed such as the framework of McComb and Smith (1991) to identify system failure factors, which included 15 key risk areas distributed between project planning and execution in one dimension and technical and human factors in the other.

Risk-based features: Barki et al. (1993), based on a literature survey of 120 projects, compiled a list of 35 features that are connected with software development risk.

Risk assessment: Thomsett (1992) developed his risk assessment questionnaire model where all the questions are divided into three areas and each question has a specific value and is later used in forming the final risk score. He proposed a new project management paradigm that recognized people-oriented values as very important in the traditional organization structure and with this he is one of the first to put an accent on people in the process of risk management.

Risk evaluation: SEI risk taxonomy, mentioned above, is an important contribution in the field of risk management because it gives a very comprehensive questionnaire and software risk evaluation method (Carr et al. 1993; Sisti and Joseph 1994).

Performance-oriented risk management: This risk assessment framework developed by Lyytinen, Mathiassen, and Ropponen (1996) and afterward supplemented by Keil et al. (1998) presents a three-level structure of management, project, and system environment, giving a performance based on how actors, structure, and technology are assembled.

Risk degrees and experience: Applegate, McFarlan, and McKenney (1996) published a book about IS (information systems) management, where the project risk assessment questionnaire is the tool to evaluate the risk-degree in the different IT applications. Further approaches were developed by Moynihan (1997, 2002), who collected a list of risks and planned their mitigation after interviewing experienced project managers.

Risk assessment questionnaires: Questionnaire-based frameworks include, for example, the One-minute Risk Assessment Tool from Tiwana and Keil (2004–2005). A comparison of selected risk management approaches can be found in Lyytinen, Mathiassen, and Ropponen (1998). Questionnaires and risk lists as a form of risk identification appear from the very beginning and are still the most relevant and used techniques. The first lists comprised less than 50 issues (McComb and Smith, 1991; Barki et al., 1993).

Risk factors: A list of 60 software project risk factors can be found in Jones (1994), where each factor is analyzed for its frequency, impact, root causes, mitigation strategies, and others.

Risk management teamwork: The Software Engineering Institute stresses their research on the importance of teamwork in risk management as the team risk management method (Higuera et al., 1994). The effectiveness of group work (including brainstorming) has been investigated by Kontio. He developed the Riskit method using communicative and easily distinguishable elements of risk scenarios, which were visualized in a risk analysis diagram (Kontio, 1997, 2001).

Quantitative versus qualitative risks analysis: Distinguishing between qualitative and quantitative methods, the qualitative techniques estimate the risk in terms of likelihood and impact and apply ordinal scales and risk matrices as well as some means of weighting and averaging the obtained score (Charette, 1990; Sisti and Joseph, 1994) and quantitative risk analysis calculates the risk based on the theories of the probability calculus such as Monte Carlo analysis or Bayesian belief networks (Grey, 1995; Vose, 2008; Schuyler, 2001). The failure mode and effect analysis method (FMEA; well-known in the engineering field) was applied to the analysis of project risk in Deept and Ramanamurthy (2004).

Generic project risk management: The general process and principles of project risk management are applicable to all kinds of software projects. Examples of generic project risk management are described in Wideman (1998), Chong and Brown (2000), (Pritchard 2001), Chapman and Ward, (2002, 2003), Kendrick (2003), Mulcahy (2003), and Smith and Merritt (2002).

Project risk management: Well-known risk management solutions for software projects have been created by Boehm (1991), Karolak (1996), and Hall (1998). At a later stage Boehm et al. (2003) proposed a risk approach of COTS (commercial off-the-shelf)-intensive projects.

Risks perception: Adams (1995) gives very important observations on everyday risk perception and management. A practitioner's view of project risk management can be found in Conrow (2003). Several works are admitted as actually used and accepted in the software development industry (Ropponen and Lyytinen, 2000; Moynihan 2002).

Business risks: Risk management over safety, environmental, or business risks is described in Waring and Glendon (1998) and Cooper et al. (2004) or to address the issue of "positive risk" of a business opportunity (Hillson, 2004). Case studies of business risk management are described in Schmietendorf (2009).

Risks management strategies: Cockburn (1997) has summarized some of the current knowledge on effective risk management strategies into reusable risk resolution patterns.

Risks management database: Kontio presented a detailed design of a risk management database (Kontio and Basili, 1996; Kontio, 2001) but its scope is limited to capturing the information on risk in actual projects and lacks the capabilities to develop generalized knowledge.

Risk management in software engineering: Risk management is an essential part of the management of a successful software project, and because of this it is covered by all the "bibles" of software engineering and project management such as Chrissis, Konrad, and Shrum (2003), Thayer and Dorfman (2002), Pressman (2004), Sommerville (2008), McConnell (2004), Abran and Moore (2004), and PMBOK (2004).

Risk management standards: The area of risk management is intensely standardized and the most widely recognized risk management standard is ISO 14971 (14971 2001) complemented by IEC 62304 (62304 2004). Although ISO 14971 covers the risk of medical devices, it is generally accepted as a mature standard on general-purpose risk management. Based on ISO 14971, Standards Australia has proposed a new extended standard AS/NZS 4360 (4360 2004), which is expected to replace ISO 14971. ISO has also published a risk management standard ISO 16085 dedicated to software engineering (16085 2006), which is based on the earlier work from IEEE, the IEEE 1540 (1540 2001).

Risks and human factors: There exist different types of human factors studies: human error analysis, human factors engineering, and human reliability analysis (Baybutt, 1996). Because of this a basic classification of human errors (Baybutt, 1996) can appear as slips, mistakes, violations, sociotechnical, and coming from the management.

Observing the described risk assessment methods we can make the following statement: all of them take as input different types of data that could be generalized

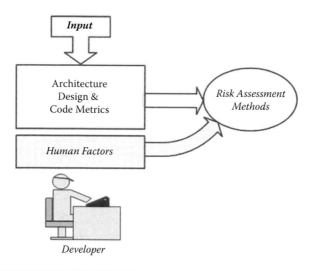

Figure 2.2   Input for the risk assessment methods.

as architecture, design, and code metrics data as visualized in Figure 2.2. Only a few of these methods (Young et al., 2007; Nogueira and Bhattacharya, 2000) consider some types of human factors. Although this attempt does not seem to be comprehensive, it is a good example that gives as much importance to human factors as to the others in the process of assessing software risks.

As shown in Figure 2.3, risk sources in the software production process are people *P*, development process *D*, software *S*, and hardware resources *H*. These four elements give us the complete software development or software production process *SPP* and software system *SS* (as *IT* area), which should be analyzed in its full complexity in order to achieve an adequate risk management process *RM* including the risk assessment *RA* and the risk controlling *RC*.

This can be expressed with the following equations according to Boehm (1991) and Figure 2.3:

$$IT = \{SPP,\ SS\} \tag{2.1}$$

$$SPP_{riskSources} = \{P_{dev},\ D_{dev},\ S_{dev},\ H_{dev}\},$$

$$SS_{riskSources} = \{P_{sys},\ S_{sys},\ H_{sys}\}$$

Furthermore, the risk assessment could be considered for both software development or production and software system as

$$RA_{SPP} : personnel_{dev} \times development_{dev} \times software_{dev} \times hardware_{dev} \tag{2.2}$$

$$\rightarrow riskAssessment_{dev}$$

$$RA_{SS} : personnel_{sys} \times software_{sys} \times hardware_{sys} \rightarrow riskAssessment_{sys}$$

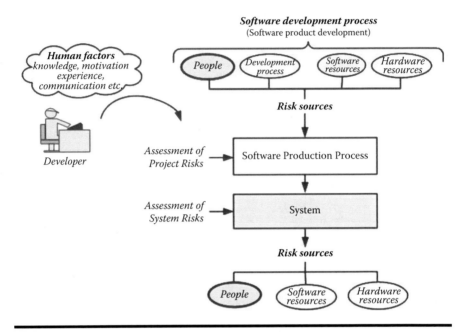

Figure 2.3   Risk in the different stages of the development process.

And finally, the general components of risk management as risk assessments and risk controlling as *RM* = {*RA, RC*} are:

$$RA = \{riskIdentification, riskAnalysis, riskPrioritization\}, \qquad (2.3)$$

$$RC = \{riskMgmtPlanning, riskResolution, riskMonitoring\}.$$

Taking into consideration the information obtained from the analyzed risk assessment methods, which is that they do not consider people as a major source of risk, and analyzing the software system in its complete form and knowing how crucial the role of the human being in every activity can be (Georgieva, 2009c), we can conclude that there exists an incompleteness of existing methods for risk assessment and new methods should be developed that cover human factors.

2.4 Human Factors in Software Engineering

Humanity is what makes the world move forward in a technical, experimental, and achieving way. Human skills, ideas, and imagination are the inspirations for all surrounding inventions and technologies, and cultural, traditional, and intellectual

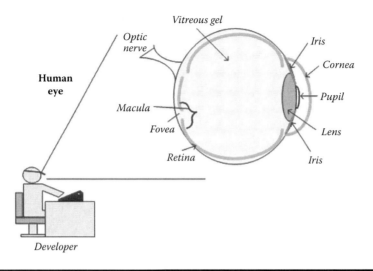

Figure 2.4 The human eye.

progress. Humans develop the technology to a newer level, always higher, always faster and, it is hoped, always better. The trace of human touch and sense is in every emerging technology, theory, business solution, and machine and of course when there is a human act, there might be a human error too.

In order to understand the complexity of the human being we start with a small example from our biological nature. Let us observe the human retina (Figure 2.4). This transparent, paper-thin layer of nerve tissue on which is projected an image of the world, that is less than 1-cm square and ½-mm thick has about 100 million neurons. The retina processes about 10 one-million-point images per second. If we want to simulate this activity with a computer, it would take 100 MIPS (million instructions per second) to do a million detections, and 1,000 MIPS to repeat them 10 times per second in order to match the retina (Moravec, 1997).

Having this information in mind, let us see what is happening in our brain (Figure 2.5). The 1,500-cubic centimeter human brain is about 100,000 times larger than the retina; this means that matching the brain activity will take about 100 million MIPS of computer power (Moravec, 1997). This small observation shows the complexity of the human brain that we have to take into consideration when speaking about human factors. Here we are just observing the technical parameters of the brain, but when we also take influencing factors such as health, emotions, motivations, ambitions, and qualification, the overall picture becomes much more complex. This is what motivated us to analyze the connection between personal characteristics and human productivity in the software development process.

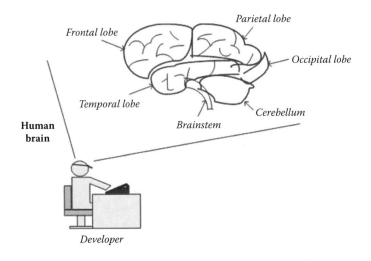

Figure 2.5 The human brain.

2.4.1 Human Errors, Mistakes, and Failures

Human error examples might be found everywhere: small quarrels with relatives affected by a complicated character; design problems in a usability form; machine construction and usage; people-to-people and human-to-machine interaction. Consequences are also numerous from small frowns and bad attitudes to catastrophic life-threatening events.

Human error is the difference that occurs from what a human is supposed to do (planned, proposed, intended) and what the result (or lack of it) is. In some cases the difference is so unnoticeable that it stays hidden; sometimes it is discovered and mitigated or remains hidden with unpredictable results when emerging. The factors affecting the result and production of an error are also classified as being a human kind. In the following we have summarized the leading classifications regarding human factors.

The pioneer in the field of human factors is Rasmussen. He published his classification in 1982 and distinguished between three types of problems that could be divided into skill-based, rule-based, and knowledge-based levels (Rasmussen, 1982). *Skill-based* performance is explained with automatic, unconscious, and parallel actions. *Rule-based* is associated with recognizing situations and following associated procedures. Finally, *knowledge-based* refers to conscious problem solving. Rasmussen also proposed a list of factors that influence human behavior and actions: social and management climate, type of the overworked information, emotional condition, physiological stressors, and physical workload. He pioneered a multifaceted taxonomy for the description and analysis of events involving human malfunction. In this taxonomy, he defined the causes of human malfunctions as: "external" (distraction, etc.), "excessive task demand" (force, time, knowledge, etc.), "operator incapacitated" (sickness, etc.), and "intrinsic human variability." As we show in the next sections, his ideas were adopted completely and slightly modified and extended by Reason and Shappell.

Reason (1990) defined human error as a planned sequence of mental or physical activities to achieve its intended outcome. He distinguished between *mistakes* and *slips*. In his view, slips are actions that proceed as planned but end with undesired actions, and mistakes are desired actions that go as they are supposed to but are not fulfilling the planned goal, so they are classified as planning failures or latent failures. Latent failures, unlike their active counterparts, may remain unnoticed for a long period before emerging in an unsuspecting situation.

From Reason's (1990) descriptions of latent and active failures, Shappell (2000) distinguished four levels of failures: *unsafe acts, predictions for unsafe acts, unsafe supervision, and organizational influences.* Although Shappell's "'Swiss cheese' model of accident causation" is meant to be used for aviation, it could be applied in the field of software engineering with great success. Anyway, almost all of the definitions and research work about human factors does not originate from the software field because the software industry emerged only in the last decades and was not as popular as the other already developed industries.

Reason separated two types of unsafe acts: *errors* and *violations*. Errors are described as mental or physical actions of an individual that do not accomplish desired outcomes. And violations are specified as determination not to obey the rules and recommendations that impose safety.

To determine more correctly a specific failure investigation these two categories are expanded as shown in Figure 2.6 into three types of errors (skill-based, decision, and perceptual) and two violation forms. Examples of these errors and violations are

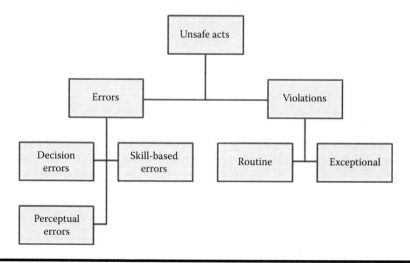

Figure 2.6   Unsafe acts categories. (Reprinted from S. A. Shappell, *The Human Factors Analysis and Classification System—HFACS*. Washington, DC: Wiegmann and Shappel, 2000. With permission.)

Table 2.1   Selected Examples of Unsafe Acts

Errors	Violations
Skill-Based Errors • Failed to prioritize attention • Omitted step in procedure • Omitted checklist item • Poor technique	• Failed to adhere to brief • Violated training rules • Not currently qualified for work
Decision Errors • Improper procedure • Misdiagnosed emergency • Wrong response to emergency • Exceeded ability • Poor decision	
Perceptual Errors • Visual illusion • Disorientation	

Source: S. A. Shappell, *The Human Factors Analysis and Classification System—HFACS*. Washington, DC: Wiegmann and Shappel, 2000. With permission.

shown in Table 2.1. We see that all these different errors are based on the individual's skills, decision, or knowledge at a special moment, so regardless of why these errors occur, they are based on an individual perception of the world. This gives us motivation to develop our performance prediction model based exactly on these individual features that, from the point of view of their performance, produce absolutely different employees from people with the same knowledge and experience.

Technical failures (Shappell, 2000), also specified as *skill-based* errors, are based on individual experience and education. *Decision errors* describe intentional behavior that ends with inappropriate or inadequate action for the situation. *Knowledge-based* errors (perceptual errors) occur when one's perception of the surrounding is different from the reality. Rasmussen defines so-called *rule-based* mistakes (Rasmussen, 1982) or procedural errors (Orasanu, 1993); they occur when a structured task is faced but the wrong procedures are performed. *Violations* are produced during intentional disregard of laws and orders. We can have routine and exceptional violations that occur as rare withdrawals from standard regulations, not demonstrating an individual's typical behavior (Shappell, 2000).

In observing all these different unsafe acts, it is important to understand why they happen, and Shappell gives the explanation with different preconditions. For example, they can be substandard conditions that represent the different mental and physiological states that people can be in and the resultant behavior. There is one more level of failures: *unsafe supervision and organizational influences*; it is extremely important to understand that although people and their mental states and cooperation are very important, the manner in which the company or team is led is also important, as is the atmosphere during the working process. We can see an example in Georgieva et al. (2010a) and Georgieva (2009d).

2.4.2 Influencing Factors

We cannot describe human factors in the software process only as errors, mistakes, and failures. We also have to describe the many different factors that influence people in their daily work and that lead them either to success or nonfulfillment of their work. The problems that people cause are only one facet of the problem we want to solve. We are actually searching for those special human features that lead to a larger or smaller number of problems. To this end we now look over the other human factors. We listed some of these factors stated by Shappell, Reason, and Rasmussen in the previous section and we now continue with the following authors.

Fisher (2001) tried to summarize the important points for creating a successful user software system. He identified the following necessary human and technical skills: graphic design, communication, organization of information, illustration, interface design, and usability testing.

Wang (2005) proposed a taxonomy of human factors in software engineering and built a behavioral model of human errors, expressed in an evaluation of the performed task. This model concentrated on the human-conducted actions in the process of performing a certain task. In 2008 Wang broadened his taxonomy and categorized the personality traits into eight groups (Wang, 2008). These can be seen in Table 2.2.

In their paper, Hillson and Webster (2006) spoke about the connection between emotions and risk behavior and tried to show the relation between emotional literacy and work attitude.

Dhillon (2007) summarized the important factors affecting the productivity of the individual worker and named them "stressors." He categorized stressors into four types:

- Occupational change-related stressors
- Occupational frustration-related stressors
- Workload-related stressors
- Miscellaneous stressors

He also defines different reasons for the occurrence of human errors:

> Poor training or skill, poor equipment design, complex task, poor work layout, high temperature or noise level in the work area, distraction in the work area, poor lighting in the work area, poorly written equipment operating and maintenance procedure, improper work tools, poor verbal communication, poor motivation, crowded work space and poor management. (Dhillon, 2007, p. 47)

Table 2.2 Taxonomy of Personal Traits and Attributes

Emotion and Motivation	Attitude	Cognitive Ability	Interpersonal Ability
Comfort/fear	Proud of job	Knowledge	Pleasant
Joy/sadness	Responsible	Skills	Tolerant
Pleasure/anger	Disciplined	Experience	Tactful
Love/hate	Thorough	Instructiveness	Helpful
Ambition	Careful	Learning ability	Scope of contact
Impulsiveness	Assertive	Expressiveness	Variety of contact
Trying in uncertainty	Energetic	Knowledge transferability	Consultative
Following rules	Enthusiastic	Reaction to events	Responsible
Self-expectation	Tolerant	Efficiency	Respectful
	Tactful	Attention	Trustworthy
	Confident	Abstraction	Sympathetic
	Individual	Searching	Modest
	Team Oriented	Categorization	Loyal
	Productive	Comprehension	Flexible
	Persistent	Planning	Independent
		Decision making	
		Problem solving	
		Analysis	
		Synthesis	
Sociability	*Rigorousness*	*Creativity*	*Custom*
Collaboration capability	Contingent error rate	Abstraction capability	Exterior hobby
Communication capability	Repeatable error rate	Imagination	Interior hobby
Extroversion	Error-correction capability	Analogy capability	Quietness

Table 2.2 (continued) Taxonomy of Personal Traits and Attributes

Sociability	Rigorousness	Creativity	Custom
Introversion	Pinpoint capability	Curiousness	Activeness
Culture factor	Concentration capability	Design ability	Literature
Leadership	Logical inference capability	Hands-on capability	Vision
Group orientation	Reliability	Broad mind	
Organization capability	Precision		
Concern of others	Perception		
Dependability	Consistency		
Compatibility	System		
	Talent		

Source: Y. Wang, *Journal of Cognitive Informatics and Natural Intelligence,* 2(4): 70–84, 2008. With permission.

Although the book concerns transportation systems, in our opinion all these factors can also be applied to the software development process.

Dayer (2007) summarized the factors that influence human reliability into two groups: internal and external. The internal is formed by the company's working atmosphere and the external by the individual's personal life. Internal factors are, for example, trust and working climate whereas external factors refer to family, health, and Maslow's pyramid of needs (Maslow, 1987).

Islam and Dong (2008) summarized human risk factors as: "personal competency, experience and leadership, team performance, availability of skilled personnel, commitment, personnel loyalty and different specific working skills."

Yanyan and Renzuo (2008) explained the psychological background of human behavior as a mixture of human knowledge, emotion, and intention. They tried to find the relationship between software engineering and knowledge and at the same time include the human factors that influence this knowledge.

Analogically to Dayer, Flouris and Yilmaz (2010) built a framework for human resource management where they divided human characteristics into internally and externally influenced ones. The internal and external performance-influencing factors are listed below:

Internal Performance Influencing Factors (Flouris and Yilmaz, 2010):
- Emotional state
- Intelligence
- Motivation/attitude
- Perceptual abilities
- Physical condition
- Sex differences
- Skill level
- Social factors
- Strength/endurance
- Stress level
- Task knowledge
- Training/experience

External Performance Influencing Factors (Flouris and Yilmaz, 2010):
- Inadequate workspace and layout
- Poor environmental conditions
- Inadequate design
- Inadequate training and job aids
- Poor supervision

Another taxonomy that we consider is that of Kim and Jung (2003). They performed a study of 18 performance-shaping factor taxonomies and summarized the human factors as shown in Table 2.3.

Table 2.3 Kim and Jung's Human Factor Taxonomy

Subgroup	Detailed Items	
Cognitive Characteristics	**Cognitive States**	**Temporal Cognitive States**
	• Attention	• Memory of recent actions
	• Intelligence	• Operator diagnosis
	• Skill level	• Perceived importance
	• Knowledge	• Perceived consequences
	• Experience	• Operator expectations
	• Training	• Confidence in diagnosis
		• Memory of previous actions

continued

Table 2.3 (continued)   Kim and Jung's Human Factor Taxonomy

Subgroup	Detailed Items	
Physical and Psychological Characteristics	**Physical States**	**Psychological States**
	• Gender/age • Motor skills • Physical disabilities • Impediment • Clarity in speaking • Fatigue/pain • Discomfort • Hunger, thirst	• Emotion/feeling • Confusion • Task burden • Fear of failure/consequences • High jeopardy risk
Personal and Social Characteristics	**Personal**	**Social**
	• Attitude • Motivation • Risk taking • Self-esteem • Self-confidence • Sense of responsibility • Sensation seeking • Leadership ability • Sociability • Personality • Anticipation	• Status • Role/responsibility • Norms • Attitudes, influenced by other people

Source: J. W. Kim and W. Jung, *Journal of Loss Prevention in the Process Industries,* 16(6): 479–495, 2003. With permission.

2.5 Summary of Human Factors

The overview of the scientific work conducted on human factors in the software process as HF_{IT} has several different perspectives:

- We have slips and mistakes occurring in everyday human work including their base (e.g., skill, rule or knowledge-based).
- Then we have malfunctions and their relation to the behavioral model of the human being with regard to performing or not performing a certain task.
- The connection between emotions and risk behavior is clearly recognized and different stressors that influence the people are categorized.
- We have different levels of failures and different factors that influence human actions.
- We have observed different types of frameworks and taxonomies that list all different personal characteristics that influence the working process.

Having all this in mind we can say that there are many scientific attempts to connect human behavior with mistakes in the work process, but thus far nobody has tried to observe personal traits and their influence over an individual's work performance. By personal traits, we understand the individual's characteristics that are important for every employee and influence the working process as well as the occurrence of mistakes or different problems. Based on this, we try to find the most important human features that affect work quality in the software development process, to evaluate the most critical ones, and to build a prediction model of the human performance.

We can say that all these different types of human factors are actually the human risks in the software development process with which we have to cope (Neumann et al., 2010a; Georgieva et al., 2010b). In order to be able to manage the different types of slips, mistakes, and errors we first have to manage the factors that cause them. We visualize this in the following way. From our research we can say that the human risk factors HRF can be divided into the following groups:

- Cognitive human risk factors HRF_{cog}
- Physical human risk factors HRF_{phys}
- Personal human risk factors HRF_{pers}
- Social human risk factors HRF_{social}

When we try to evaluate them in the software development process we have to take them as a whole but we can say that the different factors are connected with the variety of roles and their responsibilities or their involvement in the IT process. Because of this we can establish the following relations:

$$personnel_{IT} = \{P_{dev},\ P_{sys}\} \tag{2.4}$$

$$HF_{IT}\colon personnel_{IT} \times processInvolvement \times role_{IT} \rightarrow HF_{IT}$$

$$processInvolvement = \{f(P_{dev}) \cup f(P_{sys})\}$$

$$HF_{IT} = \{attention,\ communication,\ competence,\ concentration,\ cooperation,$$
$$hardworking,\ intelligence,\ self\text{-}management,\ talkativeness,$$
$$understanding,\ creativity,\ tolerance,\ positive,\ knowledge,\ motivation\}$$

where f denotes any team or business aspects in concrete industrial environments. Note that we consider the different roles, the so-called $role_{IT}$, later. Addressing risk implications, we can characterize:

$$HRF_{IT}\colon HF_{IT} \times processInvolvement \times humanRisks_{IT} \rightarrow personnelRisks \tag{2.5}$$

$$humanRisks_{IT} = \{errors_{IT},\ violations_{IT},\ failures_{IT}\}$$

$$errors_{IT} = \{skillBasedErrors,\ decisionErrors,$$

$$perceptualErrors,\ knowledgeBasedErrors\}$$

$$violations_{IT} = \{trainingRules,\ qualifications,\ socialFactors\}$$

$$failures_{IT} = \{unsafenessTasks,\ performanceSlips,\ organizationalMistakes\}$$

and furthermore

$$HRF_{IT} = \{HRF_{IT}^{cog},\ HRF_{IT}^{phys},\ HRF_{IT}^{pers},\ HRF_{IT}^{social}\}$$

$$HRF_{IT}^{cog} = \{attention,\ intelligence,\ skillLevel,\ knowledge,\ experience\} \tag{2.6}$$

$$HRF_{IT}^{phys} = \{gender,\ age,\ motorSkills,\ physicalDisabilities,$$

$$fatigue,\ discomfort,\ impediment\}$$

$$HRF_{IT}^{pers} = \{attitude,\ motivation,\ selfEsteem,\ selfConfidence,\ riskTaking,$$

$$sensationSeeking,\ leadershipAbility,\ socialibility,\ anticipation\}$$

$$HRF_{IT}^{social} = \{status,\ role,\ responsibility,\ norms,\ attitudes\}$$

Following we consider the HF_{IT} in general including their exploration for risk situations (as HRF_{IT}) or in a positive manner as reasonable characteristics for IT processes.

References

14971, I 2001. *ISO/FDIS 14971:2001 International Standard: Medical Devices—Application of risk management to medical devices.* International Organization for Standardization. Geneva, Switzerland.

1540, I 2001. *IEEE Standard for Software Life Cycle Processes—Risk Management.* Los Alamitos, CA: IEEE Computer Society Press.

16085, BI 2006. *Systems and software engineering—Life cycle processes—Risk management.* British Standard.

4360, A 2004. AS/NZS 4360:2004 *Australian Standard: Risk Management.* Standards Australia.

Abran, A. and Moore, J. (2004). *Guide to the Software Engineering Body of Knowledge—SWEBOK.* Los Alamitos, CA: IEEE Computer Society Press.

Adams, J. (1995). *Risks.* London, UK: University College Press.

Alter, S. and Ginzberg, M. (1978). Managing uncertainty in MIS implementation. *Sloan Management Review*, 20(1): 23–31.

Applegate, L., McFarlan, F., and McKenney, J. (1996). *Corporate Information Systems Management.* Irwin. Text and Causes.

Barki, H., Rivard, S., and Talbot, J. (1993). Toward an assessment of software development risk. *Journal of Management Information Systems*, 10(2): 203–225.

Baybutt, P. (1996). Human factors in process safety and risk management: Needs for models, tools and techniques. In *International Workshop on Human Factors in Offshore Operations, US Mineral Mangement Service*, New Orleans, December, pp. 412–433.

Berny, J. and Townsend, P. (1993). Macrosimulation of project risks—A practical way forward. *International Journal of Project Management*, 11(4): 201–208.

Boehm, B.W. (1988). A Spiral Model of Software Development and Enhancement. *IEEE Computer*, 21(5): 61–72.

Boehm, B. (1998). Using WinWin Spiral Model: A Case Study. *IEEE Computer*, 31(7): 33–44.

Boehm, B. (1991). Software risk management: Principles and practices. *IEEE Software*, 8(1): 32–41.

Boehm, B. and Ross, R. (1989). Theory W software project management: Principles and examples. *IEEE Transactions on Software Engineering*, 15(7): 902–916.

Boehm, B., Port, D., Yang, Y., and Bhuta, J. (2003). *Not All CBS Are Created Equally: COTS-Intensive Project Types*, LNCS 2580. Berlin: Springer.

Bowers, J. (1994). Data for project risk analyses. *International Journal of Project Management*, 12(1): 9–16.

Carr, M., Konda, S., Monarch, I., Ulrich, F., and Walker, C. (1993). Taxonomy-based risk identification. *Technical Report.* Pittsburgh: Carnegie Mellon University.

Chapman, C. and Ward, S. (2003). *Project Risk Management: Processes, Techniques and Insights*, 2nd ed. New York: John Wiley & Sons.

Chapman, C. and Ward, S. (2002). *Managing Project Risk and Uncertainty: A Constructively Simple Approach to Decision Making*. New York: John Wiley & Sons.

Charette, R. (1990). *Applications Strategies for Risk Analysis*. New York: McGraw-Hill.

Charette, R. (1989). *Software Engineering Risk Analysis and Management*. New York: McGraw-Hill.

Chee, C., Vij, V., and Ramamoorthy, C. (1995). Using influence diagrams for software risk analysis. In *TAI '95: Proceedings of the Seventh International Conference on Tools with Artificial Intelligence*, Los Alamitos, CA: IEEE Computer Society Press, pp. 128–131.

Chittister, C., Kirkpatrick, R., and Van Scoy, R. (1992). Risk management in practice. *American Programmer*, 5: 30–35.

Chong, Y. and Brown, E. (2000). *Managing Project Risk: Business Risk Management for Project Leaders*. Upper Saddle River, NJ: Prentice Hall.

Chrissis, M., Konrad, M., and Shrum, S. (2003). *CMMI: Guidelines for Process Integration and Product Improvement*. Reading, MA: Addison-Wesley.

CMMI (2002). CMMI for systems engineering/software engineering/integrated product and process development. *CMU/SEI-2002-TR-004*, Software Engineering Institute. Pittsburgh: Carnegie Mellon University.

Cockburn, A. (1997). *Surviving Object-Oriented Projects*. Reading, MA: Addison-Wesley.

Conrow, E. (2003). *Effective Risk Management: Some Keys to Success,* 2nd ed. Reston, VA: American Institute of Aeronautics & Ast.

Conrow, E. and Shishido, P. (1997). Implementing risk management on software intensive projects. *IEEE Software*, 14(3): 83–89.

Cooper, D., Grey, S., Raymond, G., and Walker, P. (2004). *Project Risk Management Guidelines: Managing Risk in Large Projects and Complex Procurements*. New York: John Wiley & Sons.

Davis, G. (1982). Strategies for information requirements determination. *IBM Systems Journal*, 21(1): 4–30.

Dayer, J.M. (2007). *Consideration of Human Errors in Risk Management*. Swiss Federal Institute of Technology Zurich (ETHZ). Zurich: Switzerland. White paper.

Deept, I. and Ramanamurthy, N. (2004). Effective risk management: Risk analysis using an enhanced FMEA technique. In *Proceedings of the Annual Project Management Leadership Conference, Bangalore, India*, pp. 210–223.

Deursen, A. van and Kuipers, T. (2003). Source-based software risk assessment. In *ICSM '03: Proceedings of the International Conference on Software Maintenance*. Los Alamitos, CA: IEEE Computer Society Press.

Dhillon, B. (2007). Basic human reliability and error concepts. In *Human Reliability and Error in Transportation Systems*. London: Springer.

Dorofee, A., Walker, J., Alberts, C., Higuera, R., Murray, T., and Williams, R. (1996). *Continuous Risk Management Guidebook*. Pittsburgh: Software Engineering Institute.

Eslinger, S., Ellis, C., Hoting, S., and Walden, G. (1993). PACE system risk analysis: An application. In *Second SEI Conference on Software Risk Management*, Pittsburgh.

Fairley, R. (1994). Risk management for software projects. *IEEE Software*, 11(5): 57–67.

Fisher, J. (2001). User satisfaction and system success: Considering the development team. *Australian Journal of Information Systems*, 9(1): 21–32.

Flouris, T. and Yilmaz, A.K. (2010). The risk management framework to strategic human resource management. *International Research Journal of Finance and Economics*, 36: 26–45.

Gemmer, A. and Koch, P. (1994). Rockwell case studies in risk management. In *Third SEI Conference on Software Risk Management,* Pittsburgh.

Georgieva, K. (2009c). The incompleteness of the risk assessment methods. *Softwaretechnik-Trends,* 29(2): 42–47.

Georgieva, K. (2009d). Human factors and software development process. In *International Workshop on Empirical Software Engineering in Practice (IWESEP),* Osaka.

Georgieva, K., Farooq, A., and Dumke, R.R. (2009a). A risk taxonomy for the software testing process. In G. Büren and R. R. Dumke, *Praxis der Software-Messung—Tagungsband des DASMA Software Metrik Kongresses (MetriKon 2009).* Aachen: Shaker, pp. 247–260.

Georgieva, K., Farooq, A., and Dumke, R.R. (2009b). Analysis of the risk assessment methods—A survey. In *Software Process and Product Measurement. International Conferences IWSM 2009 and Mensura 2009.* Berlin: Springer, pp. 76–86.

Georgieva, K., Neumann, R., and Dumke, R. (2010a). Applying human error assessment and reduction technique (HEART) in the software development process. In *Proceedings of the Joined International Conferences on Software Measurement (IWSM/MetriKon/Mensura 2010).* Aachen: Shaker, pp. 617–632.

Georgieva, K., Neumann, R., and Dumke, R. (2010b). The influence of personal features on the project success. In *5. Hochschul-Roundtable der CECMG/DASMA, Industrielle und gesellschaftliche Herausforderungen beim flexiblen Sourcing von IT-Projekten/-Dienstleistungen.* Aachen: Shaker, pp. 61–72.

Grey, S. (1995). *Practical Risk Assessment for Project Management,* 1st ed. New York: John Wiley & Sons.

Gupta, D. and Sadiq, M. (2008). Software risk assessment and estimation model. In *International Conference on Computer Science and Information Technology.* Los Alamitos, CA: IEEE Computer Society Press, pp. 963–967.

Hall, E. (1998). *Managing Risk: Methods for Software Systems Development.* Reading, MA: Addison Wesley.

Hefner, R. (1994). Experience with applying SEI's risk taxonomy. In *Third SEI Conference on Software Risk Management.* Pittsburgh: SEI Press.

Higuera, R. and Haimes, Y. (1996). *Software Risk Management.* Pittsburgh: Carnegie Mellon University.

Higuera, R., Gluch, D., Dorofee, A., Murphy, R., Walker, J., and Williams, R. (1994). *An Intoduction to Team Risk Management.* Pittsburgh: Carnegie Mellon University Press.

Hillson, D. (2004). *Effective Opportunity Management for Projects: Exploiting Positive Risk.* Boca Raton, FL: Marcel Dekker.

Hillson, D. and Webster, R. (2006). Managing risk attitude using emotional literacy. In *PMI Global Congress EMEA Proceedings,* Madrid, Spain, pp. 1–7.

Islam, S. and Dong, W. (2008). Human factors in software security risk management. *LMSA '08: Proceedings of the First International Workshop on Leadership and Management in Software Architecture.* New York: ACM, pp. 13–16.

ISO (2009). ISO/FDIS 31000 *Risk Management—Principles and Guidelines.* Geneva, Switzerland: Geneva Publ.

Jones, C. (1994). *Assessment and Control of Software Risks.* Upper Saddle River, NJ: Yourdon Press.

Karolak, D. (1996). *Software Engineering Risk Management.* Los Alamitos, CA: IEEE Computer Society Press.

Keil, M., Cule, P., Lyytinen, K., and Schmidt, R. (1998). A framework for identifying software project risks. *Communications of the ACM,* 41(11): 76–83.

Kendrick, T. (2003). *Identifying and Managing Project Risk: Essential Tools for Failure-Proofing Your Project*. New York: American Management Association.

Kim, J.W. and Jung, W. (2003). A taxonomy of performance influencing factors for human reliability analysis of emergency tasks. *Journal of Loss Prevention in the Process Industries*, 16(6): 479–495.

Kontio, J. (2001). Software engineering risk management: A method, improvement framework and empirical evaluation, PhD Thesis, Helsinki University of Technology, Helsinki.

Kontio, J. (1997). The Riskit Method for Software Risk Management, version 1. *CS-TR-3782*, Department of Computer Science, University of Maryland.

Kontio, J. and Basili, V. (1996). *Risk Knowledge Capture in the Riskit Method*. College Park, MD: SEL Software Engineering Workshop.

Lyytinen, K. (2000). A source based questionnaire of main software risks. *Technical Report*. Ulm, Germany: *Daimler Chrysler*.

Lyytinen, K., Mathiassen, L., and Ropponen, J. (1996). A framework for software risk management. *Journal of Information Systems*, 11(4): 275–285.

Maslow, A. (1987). *Motivation and Personality*. New York: Harper Collins.

McComb, D. and Smith, J. (1991). System project failure: The heuristics of risk. *Journal of Information Systems Management*, 8: 1.

McConnell, S. (2004). *Professional Software Development*. Reading, MA: Addison-Wesley.

McConnell, S. (1996). *Rapid Development: Taming Wild Software Schedules*. Redmond, WA: Microsoft Press.

McConnell, S. (1993). *Code Complete*. Redmond, WA: Microsoft Press.

McFarlan, F. (1974). Portfolio approach to information systems. *Harvard Business Review*. 52(5): 142–150.

Meyers, D.J. and Trbovich, D. (1993). One project's approach to software risk management. In *Second SEI Conference on Software Risk Management*, Pittsburgh.

Michaels, J. (1996). *Technical Risk Management*. Upper Saddle River, NJ: Prentice Hall.

Moravec, H. (1997). When will computer hardware match the human brain? *Journal of Evolution and Technology*, 1.

Morin, J.M. (1993). Risk driven project management: A practical approach. In *Second SEI Conference on Software Risk Management*, Pittsburgh.

Moynihan, T. (2002). *Coping with IS/IT Risk Management: The Recipes of Experienced Project Managers*. Berlin: Springer.

Moynihan, T. (1997). How experienced project managers assess risk. *IEEE Software*, 14(3): 35–41.

Mulcahy, R. (2003). *Risk Management, Tricks of the Trade for Project Managers*. Washington, DC: RMC.

Neumann, D.E. (2002). An enhanced neural network technique for software risk analysis. *IEEE Transactions on Software Engineering*, 28: 904–912.

Neumann, R., Georgieva, K., and Dumke, R. (2010a). Recruiting excellence for global players—How the most successful software company on earth sources talent. In CECMG/DASMA, *Industrielle und gesellschaftliche Herausforderungen beim flexiblen Sourcing von IT-Projekten/-Dienstleistungen*. Aachen: Shaker, pp. 68–76,

Nogueira, J. and Bhattacharya, S. (2000). A risk assessment model for software prototyping projects. In *RSP '00: Proceedings of the 11th IEEE International Workshop on Rapid System Prototyping (RSP 2000)*. Los Alamitos, CA: IEEE Computer Society Press.

Nolan, R. (1979). Managing the crises in data processing. *Harvard Business Review*, 57(3): 68–76.

Nolan, R. (1973). Managing the computer resource: A stage hypothesis. *Communications of the ACM*, 16(7): 399–405.

Orasanu, J. (1993). *Decision-Making in the Cockpit*. San Diego, CA: Academic Press.

Ould, M. (1990). *Strategies for Software Engineering, The Management of Risk and Quality*. New York: John Wiley & Sons.

Pandelios, G., Rumsey, T., and Dorofee, A. (1996). Using risk management for software process improvement. In *SEPG Conference*. Pittsburgh: Software Engineering Institute Press.

PMBOK (2004). *A Guide to the Project Management Body of Knowledge*, 3rd ed. Newtown Square, PA: Project Management Institute.

Pressman, R. (2004). *Software Engineering: A Practitioner's Approach*. New York: McGraw-Hill.

Pritchard, C. (2001). *Risk Management: Concepts & Guidance*, 2nd ed. Frankfurt: ESI International.

Rasmussen, H. (1982). Human errors: A taxonomy for describing human malfunction in industrial installations. *Journal of Occupational Accidents*, 4: 311–333.

Reason, J. (1990). *Human Error*. Cambridge, UK: Cambridge University Press.

Ropponen, J. and Lyytinen K. (2000). Components of software development risk: How to address them? A project manager survey. *IEEE Transactions on Software Engineering*, 26(2): 98–112.

Schmietendorf, A. (2009). *Compliance and Risk Management in the Context of Complex and High-Integrated Business Architectures* (German). Aachen: Shaker.

Schuyler, J. (2001). *Risk and Decision Analysis in Projects*, 2nd ed. Newtown Square, PA: Project Management Institute.

SEI (2011). *SEI*, viewed 1 July 2014, http://www.sei.cmu.edu/architecture/research/previousresearch/duties.cfm

Shappell, S.A. (2000). *The Human Factors Analysis and Classification System—HFACS*. Washington, DC: Wiegmann and Shappel.

Sisti, F. and Joseph, S. (1994). *Software Risk Evaluation Method*. Pittsburgh: Carnegie Mellon University Press.

Smith, P. and Merritt, G. (2002). *Proactive Risk Management: Controlling Uncertainty in Product Development*. Boca Raton, FL: Productivity Press.

Sommerville, I. (2008). *Software Engineering*, 8th ed. Reading, MA: Addison Wesley.

Sommerville, I. (2004). *Software Engineering*, 7th ed. Reading, MA: Addison-Wesley.

Thayer, R. and Dorfman, M. (2002). *Software Engineering Volume 1: The Development Process*. Los Alamitos, CA: IEEE Computer Society Press.

Thomsett, R. (1992). *Third Wave Project Management*. Upper Saddle River, NJ: Prentice Hall.

Van Scoy, R. (1992). *Software Development Risk: Opportunity, Not Problem*. Pittsburgh: Carnegie Mellon University Press.

Vose, D. (2008). *Risk Analysis: A Quantitative Guide*, 3rd ed. New York: John Wiley & Sons.

Vucovich, J.P., Stone, R.B., Liu, X., and Tumer, I.Y. (2007). Risk assessment in early software design based on the software function-failure design method. In *COMPSAC '07: Proceedings of the 31st Annual International Computer Software and Applications Conference*. Los Alamitos, CA: IEEE Computer Society Press, pp. 405–412.

Wang, Y. (2008). On cognitive properties of human factors and error models in engineering and socialization. *Journal of Cognitive Informatics and Natural Intelligence*, 2(4): 70–84.

Wang, Y. (2005). On cognitive properties of human factors in engineering. *Theoretical and Empirical Software Engineering Research Centre.* Calgary: University Press.

Waring, A.E. and Glendon, A.I. (1998). *Managing Risk: Critical Issue for Survival and Success into the 21st Century.* Boston: Cengage Learning EMEA.

Wideman, R. (1998). Project and Program Risk Management: A Guide to Managing Project Risks and Opportunities. Newtown Square, PA: Project Management Institute.

Williams, R.C., Pandelios, G.J., and Behrens, S.G. (1999). Software Risk Evaluation Method Description (version 2). *CMU/SEI-99-TR-029, ESC-TR-99-029.* Pittsburgh: Software Engineering Institute Press.

Williamson, J. (1994). Experiences with an independent risk assessment team. In *Third SEI Conference on Software Risk Management*, Pittsburgh.

Yacoub, S.M. and Ammar, H.H. (2002). A methodology for architecture-level reliability risk analysis. *IEEE Transactions on Software Engineering*, 28: 529–547.

Yanyan, Z. and Renzuo, X. (2008). The basic research of human factor analysis based on knowledge in software engineering. In *International Conference on Computer Science and Software Engineering.* Los Alamitos, CA: IEEE Computer Society Press.

Young, H., Juhua, C., Huang, J., Liu, M., and Xie, K. (2007). Analyzing software system quality risk using Bayesian belief network. In *GRC '07: Proceedings of the 2007 IEEE International Conference on Granular Computing.* Los Alamitos, CA: IEEE Computer Society Press.

Young, H., Juhua, C., Zhenbang, R., Liu, M., and Kang, X. (2006). A neural networks approach for software risk analysis. In *ICDMW '06: Proceedings of the Sixth IEEE International Conference on Data Mining—Workshops*, Los Alamitos, CA: IEEE Computer Society Press.

Chapter 3

Software Engineering, Team, and Responsibilities

Our research is devoted to the software engineering world and therefore we give a short explanation of its main parts in this chapter. We examine the software process, product, and resources and try to distinguish the importance of the human performance within. Later we focus on the software team roles and their responsibilities and describe them in order to understand the importance and complexity of human beings in the software engineering process. The chapter ends with summarizing the personal characteristics of the different roles, which is the input for the further research in the next chapter.

3.1 Software Engineering Background

3.1.1 Software Engineering Characterization

Basically, software engineering can be defined with the following classical IEEE (1990) description; that is: "Software engineering is the application of a systematic, disciplined, quantifiable approach to the development, operation, and maintenance of software; that is, the application of engineering to software." This definition leads us to the simple visualization of the software engineering components in Figure 3.1 (based on Dumke (2003), Laplante (2011), Pfleeger (1998), Dumke, Mencke, and Wille (2010), and Georgieva et al. (2010c)).

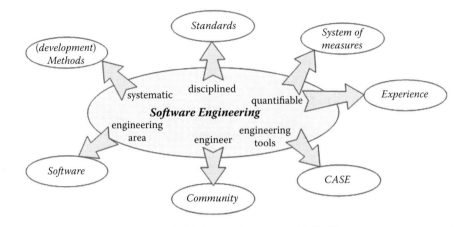

Figure 3.1   Basic characteristics of software engineering.

Considering this characterization, we can formulate in the following simple structure of the software engineering *SE* area as a system in general (see Skyttner (2005) and Wang and King (2000)):

$$SE = (M_{SE}, R_{SE}) = (\{SE\text{-}Methods, CASE, SE\text{-}SystemOfMeasures^*, SE\text{-}Standards,$$

$$SE\text{-}SoftwareSystems, SE\text{-}Experience, SE\text{-}Communities\}, R_{SE)} \qquad (3.1)$$

where R_{SE} represents the set of all relations between the elements of the set M_{SE} where the elements of M_{SE} mean in detail:

SE-Methods: "Structured approaches to software development, which include system models, notations, rules, design advice and process guidance" (Sommerville, 2008).

CASE (computer-aided software engineering): "Software systems which are intended to provide automated support for software process activities" (Sommerville, 2008).

SE-SystemOfMeasures: A set of metrics and measures in order to measure and evaluate all aspects, components, and methodologies of the software engineering areas (see Zuse (1998), Dumke et al. (2009a), Georgieva et al. (2009e), and Dumke et al. (2009b, 2008)).

SE-Standards: The software engineering standards are a set of rules and principles as a foundation of control and examination of components achieving special defined characteristics certified by a consortium such as IEEE or ISO (see Dumke (2003) and Georgieva, Neumann, and Dumke (2008)).

---

* We use this kind of notification adapted from the OO area for more mnemonics.

SE-SoftwareSystems: A software system, respectively, a software product "is a purposeful collection of interrelated components that work together to achieve some objectives" and requirements. It includes the computer programs and the associated documentation (Sommerville, 2008).

SE-Experience: The experience summarizes the general aspects of laws, principles, criteria, methodologies, and theories in software engineering in the different forms of aggregation, correlation, interpretation, and conclusion based on a context-dependent interpretation (see Basili (2007), Davis (1995), Endres and Rombach (2003), and Kandt (2006)).

SE-Communities: The software engineering community involves people, organizations, events, and initiatives in which interpersonal relationships are an integral part, considering aspects or paradigms in software engineering (see Dumke and Abran (2011a) and Figallo (1998)).

Based on (3.1) we can formulate the following examples, components, and elements of R_{SE}:

■ The process of producing new or extended experience in software engineering:

$$r_{SE}^{(SE\text{-}Experience)} \in R_{SE}: SE\text{-}Methods \times CASE \times SE\text{-}SoftwareSystems$$

$$\rightarrow SE\text{-}Experience \qquad (3.2)$$

■ The general activities in order to define new standards in the SE:

$$r_{SE}^{(SE\text{-}Standards)} \in R_{SE}: SE\text{-}Methods \times SE\text{-}SoftwareSystems \times SE\text{-}Communities$$

$$\rightarrow SE\text{-}Standards \qquad (3.3)$$

■ The process of extension of the set of measures during software development, maintenance, or application:

$$r_{SE}^{(SystemOfMeasures)} \in R_{SE}: SE\text{-}Methods \times SE\text{-}SoftwareSystems$$

$$\times systemOfMeasures \rightarrow systemOfMeasures \qquad (3.4)$$

■ The process of risk management:

$$r_{SE}^{(RiskManagement)} \in R_{SE}: SE\text{-}RiskAssessment \times SE\text{-}RiskControl$$

$$\rightarrow RiskManagement \qquad (3.5)$$

■ The characterization of the software quality personnel:

$$r_{SE}^{(RiskCommunity)} \in R_{SE}: \text{SE-Communities} \times \text{systemOfRiskMeasures}$$

$$\times \text{RiskManagement} \to \text{RiskMeasurementStaff} \tag{3.6}$$

3.1.2 Software Product

The main intention of software engineering is to create or produce high-quality software products for the customers. A software system or software product *SP* was developed by the software process as development *SD* shown in Figure 3.2 and is based on the supporting resources *SR*.

We first define the software product as a (software) system:

$$SP = (M_{SP}, R_{SP}) = (\{programs, documentations, data\}, R_{SP}) \tag{3.7}$$

where the three sets are divided into the following elements or components (without achieving completeness):

$$programs \subseteq \{sourceCode, objectCode, template, macro, library, \tag{3.8}$$

$$script, plugIn, setup, demo\}$$

$$documentations = \{userManual, referenceManual, developmentDocumentation\}$$

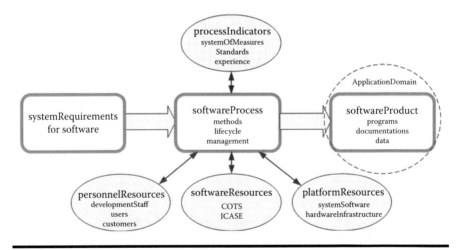

Figure 3.2 General software development process.

$$data = \{singleData, eventData, sensorData, dataBases,$$

$$dataWarehouses, dataInfrastructures, knowledge\}$$

$$dataRisks = \{missing, incorrect, incomplete, not synchronized, misleading\}$$

and R_{SP} describes the set of relations over the *SP* elements. The given subsets could be described in the following:

$$developmentDocumentation = \{documentationElements\} = \qquad (3.9)$$

$$\{productRequirements, productSpecification, productDesign,$$

$$implementationDescription\}$$

$$documentationElements \subseteq \{model, chart, architecture, diagram,$$

$$estimation, review, audit, verificationScript, testCase,$$

$$testScript, pseudoCode, extensionDescription, qualityReport\}$$

$$productRequirements = systemRequirement \subseteq \{functionalRequirements,$$

$$qualityRequirements, platformRequirements, processRequirements\}$$

$$functionalRequirements \subseteq \{execution, mapping, information,$$

$$construction, controlling, communication, learning, resolution,$$

$$cooperation, coordination\}^{*}$$

$$qualityRequirements \subseteq \{functionality, reliability, efficiency, usability,$$

$$maintainability, portability\}^{\dagger}$$

---

[*] The kind of functional requirements depends on the kind of software system that we characterize.
[†] This set of quality characteristics is related to the ISO 9126 product quality standard.

platformRequirements ⊆ {*systemSoftware, hardwareComponent,*

hardwareInfrastructure, peripheralDevice, host}

processRequirements ⊆ {*developmentMethod, resources, cost, timeline,*

milestone, criticalPath, developmentManagement, lifecycleModel}

A simplified view of the software product aspects during development and application that must be defined through the product requirements can be seen in Figure 3.3. This visualization could help us with further investigations of the detailed components and aspects of the software product. Here, we can define a software product as a software system as the following (see Chung et al. (2000), Dumke (2011), Laplante (2011), Maciaszek (2001), Mikkelsen and Phirego (1997), and Neumann (2013)).

SE-SoftwareSystems ⊆ {*informationSystem, constructionSystem,*   (3.10)

embeddedSystem, communicationSystem, distributedSystem,

knowledgeBasedSystem}

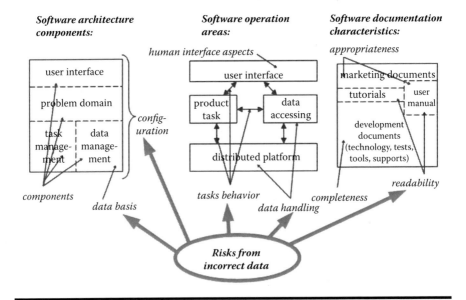

Figure 3.3 Simplified visualization of product characteristics and risk involvements.

Some of the examples of the relations in R_{SP} could be derived as:

■ The software testing process on some software product components, examples (Farooq et al., 2008a,b; Fisher 2007):

$$r_{SP}^{(test)} \in R_{SP}: sourceCode \times verificationScript \times testScript \qquad (3.11)$$

$$\rightarrow testDescription$$

■ The elements of the product design considering the necessary components:

$$r_{SP}^{(design)} \in R_{SP}: architecture \times review \times template \times library \qquad (3.12)$$

$$\times pseudoCode \rightarrow productDesign$$

■ A special kind of a programming technique could be defined as the following:

$$r_{SP}^{(programmingTechnique)} \in R_{SP}: template \times macro \rightarrow sourceCode \qquad (3.13)$$

■ The software testing process on some software product components:

$$r_{SP}^{(implementation)} \in R_{SP}: coding \times unitTest \times integrationTest \qquad (3.14)$$

$$\rightarrow implementation$$

■ The process of risk identification:

$$r_{SP}^{(riskIdentification)} \in R_{SP}: dataRisks \times applicationAnalysis \qquad (3.15)$$

$$\rightarrow riskIdentification$$

Figure 3.4 summarizes the components and elements of the software product described in the text above.

3.1.3 Software Development Process

Now, we define the software development process *SD* itself (note that the concrete software process is known as the *software project*). Some special software enterprise applications can be seen in Neumann, Georgieva, and Dumke (2010b), Asfoura et al. (2011), and Dumke and Abran (2011a). To begin we show the general processt

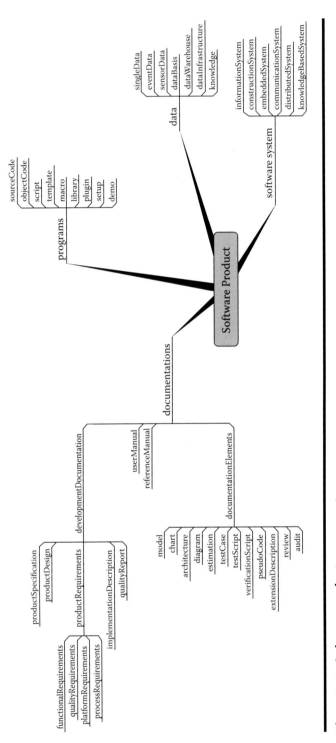

Figure 3.4 Software product components.

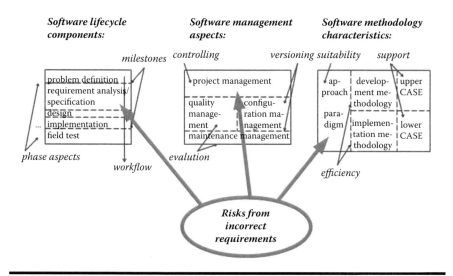

Figure 3.5 Simplified visualization of the process characteristics and risk involvements.

aspects in Figure 3.5. Thus we can define the software process *SD* as the following (including the essential details of every development component; Keyes (2003)):

$$SD = (M_{SD}, R_{SD}) = (\{developmentMethods, lifecycle, softwareManagement\} \quad (3.16)$$

$$\cup\ M_{SR}, R_{SD})$$

$$developmentMethods \subseteq \{formalMethods, informalMethods\} = SE\text{-}Methods$$

$$formalMethods \in \{CSP, LOTOS, SDL, VDM, Z\}$$

We can see a plenty of "classical" informal development methods (Günther et al., 2011) as structured/procedural methods *SAM*. Actually, the informal methods are based on the objects *OOSE* (Sommerville, 2008), the components *CBSE* (Laplante, 2011), the agents *AOSE* (Dumke, Mencke, and Wille, 2010), or the services *SOSE* (Neumann et al., 2011a,b). Therefore, we can define:

$$informalMethods \in \{SAM, OOSE, CBSE, AOSE, SOSE\} \quad (3.17)$$

and especially

$$SAM \in \{SA/SD, Jackson, Warnier, HIPO\}$$

$$OOSE \in \{UML, OMT, OOD, RDD, Fusion, HOOD, OOSA\}$$

$$CBSE \in \{DCOM, EJB, CURE, B\text{-}COTS, SanFrancisco\}$$

$$AOSE \in \{AAII, AUML, DESIRE, MAS, MaSE, MASSIVE, SODA\}$$

$$SOSE \in \{SOA, GRID, WebServices, Cloud\}$$

The life-cycle aspects could be explained by the following descriptions:

$$lifecycle = \{lifecyclePhase, lifecycleModel\} \tag{3.18}$$

$$lifecyclePhase \in \{problemDefinition,^* requirementAnalysis,$$

$$specification, design, implementation, acceptanceTest, delivering\}$$

$$lifecycleModel \in \{waterfallModel, Vmodel, prototyping,$$

$$evolutionaryDevelopment, incrementalDevelopment,$$

$$spiralModel, \dots , winWinModel\}$$

$$requirementsRisks = \{incomplete, unrealistic, subjective, dependability,$$

$$dynamic, incompatible, not\ measurable\}$$

Finally, the software management component of the M_{SD} could be described in the following manner:

$$softwareManagement = developmentManagement \tag{3.19}$$

$$\subseteq \{projectManagement, qualityManagement,$$

$$configurationManagement, riskManagement\}$$

Note that the software development process (Dumke et al., 2009c) could be dependent or addressed to a special kind of software system. Hence, we can make the following characterization:

$$SD_{informationSystem} \neq SD_{embeddedSystem} \neq SD_{distributedSystem} \tag{3.20}$$

$$\neq SD_{knowledgeBased\ System}$$

---

* The problem definition is a verbal form of the defined system or product requirements.

■ The process of risk management on a particular product (Boehm, 1991):

$$r_{SP}^{(riskManagement)} \in R_{SP}: riskIdentification \times riskAnalysis \qquad (3.21)$$

$$\times riskPrioritization \times riskMgmtPlanning \times riskResolution$$

$$\times riskMonitoring \rightarrow riskManagement$$

Furthermore, some examples of the relations in R_{SD} could be derived in the following way:

■ The process of building an appropriate life-cycle model:

$$r_{SD}^{(lifecycle)} \in R_{SD}: lifecyclePhase_{i_1} \times \dots \times lifecyclePhase_{i_n} \qquad (3.22)$$

$$\rightarrow lifecycleModel$$

The defining of software development based on the waterfall model:

$$r_{SD}^{(waterfallRisks)} \in R_{SD}: problemDefinition \times specification \times design \qquad (3.23)$$

$$\times implementation \times acceptanceTest \times riskManagement$$

$$\rightarrow waterfallModel$$

■ The defining of software development based on the V-model:

$$r_{SD}^{(VmodelRisks)} \in R_{SD}: (problemDefinition, softwareApplication, \qquad (3.24)$$

$$riskManagement) \times (specification, acceptanceTest,$$

$$riskManagement) \times (design, integrationTest, riskManagement)$$

$$\times (coding, unitTest, riskManagement) \rightarrow Vmodel$$

The characterization of the tool-based software development based on UML:

$$r_{SD}^{(UMLdev)} \in R_{SD}: UML \times developmentEnvironment_{UML} \qquad (3.25)$$

$$\times systemOfMeasures_{UML} \times experience_{UML} \times standard_{UML}$$

$$\rightarrow developmentInfrastructure_{UML}$$

Finally, the components and aspects of the software engineering process are shown in Figure 3.6.

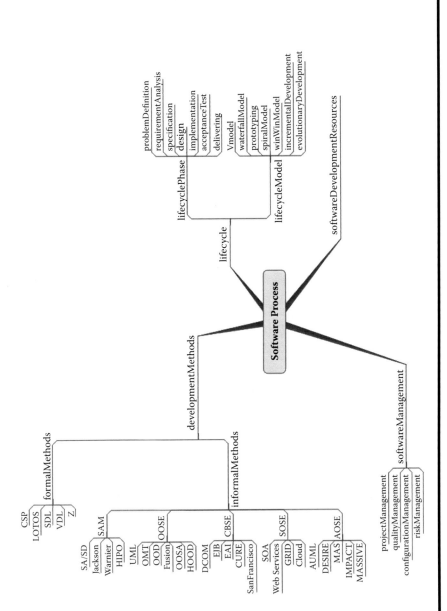

Figure 3.6   Software engineering process components.

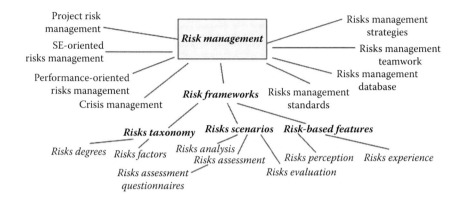

Figure 3.7   Risk management components.

The *Risk Management* components that are an unavoidable part of the software process are shown in Figure 3.7. We go into some more detail about the project risk management, because as we have already said: the concrete software process is known as the software project. The software project risks as a part of the development process can be divided into different groups of risks, as follows (see Gaulke (2002)):

Business Focus Group Risks: Here the risks are grouped that are connected with the weak points in the matching between the project and the business goals and requirements of the company and also the external risks. The risk of weak management from the business IT project is the problem that some specific parts of the project may not have enough resources and therefore won't be able to be correctly developed.

Stability of the Organization Risks: Changes in the company organization can be critical for the project. This could mean a change in resources or even closure of the project. The restructuring of an organization because of external or internal circumstances, for example, a new business field or efficient control, means extreme danger for the IT project. The instability and the changes can have a critical influence on employees' motivation and this can be the point that brings a project to the end.

Dynamic of the Marketplace Risks: The risk in the dynamic marketplace is that in a case of change it could be that the project is no longer relevant or should be changed entirely. This leads to an extreme loss of money and time and therefore it is very important to start with a rich analysis of the marketplace in order to be sure that the IT project will be successful.

Criticality of the IT-System Risks: The risk of implementing systems with high criticality is that the expected security, performance, or some feature could fail. The criticality of a system can be connected with the special function that should be fulfilled, for example, a bank transfer, military communication, or also with business risk.

Special Risks: These are external and unexpected for project factors that have a negative influence over them. For example, financial risks, even liquidity crises in the marketplace, or reputation loss (loss of personnel) can lead to extremely heavy problems for a project.

The software project/process risk can be expressed in the following way:

$$r_{SD}^{(processRisk)} \in R_{SD} = businessFocus \times organizationStability \times \qquad (3.26)$$

$$marketDynamic \times systemCriticality \times specialRisk \to processRisks$$

3.1.4 Software Development Resources

In order to develop a software product we need resources such as the developer (software team), CASE tools, and variants of hardware. Therefore, we define the software development resources *SR* as:

$$SR = (M_{SR}, R_{SR}) = (\{personnelResources, softwareResources, \qquad (3.27)$$

$$platformResources\}, R_{SR})$$

where the software resources play a dual role in software development: as part of the final system (such as COTS or software components) and as development support (such as CASE or integrated CASE as ICASE). Figure 3.8 shows a possible distribution of the different characteristics addressed to the main parts of the software development resources.

We continue our definition as the following:

$$softwareResources = \{COTS\} \cup \{ICASE\} \qquad (3.28)$$

$$\text{and } ICASE = CASE \cup CARE \cup CAME$$

where *CARE* stands for computer-aided re-engineering and *CAME* means computer-assisted measurement and evaluation tools. Considering the WWW aspects and possibilities for software development infrastructure based on CASE environments, the set of CASE tools could be divided as:

$$CASE_{infrastructure} = \{(\{UpperCASE\} \cup \{LowerCASE\})_{environment}\} \qquad (3.29)$$

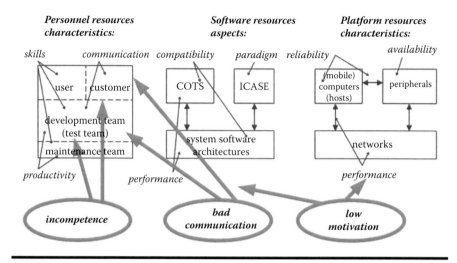

Figure 3.8 Simplified visualization of resource characteristics and risk involvement.

Furthermore, we can define

$$UpperCASE = \{modelingTool, searchTool, documentationTool, diagramTool,$$

$$simulationTool, benchmarkingTool, communicationTool\}$$

$$LowerCASE = \{assetLibrary, programmingEnvironment, compiler,$$

$$programGenerator, debugger, analysisTool, configurationTool\}$$

Especially, we can describe the following types of software development resources as:

$$personnelResources = person_{IT} \cup person_{customer} \cup person_{applicatiuon} \qquad (3.30)$$

$$person_{IT} = \{analyst, designer, developer, acquisitor, reviewer,$$

$$programmer, tester, administrator, qualityEngineer, project leader,$$

$$systemProgrammer, chiefProgrammer\}$$

$$person_{customer} = \{stakeholder, manager, acquisitor\}$$

$$person_{application} = \{user, operator, client, consumer\}$$

$$personnelRisks = HRF_{IT}$$

$$softwareResourcesRisks = \{notAvailability, highCosts, incomplete,$$

$$incompatible, veryComplex, difficultyByChanges\}$$

$$hardwareResourcesRisks = \{lowPerformance, deadlocks, highCosts, incompatibility\}$$

and

$$SE\text{-}Communities = \{personnelResources, ITadministration, \qquad (3.31)$$

$$softwareUser, computerSociety\}$$

Accordingly, some of the examples of the relations in R_{SR} could be derived in the following manner:

■ The process of building an appropriate development environment:

$$r_{SR}^{(devEnv)} \in R_{SR}: ICASE \times platformResources \qquad (3.32)$$

$$\rightarrow developmentEnvironment$$

■ The defining of software developer teams for agile development, for example:

$$r_{SR}^{(agile)} \in R_{SR}: programmer \times programmer \times customer \qquad (3.33)$$

$$\rightarrow agileDevelopmentTeam$$

■ The assessment of potential risks based on personnel resources (see (2.4)):

$$r_{SR}^{(personnelRisks)} \in R_{SR}: HF_{IT} \times processInvolvement \times role_{IT} \rightarrow personnelRisks$$

■ The assessment of human performance.

We have adopted the definition of productivity (in our case synonymous with performance), "Productivity is defined as output over input" (Ebert and Dumke, 2007), where the output can be

1. Counted function points, developed components, written documents, or artifacts or delivered source statements
2. Quality or complexity aspects for point 1
3. Certain skills, pressure, tool support, computing platform, frequency of requirements changes such as environmental setting
4. Aspects of the application-domain and chosen technology

And, "input is the way you create this output. It relates how well you are working" (Ebert and Dumke, 2007). Examples are

1. The productivity as adjusted size/effort, where adjusted size is based on the history and constraints estimation and expresses productivity as comparing estimated to the actual effort.
2. Furthermore, the productivity can be measured as a dimensionless indicator using any method or tools such as qsm slim, cocomo, or knowledge-plan.
3. Finally, productivity can be executed by earned value divided by actual effort.

Having these explanations in our performance evaluation we decided to use three different components based on the personnel, supervisor, and colleague assessment based on the observed input–output dependence.

$$humanPerformance = \{HF_{IT}, softwareDevelopmentProcess\} \qquad (3.34)$$

$$humanPerformanceEvaluation = \{personalAssessment,$$

$$supervisorAssessment, colleagueAssessment\}$$

$$r_{SR}^{(personalAssessment)} \in R_{SR}: person_{IT} \times assessment \times workingProcess$$

$$\rightarrow personalAssessment$$

$$r_{SR}^{(supervisorAssessment)} \in R_{SR}: person_{IT} \times supervisor \times assessment$$

$$\times workingProcess \rightarrow supervisorAssessment$$

$$r_{SR}^{(colleagueAssessment)} \in R_{SR}: person_{IT} \times colleague \times assessment$$

$$\times workingProcess \rightarrow colleagueAssessment$$

Now we summarize the different elements and components of the resources as the basics of software development and maintenance in Figure 3.9.

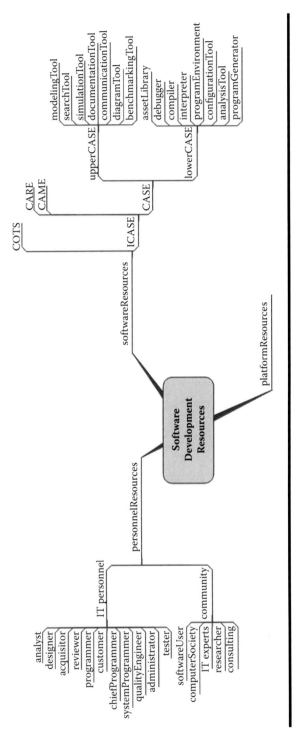

Figure 3.9 Software development resource components.

3.1.5 Software Product Use

After software development, the software product goes in two directions: first (the original sense of a software product) to the software application *SA*, second to the software maintenance *SM*. We define the different aspects:

$$SA = (M_{SA}, R_{SA}) = (\{applicationTasks, applicationResources, \quad (3.35)$$

$$applicationDomain\} \cup M_{SP}, R_{SA})$$

where

applicationTask ∈ {*delivering, operation, migration, conversion, replacement*}
applicationResources = {*applicationPlatform, applicationPersonnel,*
    applicationDocuments}
applicationPersonnel ⊆ {*customer, user, operator, administrator, consultant, trainer*}
applicationDomain ⊆ {*organizationalDocument, law, contract, directive,*
    rightDocument}
applicationDocument ⊆ {*userManual, trainingGuideline, acquisitionPlan,*
    setup, damageDocument, troubleReport}

The risks connected with the Personnel application in the process of use of the software product can be summarized as:

$$risksInUse \subseteq \{lackOfExperience, lackOfResources, strongDependencies, \quad (3.36)$$

$$lackOfUnderstanding, notFlexibleOrganization, lackOfGoalValidation,$$

$$highSystemComplexity, lackOfData, badInformationStructure\}$$

Based on these definitions, some of the examples of the relations in R_{SA} could be derived in the following manner:

■ The process of the first introduction of the software product as delivery:

$$r_{SA}^{(delivery)} \in R_{SA}: SP \times trainer \times applicationPersonnel \quad (3.37)$$

$$\times applicationPlatform \rightarrow delivery$$

■ The defining of software migration based on essential requirements:

$$r_{SA}^{(migration)} \in R_{SA}: productExtension \times SP \times migrationPersonnel \quad (3.38)$$

$$\rightarrow migration$$

■ The characterization of software operation:

$$r_{SA}^{(operation)} \in R_{SA}: applicationPersonnel \times applicationPlatform \qquad (3.39)$$

$$\times SP \times user \rightarrow operation$$

■ The defining of the software operation outsourcing by external IT contractors:

$$r_{SA}^{(outsourcing)} \in R_{SA}: systemInputs \times contractors \times systemFeedback \qquad (3.40)$$

$$\rightarrow outsourcing$$

The source of risks for the software application can be summarized from these relations (Georgieva, Farooq, and Dumke, 2009f) in the following manner:

$$r_{SA}^{(applicationRisk)} \in R_{SA}: deliveryRisk \times migrationRisk \times operationRisk \qquad (3.41)$$

$$\times outsourcingRisk \rightarrow applicationRisk$$

We can see all parts of the software product application in Figure 3.10.

3.1.6 Software Maintenance

The different aspects and characteristics of software maintenance are summarized by the following formulas:

$$SM = (M_{SM}, R_{SM}) = (\{maintenanceTasks, maintenanceResources\} \cup SP) \quad (3.42)$$

where
maintenanceTasks = {extension, adaptation, correction, improvement, prevention}
maintenanceResources = ICASE ∪ {maintenancePersonnel, maintenancePlatform}
maintenancePersonnel = {maintainer, analyst, developer, customer, user}

Accordingly, some of the examples of the relations in R_{SM} could be derived as follows:

■ The process of building the extension activity of the maintenance:

$$r_{SM}^{(extension)} \in R_{SM}: SP \times functionalRequirements \rightarrow SP^{(extended)} \qquad (3.43)$$

■ The defining of software correction:

$$r_{SM}^{(correction)} \in R_{SM}: SP \times qualityRequirements \rightarrow SP^{(corrected)}$$

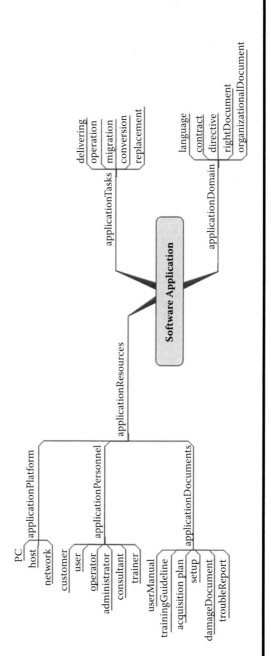

Figure 3.10 Software product applications components.

- The defining of software adaptation:

$$r_{SM}^{(adaptation)} \in R_{SM} : SP \times platformRequirements \rightarrow SP^{(adapted)}$$

- The defining of software improvement:

$$r_{SM}^{(perform)} \in R_{SM} : SP \times performanceRequirements \rightarrow SP^{(improved)}$$

- The defining of software prevention:

$$r_{SM}^{(prevention)} \in R_{SM} : SP \times preventionRequirements \rightarrow SP^{(modified)}$$

- The characterization of a special kind of software maintenance as remote maintenance:

$$r_{SM}^{(remoteMaint)} \in R_{SM} : ICASE_{remote} \times maintenanceTasks \qquad (3.44)$$

$$\times\, maintenancePersonnel \rightarrow remoteMaintenance$$

- The risk in software maintenance can be summarized as:

$$r_{SM}^{(maintenanceRisk)} \in R_{SM}: extensionRisk \times correctionRisk \qquad (3.45)$$

$$\times\, adaptationRisk \times improvementRisk \times preventionRisk$$

$$\times\, remoteMaintRisk \rightarrow maintenanceRisk$$

We can see the software maintenance components in Figure 3.11. Finally, the software engineering background in our human factor considerations can be characterized as shown in Figure 3.12.

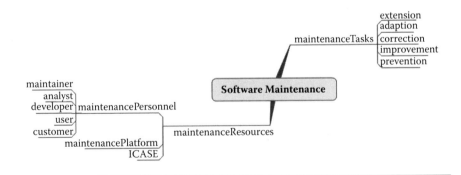

Figure 3.11   Software maintenance components.

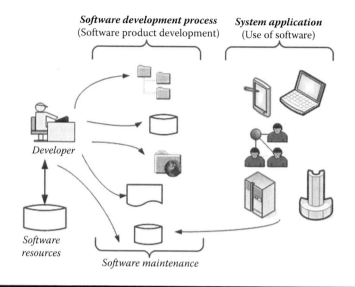

Figure 3.12   Software engineering characteristics.

3.2 Software Team

At the core of every software development process are the people. If software development is considered as a project, then the people either build the project successfully or not. Independent of the methodology chosen for a particular project, a group of people called the project team is involved in it. The generalized roles involved in the software development process are provided in Figure 3.13 (see Kurble (2008), Laporte et al. (2007), and Bogue (2005)).

In order to achieve the project goals, the project team has to be organized in a specific manner, called the project team structure. This structure is primarily a function of project resource ownership and project manager authority. The project manager's responsibility for achieving project performance objectives must be supported by an appropriate level of authority to control project resource utilization, assign and manage project task performance, and enforce accountability of the project team members. Otherwise, the designated project leader is merely serving as a project coordinator or project report administrator and cannot reasonably be held responsible for project outcomes.

The software development process is executed within the organization. Each organization has its own organizational structure. Therefore the project team structure depends on the organizational structure of the company in which the software is developed. Availability of resources, manager's authority, budget control, and many more factors depend on the organization of the company. Therefore, the possible organizational structures are discussed in detail and the most appropriate organizational structure is specified for software development.

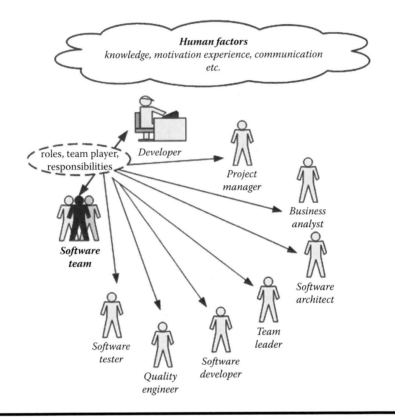

Figure 3.13 Considered team roles.

3.2.1 Organizational Structures in IT

An organizational structure is the "formal system of task and reporting relationships that controls, coordinates, and motivates employees so that they cooperate to achieve an organization's goals" (Kurble, 2008). There are three basic types of organizational structures (see Heldman (2009) and PMI (2008)):

■ Functional organization
■ Projectized organization
■ Matrix organization

3.2.1.1 Functional Organization

The functional organization, shown in Figure 3.14, is an organization structured according to functions such as analysis, design, implementation, testing, quality, and so on. Here software personnel are grouped by specialty; that is, people with

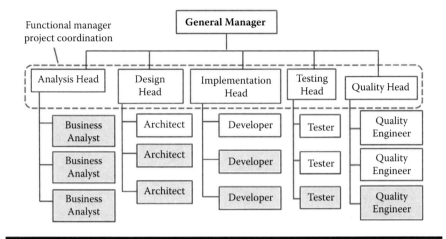

Figure 3.14 Functional organization. Gray boxes represent the people engaged in the same project. (Reprinted from PMI, *A Guide to the Project Management Body of Knowledge*® 4th ed. Newtown Square, PA: Project Management Institute, 2008. With permission.)

similar skills are placed in the same group. Each group has one head called the functional manager, and each employee has one clear superior (Heldman, 2009). Each group is managed independently and has a limited span of control (Kerzner, 2009).

Whenever a project has to be carried out in a functional organization, personnel from several functional areas work together. In this type of organization, a project manager is optional. Even if a project manager is assigned to a project, the project manager has little or no authority over project resources. Instead, the functional manager has complete authority over the project resources in a business unit.

The projects are typically undertaken in a divided approach (Heldman, 2009); that is, for a project in the design phase, the design department will work on its portion of the project and then hand it off to the implementation department to complete its part and so on. Here a chain of command is followed. For example, when questions about design arise in the implementation phase, they are passed up the organizational hierarchy to the department head, who consults with the head of the design department. The design department head then passes the answer back down the hierarchy to the implementation functional manager. In a real organization— in a multilevel hierarchy—the path up and down the organizational tree can be long and time consuming.

Although functional organizations have the advantage of being simple to understand with clear lines of command, they also have some disadvantages. The following are the advantages and disadvantages of a functional structure (adapted from Kerzner (2009)):

- Advantages:
  - Education and training of technical competency in specialized areas
  - Confidence among the personnel
  - Concentration on the functional objectives
  - Engaging of permanent and relevant objectives
  - Easy compatibility of internal objectives
  - Clear horizontal relations
  - Accurate specifications of roles and responsibilities
  - High efficiency based on standardization
  - Stability in team relationships
  - Clearly defined personnel careers
  - Easy learning organizational aspects
  - Efficient quality management and performance control
  - Efficiency in laboratory work
- Disadvantages:
  - Special views with a lack of wholeness
  - Problems in team integration and possible conflicts
  - Difficulty in motivation of project goals
  - Difficulty of concentration on main objectives
  - Problems in effectiveness between quality and timelines
  - All team members responsible for project objectives
  - Subordination of technical point of view
  - Difficulty in adaptation of objectives
  - Lack of communication of internal information
  - Problems of user transparency
  - Lack of personnel capabilities

3.2.1.2 Projectized Organization

Projectized organizations (Heldman, 2009) are almost the opposite of the functional ones. The idea behind them is to be loyal to the project manager and to organize the working process in the form of projects where all people are in project teams headed by a project manager to whom they report. Organizational resources are dedicated to projects and project work. Figure 3.15 depicts a typical projectized organization.

Project managers have absolute power over the project in this structure and report directly to the general manager. They are responsible for making decisions regarding the project, acquiring and assigning resources, and have the authority to choose and assign resources from other areas in the organization or from outside (Heldman, 2009). Project managers in all organizational structures are limited by triple constraints: project scope, schedule, and cost.

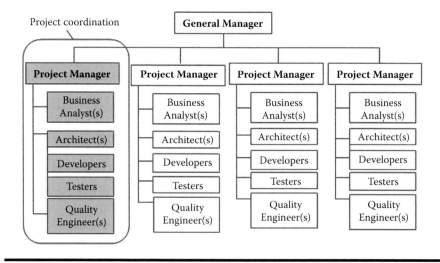

Figure 3.15 Projectized organization. Gray boxes represent staff engaged in project activities. (Reprinted from PMI, *A Guide to the Project Management Body of Knowledge*®, 4th ed. Newtown Square, PA: Project Management Institute, 2008. With permission.)

Project teams are formed from various specialists and are often colocated, which ensures good communication. Motivation for project activities is high inasmuch as the project is the main focus of the team. Even though it is a better organizational structure than the functional structure, it has some drawbacks. The following are the advantages and disadvantages of a projectized organization (adapted from Kerzner (2009)):

- Advantages:
  - Project managers are the leaders of the project.
  - Immediately tasks go to the project manager.
  - Communication efficiency.
  - Agreement of personnel on the project goals.
  - Short timelines are introduced.
  - Management of interface leads to decreased effort.
  - Common locations for team members.
- Disadvantages:
  - Necessity of more resources and effort.
  - Longer project binding of personnel as necessary.
  - Problems in technology perspectives because of lack of specialization.
  - High controlling of functional specialists would be necessary.
  - Difficulty interchanging between projects.
  - Problems in continuity of personnel careers.

3.2.1.3 Matrix Organization

The matrix organizational form is an attempt to combine the advantages of the previous two structures. Here the project team members continue within their own functional groups, reporting to their usual managers for the purposes of career development and performance evaluation (Heldman, 2009; Dinsmore, 2010). In matrix organizations project managers can focus on the project work and the project team can focus on the project objectives without being distracted by the functional department. The project manager manages the project and the employees report to one functional manager and to at least one project manager.

Functional managers are concerned with administrative duties and assign employees to the different projects and at the same time maintain the projects' quality (Kerzner, 2009). The functional managers have to ensure a unified technical base that allows an exchange of information on every project and an awareness of the latest technical accomplishments in the industry. On the other hand, the project manager has total responsibility and accountability for project success. Project managers are responsible for executing the project and assigning the tasks to the team members according to the project activities. Figure 3.16 depicts the matrix organizational structure. The gray color indicates the staff associated with a particular project manager.

Although the matrix organizational structure is more beneficial than the other two structures, it has the following pros and cons (adapted from Kerzner (2009)):

■ Advantages:
  – Total control of project resources and costs of the project manager.
  – Conflict management over projects would be done by the project manager.

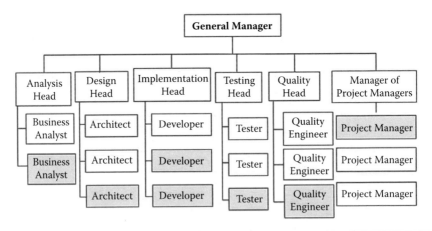

Figure 3.16 Matrix organizational structure. (Reprinted from PMI, *A Guide to the Project Management Body of Knowledge*®, 4th ed. Newtown Square, PA: Project Management Institute, 2008. With permission.)

- Efficiency of change management, conflict resolution, and project organization.
- Functional organization only supporting project objectives.
- All team members are involved in the organization after project completion.
- Key people can be shared over project changes.
- Hierarchical structure leads to minimizing conflicts.
- Efficiency in the relationships among time, cost, and performance.
- Responsibility and authority are shared.
- Efficiency leads to a strong technique and initiates more time for complex problem solving.

■ Disadvantages:
  - Work flow could be multidimensional.
  - Heterogeneous information flow.
  - Multidimensional reporting.
  - Change management involves priorities.
  - Management intentions can differ from project objectives.
  - Problems in conflict resolution.
  - Project organization includes separate operations.
  - Policies and procedures require more effort and time.
  - Functional managers work on their own priorities.
  - Functional and project organizations must be synchronized.
  - Roles of employees and managers can differ from the project goals.

In matrix organizations there exist different possibilities for the range of the organizational structure: we have weak, balanced, and strong matrices. In a strong matrix organization, the power is held by the project managers, who make the most important decisions. Of course at the other end of the organizational structure spectrum is the weak matrix, where the functional managers have all the power and the project managers are just coordinators or expeditors.

In the middle is the so-called balanced matrix organizational structure and it differentiates with the advantage of balancing between project managers and functional managers. "Each manager has responsibility for their parts of the project or organization, and employees get assigned to projects based on the needs of the project, not the strength or weakness of the manager's position" (Heldman, 2009). A balanced matrix organization is shown in Figure 3.17.

3.2.1.4 Organizational Structure of a Software Company

Having discussed the possibilities for organizational structures and their pros and cons we now observe the most suitable structure for a software company proposed in Kurble (2008): the strong matrix organization. The functional areas of a software company are analysis, design, coding, testing, and so on. These functional

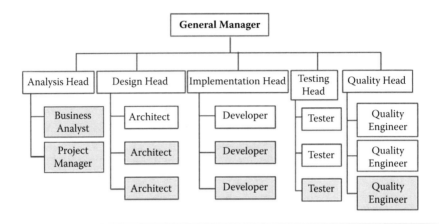

Figure 3.17 Balanced matrix organization. Gray boxes represent staff engaged in project activities. (Reprinted from PMI, *A Guide to the Project Management Body of Knowledge*®, 4th ed. Newtown Square, PA: Project Management Institute, 2008. With permission.)

areas can be arranged in a hierarchical manner and strong matrix organization is used in executing the software projects. Figure 3.18 shows the typical organizational structure of a software company. We have the following departments (see Kurble (2008)):

- *Project management*: Project manager, assistant project manager, and administrative personnel
- *Sales and marketing*: Not visualized in our case, but usually a part of a software firm
- *Analysis*: Requirements engineers or systems analysts performing requirements engineering
- *Design*: Software architects developing the architecture of the system; class, database, and GUI designers
- *Implementation*: Java; database and GUI programmers
- *Testing*: Staff performing module, integration, and system testing
- *Standards*: A quality officer or assistant to ensure that software engineering standards are met

These roles are the basic ones in the outcome of a software project. They are responsible for the success or failure of a project. Each role appears in some step of the software development life cycle and is assigned with particular responsibilities. In the next section, we discuss the responsibilities of each role.

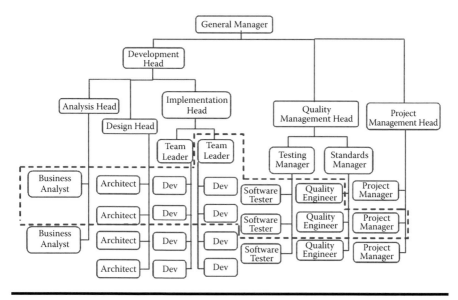

Figure 3.18 **Software development organizational structure. The people on the dotted line indicate staff engaged for a project; Dev is the developer. (Reprinted from PMI,** *A Guide to the Project Management Body of Knowledge*®, **4th ed. Newtown Square, PA: Project Management Institute, 2008. With permission.)**

3.2.2 Software Roles and Responsibilities

3.2.2.1 Project Manager

The purpose of the project manager's role is to undertake the phases, activities, and tasks within the specified time, cost, and quality constraints to deliver the required software project outcome and achieve total customer satisfaction. "A project manager's task is threefold: to supervise the team members, understand state of the art techniques, and make the software project successful" (Sodhi and Sodhi, 2001).

The project manager is responsible for controlling the software development work from the initial stages through to the end. This includes all software phases: planning, product design and development, implementation, administration, and setting and meeting of deadlines (Desmond, 2004). The project manager must have the following personal competencies and meet the following technical responsibilities for the successful outcome of the software project (adapted from Desmond (2004) and Sodhi and Sodhi (2001)):

■ Personal Competencies:
  – Communication and organizational experience are good.
  – Ability of team leadership and motivation.

- Team members respect each other.
- Team members initiate success.
- Personnel implicate structured discipline.
- Individual differences are considered and solved.
- Team members have effective communication.
- Conflicts resolved and motivate interpersonal issues.
- Personnel are open to new ideas.
- Project goals achieved in the established schedule and budget.
- Real priorities and deadlines are planned and achieved.
- Personnel realize continuous learning.
- Team has a structured roadmap in change management.
- Team members have motivation for improvements in all work aspects.

■ Technical Responsibilities:
- Profound knowledge of project planning and control techniques.
- Capability for detailed project plan milestones and changes.
- Efficiency in the use of personnel resources.
- Engagement for effective change management.
- Project challenges lead to practices for project improvement.
- Understanding of the business is given in a whole manner involving business plans.
- Software development life cycles are well known.
- Capabilities of quality assurance and control are given and applied.
- Problems can be identified early leading to corrective actions.
- Project objectives are reviewed or established in a hierarchy in order to identify higher-level project objectives.
- Project documentations and descriptions involve the specification of authority, responsibility, and relationships of the project manager and project staff.
- Implementation success evaluated leading to some changes.
- Characterization of different dependencies, risks, and control was planned and involved potential problems caused by actors and factors.
- Project documentation is the basis for common understanding of objectives, deliverables, organizational structure, and the like.
- Proposed project implementation plan was specified.
- Commitment of resources is verified with the head of department.
- Presentation for management as project review was documented.
- Inspection and acceptance procedures of the project plan are defined.
- Final project review or audit is conducted.
- Contracts are closed out and any outstanding disputes settled.
- All work orders and project accounts are to close.

3.2.2.2 Team Leader

The team leader acts as a middle-point between the software architect and the developers. Depending on the project size, the team leader is responsible for extracting details for the complete or part of the architecture and creating program specifications from which the developers work. Usually the team leaders are developers, grow up in the hierarchy in the role of supervisors, and guide the rest of the team during the software development process.

The team leader glues together the programs from the developers which form a part or the whole architecture created by the software architect. In order to lead a group of developers successfully, a team leader should possess the following personal competencies and fulfill the following technical responsibilities (adapted from Humphrey (2005) and Palmer (1998)).

- ■ Personal Competencies:
    - – Team members' responsibilities are clarified.
    - – Capability for plan and priority of work targets.
    - – Requirements performed to actionable outputs with timelines.
    - – Setting of objectives and timeframes was realistically specified.
    - – Engagement for team progress reviewing.
    - – Ability to be flexible and adaptable in an evolutionary development.
    - – Psychological and fear aspects are understood.
    - – Adaptation of new techniques, theories, methods, and so on.
    - – Communication skills are good.
    - – Ability to be an effective team member.
    - – Understanding the needs of internal and external customers.
    - – Engagement for team leading.
- ■ Technical Responsibilities:
    - – Team work planning and coordinating with the project manager.
    - – Business objectives are translated into actions.
    - – Control and motivate a good team climate.
    - – Create important issues for the project manager.
    - – Quality control assurance of the team's work.
    - – Mitigation of all identified risks.
    - – Keep assigning appropriate resources to the tasks and monitor the effectiveness of the team.
    - – Engagement that all team members have the required skills.
    - – Team supporting for finding: customer needs, specifications, design standards, techniques, and tools to support the task performance.
    - – Ability for planning meeting times, places, and agendas.

- Capability for organization of meetings for work coordinating with project management.
- Specification of status report activities against the program schedule.

3.2.2.3 Business Analyst

Requirements play a vital role in the software development process and improper requirements gathering may end with a software development process failure. It is the role of the business analyst to ensure that the requirements are captured and fully understood by the technical team before moving to implement them into solutions. The business analyst is the connection between the business part and the technical providers throughout the software development process. He or she defines and documents the requirements and this textual representation of the future system is an intermediate step between the software need and the solution design. This design process is divided into business need identification, scope definition, and elicitation (see Hass (2005) and Paul, Yeates, and Hindle (2006)).

The first step is a preanalysis, which is concerned with detailed research on the business needs, feasibility studies, solution trade-off analysis, and development of high-level business requirements. Then follows the scope definition, where are included all documents about the description of the initial requirements: the business case, project charter, or statement of work (Hass, 2005). And the last step—the requirements elicitation—is expressed in the clear description of all stakeholders', customers', and users' needs.

In order to capture the complete and accurate list of requirements the business analyst must possess a special skillset in the form of the following personal competencies and technical responsibilities (adapted from Hass (2005) and Hass (2007)):

- ■ Personal Competencies:
    - Qualified communication of technical concepts to customers
    - Engagement for conceptualization and creativity
    - Efficiency in management and personal organization
    - Ability to diagnose problems effectively
    - Knowledge for resolving issues and eliciting requirements
    - Capability for strategic and business thinking
    - Communication of business concepts to technical audiences effectively
    - Understanding of information in an accurate manner
    - Knowledge in written and verbal communication
    - Skills in effective presentations with relevant ideas
    - Ability in problem solving, negotiation, and decision making
    - Knowledge in management of customer relationship
    - Identifying fellow team members to make innovative contributions

- ■ Technical Responsibilities:
    - − Skills in system engineering concepts and principles
    - − Experience in and knowledge of complex modeling techniques
    - − Knowledge of the technical
    - − Profound skills in management
    - − Knowledge in techniques to plan and document requirements
    - − Engagement in risk assessment and management
    - − Skills in methods of cost–benefit analysis
    - − Documentation knowledge in application of standard notation and language understood by business users and other stakeholders
    - − Experience in business improvement and re-engineering
    - − Ability in business domain knowledge involving case development and business writing
    - − Motivation in order to understand customer needs including commitment negotiation
    - − Requirement analysis for business and organizational documents
    - − Capability to evaluate customer business needs involving strategic planning of information systems and technology goals
    - − Skills in identifying and understanding business problems and their impact on the proposed solution
    - − Ability to specify complex areas of project scope, objectives, added value or benefit expectations, using modern analysis and modeling techniques
    - − Engagement for customer cooperation during product delivery and testing of new services
    - − Knowledge in requirements risks involving their analysis and management
    - − Skills for root-cause analysis of essential problems during system development
    - − Knowledge in data analyses and studies (including research, case studies, and feasibility) as directed supporting potential projects
    - − Ability in measurement of new business solutions and comparison to planned goals

3.2.2.4 Software Architect

The software architect builds the software architecture. She transforms the requirements for the software into an architecture that describes the top-level structure and identifies the software components. Her responsibilities emerge from conceptualization and experimentation with alternative architectural approaches through developing models and documents to validating everything against the software requirements (Laporte et al., 2007). The software architect should possess the following personal competencies and technical responsibilities (adapted from Rozanski and Woods (2005)):

- Personal Competencies:
  - Ability for quick and effective decision making
  - Using a holistic view in understanding problems and situations
  - Skills for early problem identification and corrective action taking
  - Empowering team members
  - Knowledge in conflict resolution and interpersonal issues management
  - Ability in continuous development of people
  - Skills for effective team leading
  - Engagement for guiding or resolving performance-related problems and aspects
  - Experience in negotiating oneself
  - Capability to persuade others to one's point of view
  - Skills in effective presentations
  - Knowledge in information combining and summarizing to add clarity for others
  - Ability to develop relationships with potential as well as existing customers
  - Experience in specifying clear milestones and objectives
  - Skills in involving team members during scheduling
  - Knowledge of human strengths and limitations and their use in planning
  - Engagement for choosing the right priorities in conflict situations
  - Achieving efficient use of people and resources
  - Capability for life-long learning
  - Skills in change management over the team structure
  - Knowledge for improvements in all aspects of one's work
  - Ability for good listening in meetings and communication
  - Engagement for turning a hostile interaction into a positive outcome
- Technical Responsibilities (adapted from SEI (2011) and Laporte et al. (2007)):
  - Ability to analyze the reasons and consequences of actions
  - Should represent the best interests of the organization
  - Skills in performing high-level communication suitable for organization-wide or external consumption
  - Knowledge of a wide industrial area
  - Ability for dual viewpoint of activities, of both the developer and the customer
  - Capability for continuous review planning
  - Experience of a continuous benchmark of own work
  - Complete knowledge of the business domain
  - Skills in modern software life cycles
  - Engagement for assessment of project goals in relation to current strengths and weaknesses
  - Knowledge of software architecture modeling
  - Skills for deriving the software architecture requirements
  - Knowledge in identifying key design issues for successful development of the software

- Ability for generation of architecture alternatives and constraints
- Allocating the software requirements for architecture components and interfaces
- Experience in maintaining requirements traceability
- Capability for specification of software architecture by capturing the design results
- Identifying appropriate derived requirements that lead to effective and cost-efficient life-cycle phases
- Skills to document, approve, and track technological changes
- Knowledge in mitigation of risk strategies

3.2.2.5 Software Developer

From a technical point of view the developer is at the most basic level in the software hierarchy expected to be able to translate algorithms and technical specifications into functioning software code. He has to have good programming language skills and a logical way of thinking in order to transform the specification into particular functions. Of course this knowledge is only the basis for the other competencies that a good programmer must possess (adapted from Klipp (2009) and Humphrey (2000)).

- ■ Personal Competencies:
  - Introducing fresh perspective (an "unbiased point of view")
  - Engagement for generating new and imaginative ideas/approaches
  - Skills for specifying flexibility in aligning personal and team objectives
  - Capability of being a team player
  - Experience in tolerance of dissent and different viewpoints
  - Willingness in sharing of information and data
  - Engagement for sharing opinions and expressing self confidently
  - Skills in effective asking and answering questions
  - Ability to "give her best" for understanding and meeting customer requirements
  - Capability for effective time management
  - Knowledge for prioritizing project activities and procedures
  - Experience for growth based on failure, application for improvement
  - Ability to articulate own thoughts involving ideas of others
  - Skills in life-long learning
  - Engagement for adaptation of suggestions and new ideas
  - Taking full responsibility for own work
  - Knowledge in understanding new technologies, tools, and business processes
  - Ability for structured thinking and objectivity in analyzing complex activities

■ Technical Responsibilities:
  - Knowledge and skills of essential engineering processes
  - Ability to use relevant standards, templates, checklists, and defect prevention
  - Basic knowledge of relevant software methodologies and tools (programming techniques, operating systems, databases, testing, and measurement tools)
  - Knowledge of configuration management
  - Skills in achieving adequacy of test planning and testing
  - Ability to understand design specifications
  - Experience in accepting software only when it works correctly, is safe, and has been tested enough
  - Skills in identifying problems with the software and document or report to the client or user
  - Capability of full understanding of the software specifications
  - Engagement for a good documentation of the software
  - Ability in ensuring adequate testing, debugging, and review of software artifacts and their related documents
  - Experience in maintaining data integrity
  - Knowledge in agreements to all concerned parties avoiding conflicts of interest
  - Skills for taking responsibility for detecting, correcting, and reporting errors in software and the influenced components
  - Ability to integrate software units into the system
  - Knowledge in the testing of software elements, components, and systems

3.2.2.6 Software Tester

The job of the software tester is to perform testing of the application. "Software Testing is a process of verifying and validating that a software application or program meets the business and technical requirements and works as expected" (Bentley, Bank, and NC, 2004). The software tester works with the business analyst, the software architect, and the developer to convert the requirements and design documents into a set of testing cases and scripts and then report the problems. These testing cases and scripts can be used to verify that the system meets client needs.

The software tester is mainly responsible for creating test cases and scripts, executing them and facilitating or performing random testing of all components to ensure that there's not a random bug affecting the system. Following are the competencies and responsibilities so that she can fulfill the job with the expected accuracy (adapted from Dustin (2002), Perry (2006), and Watkins (2004)).

■ Personal Competencies:
  - Intention of creativity and openness for others' ideas
  - Skills in flexibility in tasking approaches

- Clear and open communication supporting team members
- Efficient response to customer requirements
- Willingness for learning and open-minded conversations
- Engagement for appreciating new suggestions
- Experience in discussion-relevant issues with colleagues
- Technical Responsibilities:
  - Excellent understanding of GUI design principles
  - Proficiency in software testing techniques
  - Knowledge in the business application area
  - Ability in various methods of testing techniques
  - Experience in working with testing tools
  - Skills in quality assurance for planning test strategy and test plans
  - Capability for specification of test requirements
  - Performing the functional application test
  - Engagement for performing test scripts and test cases
  - Specification, design, and implementation of test artifacts
  - Knowledge in archiving test artifacts and test data
  - Ability for executing test scripts and test results analysis
  - Engagement for documenting test results
  - Skills in identifying and documenting fault considerations
  - Efficient in performing retesting after fixed faults and errors
  - Engagement for archiving all testing documentation and artifacts

3.2.2.7 Quality Engineer

According to Kasse (2004), the quality engineer should be able to ensure visibility into the project's processes for the understanding of the management team and to determine if they are efficient and effective. Also this role is concerned with the necessary product quality, which has to satisfy customer, competitor, and organization or project quality goals. The quality engineer has to validate the developer's tests, to ensure that the work of several developers fits together and to follow different standardization methodologies. The main goal of this role is to ensure the awaited performance of a software solution. The following competencies and responsibilities have to be fulfilled for a successful quality engineer (adapted from Daughtrey (2001) and Kasse (2004)):

- Personal Competencies:
  - Capability for new ideas and flexible personality
  - Engagement for supporting team objectives
  - Skills in remaining positive and focused on opportunities
  - Experience in systematic and organized personality
  - Ability for tolerating others' opinions
  - Knowledge in effective time management and resource estimation

- Skills in project suggestions, new ideas, and others' opinion
- Capability for life-long learning
- Ability for cooperation from others
- Experience for understanding customer business
- Skills to convince the customer
- Capability to conceptualize and provide appropriate solutions
- Engagement for data presentation for decision making
- Knowledge in interacting with senior managers
- Experience to track progress according to plan and project goals
- Ability to interact with external vendors and consultants

■ Technical Responsibilities:
- Experience in monitoring quality goals and measurements
- Skills in milestone analysis and reports
- Knowledge in software engineering methodologies
- Ability to conduct project reviews and audits
- Skills and application of SWOT (strengths, weaknesses, opportunities, and threats) for business area
- Good understanding of software processes and related standards, practices, and procedures
- Knowledge in theory and practice of software measurement
- Skills in software life-cycle management and tools
- Experience in statistical techniques
- Engagement for problem solving and case-based reasoning
- Capability for resource planning
- Knowledge of track utilization of budgets
- Engagement for planning project initiatives
- Skills in identifying criticality levels of product components
- Experience in ad hoc process compliance management
- Ability in cooperation with appropriate customer representatives of quality requirements
- Knowledge in evaluating supplier's quality plan and resulting implementation
- Skills in organization's configuration management activities to ensure consistency of work products
- Engagement for software component and acceptance testing

3.3 Summary of Software Engineering and Software Roles

In the first part of the chapter the basics of software engineering were explained, which could be briefly summarized in the already mentioned formula:

$$SE = (M_{SE}, R_{SE}) = (\{SE\text{-}Methods, CASE, SE\text{-}SystemOfMeasures, SE\text{-}Standards,$$

$$SE\text{-}SoftwareSystems, SE\text{-}Experience, SE\text{-}Communities\}, R_{SE})$$

The overview of high-quality software products, as the main point of software engineering is expressed in the following: a software system/product *SP* is developed by the software process/development *SD* and is based on the supporting resources *SR*. As we have already seen, one of the major resources is the software personnel.

$$SR = (M_{SR}, R_{SR}) = (\{personnelResources, softwareResources,$$

$$platformResources\}, R_{SR})$$

Explanations of the software development process, use of the software product, and software maintenance make the software engineering overview complete and comprehensive. One of the major points is the software project risks as part of software development, where we clearly see the large number of risks connected with the personnel. For example:

- Lack of experience and specific knowledge
- A lot of outsourcing
- Lack of understanding of the business processes
- Inflexible organization structure
- Lack of goal validation

The different involvements of human risks in the software engineering area are summarized as the following. Considering software risk-based processes:

$$r_{SE}^{(RiskManagement)} \in R_{SE}: SE\text{-}RiskAssessment \times SE\text{-}RiskControl \quad (3.46)$$

$$\rightarrow RiskManagement$$

$$r_{SE}^{(RiskCommunity)} \in R_{SE}: SE\text{-}Communities \times systemOfRiskMeasures$$

$$\times RiskManagement \rightarrow RiskMeasurementStaff$$

$$r_{SP}^{(riskIdentification)} \in R_{SP}: dataRisks \times applicationAnalysis \rightarrow riskIdentification$$

$$r_{SP}^{(riskManagement)} \in R_{SP}: riskIdentification \times riskAnalysis \times riskPrioritization$$

$$\times \ riskMgmtPlanning \times riskResolution \times riskMonitoring$$

$$\rightarrow riskManagement$$

$r_{SD}^{(waterfallRisks)} \in R_{SD}$: *problemDefinition* × *specification* × *design* ×

$$implementation \times acceptanceTest \times riskManagement$$

$$\rightarrow waterfallModelRisk$$

$r_{SD}^{(VmodelRisks)} \in R_{SD}$: (*problemDefinition, softwareApplication,*

$$riskManagement) \times (specification, acceptanceTest,$$

$$riskManagement) \times (design, integrationTest, riskManagement)$$

$$\times (coding, unitTest, riskManagement) \rightarrow VmodelRisk$$

$r_{SD}^{(processRisk)} \in R_{SD} = businessFocus \times organizationStability \times specialRisk$

$$\times \ marketDynamic \times systemCriticality \rightarrow processRisks$$

$r_{SR}^{(personnelRisks)} \in R_{SR}$: $HF_{IT} \times processInvolvement \times role_{IT} \rightarrow personnelRisks$

$r_{SR}^{(personalAssessment)} \in R_{SR}$: $person_{IT} \times assessment \times workingProcess$

$$\rightarrow personalAssessment$$

$r_{SR}^{(supervisorAssessment)} \in R_{SR}$: $person_{IT} \times supervisor \times assessment$

$$\times \ workingProcess \rightarrow supervisorAssessment$$

$r_{SR}^{(colleagueAssessment)} \in R_{SR}$: $person_{IT} \times colleague \times assessment$

$$\times \ workingProcess \rightarrow colleagueAssessment$$

$r_{SA}^{(applicationRisk)} \in R_{SA}$: *deliveryRisk* × *migrationRisk* × *operationRisk* ×

$$outsourcingRisk \rightarrow applicationRisk$$

$$r_{SM}^{(maintenanceRisk)} \in R_{SM}: extensionRisk \times correctionRisk \times adaptationRisk \times$$

$$improvementRisk \times preventionRisk \times remoteMaintRisk$$

$$\rightarrow maintenanceRisk$$

and considering software process risks aspects

$$dataRisks = \{missing, incorrect, incomplete, not\ synchronized, misleading\} \quad (3.47)$$

$$requirementsRisks = \{incomplete, unrealistic, subjective, dependability,$$

$$dynamic, incompatible, not\ measurable\}$$

$$personnelRisks = HRF_{IT}$$

$$softwareResourcesRisks = \{notAvailability, highCosts, incomplete,$$

$$incompatible, veryComplex, difficultyByChanges\}$$

$$hardwareResourceslRisks = \{lowPerformance, deadlocks,$$

$$highCosts, incompatibility\}$$

$$humanPerformance = \{HF_{IP}, softwareDevelopmentProcess\}$$

$$humanPerformanceEvaluation = \{personalAssessment,$$

$$supervisorAssessment, colleagueAssessment\}$$

$$risksInUse \subseteq \{lackOfExperience, lackOfResources, strongDependencies,$$

$$lackOfUnderstanding, notFlexibleOrganization, lackOfGoalValidation,$$

$$highSystemComplexity, badInformationStructure, lackOfData\}$$

Having explained the basics of software engineering we moved forward to the software team and observed the seven basic roles that are met in every kind of software company. First we researched the possibilities for organizational structure in order to find the most common one—the matrix organization—and then we observed in detail the roles and their responsibilities. The general characterization of the considered personnel resources is defined as the following:

$$personnelResources = person_{IT} \cup person_{customer} \cup person_{applicatiuon} \qquad (3.48)$$

$$person_{IT} = \{analyst, designer, developer, acquisitor, reviewer,$$

$$programmer, tester, administrator, qualityEngineer,$$

$$projectLeader, systemProgrammer, chiefProgrammer\}$$

$$person_{customer} = \{stakeholder, manager, acquisitor\}$$

$$person_{application} = \{user, operator, client, consumer\}$$

Therefore, we summarize the chosen personnel, as seven basic roles of $person_{IT}$, and their competencies as the following:

$$HF_{ProjectManager} = \{communicative, managerial skills, disciplined, \qquad (3.49)$$

$$respects the others, resolves conflicts, open minded,$$

$$willing to develop himself, well-organized, goal-oriented,$$

$$seeks improvement\}$$

$$HF_{TeamLeader} = \{plan and prioritize the work, reviews team progress,$$

$$flexible and adaptable, communicative, an effective$$

$$advocate for the team, ability to lead and to impress\}$$

$$HF_{BusinessAnalyst} = \{communicative, conceptual thinking, creativity,$$

$$strategic and business thinking, problem solving,$$

$$negotiation and decision making, customer oriented, team player\}$$

$$HF_{SoftwareArchitect} = \{good decision maker, team player,$$

$$performance oriented, technical understanding that supports the team,$$

$$optimizing abilities, seeks new knowledge\}$$

$$HF_{SoftwareDeveloper} = \{creativity, team\ player,\ tolerant,$$

$$always\ in\ a\ learning\ mode,\ able\ to\ articulate\ own\ thoughts,$$

$$respects\ others'\ ideas,\ structured\ thinking\}$$

$$HF_{SoftwareTester} = \{creativity,\ flexibility,\ communicative,\ open\text{-}minded,$$

$$respects\ the\ others\}$$

$$HF_{QualityEngineer} = \{flexible,\ team\ oriented,\ positive\ attitude,$$

$$systematic\ and\ organized,\ respects\ the\ others,$$

$$seeking\ for\ knowledge,\ convincing\ ability,$$

$$ability\ to\ interact\ with\ managers\ and\ customers\}$$

These competencies are used in the FMEA analysis in the next chapter in order to discover those human factors that most influence the software engineering process and the corresponding failure modes.

References

Asfoura, E., Kassem, G., Georgieva, K., and Dumke, R. (2011). Developing approach for conception of appropriate business model for federated ERP systems. In *International Conference on E-Learning, E-Business, Enterprise Information Systems, & E-Government, WORLDCOMP (EEE)*. Las Vegas: CSREA Press.

Basili, V.R. et al. (2007). *Empirical Software Engineering*. LNCS 4336. Berlin: Springer.

Bentley, J., Bank, W., and NC, C. (2004). *Software Testing Fundamentals—Concepts, Roles, and Terminology*, viewed 3 February 2014, http://www2.sas.com/proceedings/sugi30/141-30.pdf

Boehm, B. (1991). Software risk management: Principles and practices. *IEEE Software*. 8(1): 32–41.

Bogue, R. (2005). *Breaking Down Software Development Roles*, viewed 19 January 2014, http://www.developer.com/mgmt/article.php/3515426/Anatomy-of-a-Software-Development-Role-Quality-Assurance.htm

Chung, L., Nixon, B.A., Yu, E., and Mylopoulos, J. (2000). *Non-Functional Requirements in Software Engineering*. Boston: Kluwer Academic.

Daughtrey, T. (2001). *Fundamental Concepts for the Software Quality Engineer*. Wisconsin: ASQ Quality Press.

Davis, A.M. (1995). *201 Principles of Software Development*, New York: McGraw-Hill.

Desmond, C.L. (2004). *Project Management for Telecommunications Managers.* Boston: Kluwer Academic.

Dinsmore, P.C. (2010). *The AMA Handbook of Project Management*, 3rd ed. New York: AMACOM.

Dumke, R. (2011). *Product Portfolios Management.* In P. A. Laplante, *Encyclopedia of Software Engineering*, Volume II. Boca Raton, FL: CRC Press, pp. 729–752.

Dumke, R. (2003). *Software Engineering—Eine Einführung für Informatiker und Ingenieure*, 4th ed. Wiesbaden: Vieweg.

Dumke, R. and Abran, A. (2011a). *COSMIC Function Points—Theory and Advanced Practices.* Boca Raton, FL: CRC Press.

Dumke, R., Mencke, S., and Wille, C. (2010). *Quality Assurance of Agent-Based and Self-Managed Systems.* Boca Raton, FL: CRC Press.

Dumke, R., Richter, K., Asfoura, E., and Georgieva, K. (2009c). Process improvement using causal networks. In *International Conference on Software Engineering Research & Practice (SERP) WORLDCOMP.* Las Vegas, pp. 451–457.

Dumke, R., Schmietendorf, A., Georgieva, K., and Yazbek, H. (2008). *Software Measurement for Agile Software Development in Computer Science and Technologies*, Volume VI/2. Los Alamitos, CA: IEEE Computer Society Press, pp. 42–47.

Dumke, R., Schmietendorf, A., Kunz, M., and Georgieva, K. (2009a). Software-Metriken für die agile Software-Entwicklung. In *Proceedings of the SQS.* Düsseldorf, Part III.

Dumke, R., Yazbek, H., Asfoura, E., and Georgieva, K. (2009b). A general model for measurement improvement. In *Proceedings of Software Process and Product Measurement, International Conferences IWSM and Mensura*, Amsterdam. Berlin: Springer, pp. 48–61.

Dustin, E. (2002). *Effective Software Testing: 50 Specific Ways to Improve Your Testing.* New York: Addison-Wesley.

Ebert, C. and Dumke, R. (2007). *Software Measurement—Establish, Extract, Evaluate, Execute.* Berlin: Springer.

Endres, A. and Rombach, D. (2003). *A Handbook of Software and System Engineering.* Munich: Pearson Education.

Farooq, A., Georgieva, K., and Dumke, R. (2008a). Challenges in evaluating SOA test processes. In *Proceedings of Software Process and Product Measurement. International Conferences IWSM, MetriKon, and Mensura.* Berlin: Springer, pp. 107–113.

Farooq, A., Georgieva, K., and Dumke, R. (2008b). A meta-measurement approach for software test processes. In *12th IEEE—International Multitopic Conference (IEEE INMIC)*, Karachi, Pakistan. pp. 333–338.

Figallo, C. (1998). *Hosting Web Communities.* New York: John Wiley & Sons.

Fisher, M.S. (2007). *Software Verification and Validation—An Engineering and Scientific Approach.* New York: Springer.

Gaulke, M. (2002). *Risikomanagement in IT-Projekten.* Oldenbourg: Oldenbourg Wissenschaftsverlag.

Georgieva, K., Dumke, R., Neumann R., and Farooq, A. (2009e). Software measurement modelling and improvement. In *Proceedings of the International Conference on Software Engineering Research & Practice (SERP), WORLDCOMP'09.* Los Alamitos, CA: IEEE Computer Society Press, pp. 396-402.

Georgieva, K., Farooq, A., and Dumke, R. (2009f). Design quality of aspect-oriented and object-oriented programs—An empirical comparison. In *Fourth International Conference on Software and Data Technologies (ICSOFT)*. Sofia, Bulgaria, pp. 287–290.

Georgieva, K., Neumann, R., and Dumke, R. (2008). Ontological Description of Software Quality Standards. *Computer Science and Technologies*, VI(2): 48–52.

Georgieva, K., Neumann, R., and Dumke, R. (2010c). Software quality standards and approaches from ontological point of view. In *Proceedings of the 7th Software Measurement European Forum (SMEF 2010)*. Rome. Milan: Libreria CLUP Soc. Coop. pp. 93–102,

Günther, D., Neumann, R., Georgieva, K., and Dumke, R. (2011). Causal networks based process improvement. In *Proceedings of the 23rd International Conference on Software Engineering & Knowledge Engineering (SEKE 2011)*, Miami Beach, FL. Illinois: Knowledge Systems Institute pp. 462–465.

Hass, K.B. (2007). *Professioinalizing Business Analysis: Breaking the Cycle of Challenged Projects*. Washington, DC: Management Concepts Inc.

Hass, K.B. (2005). *Management Concepts*. viewed January 20, 2014, http://www.managementconcepts.com/portal/server.pt?in_hi_space=SearchResult&in_hi_control=bannerstart&in_tx_query=the%20business%20analyst

Heldman, K. (2009). *Project Management Professional Exam Study Guide*, 5th edn. New York: John Wiley & Sons.

Humphrey, W. (2005). *TSP—Leading a Development Team*. Reading, MA: Addison-Wesley; Amsterdam: Longman.

Humphrey, W. (2000). *Introduction to the Team Software Process*. Reading, MA: Addison-Wesley.

IEEE. (1990). *IEEE Standard Glossary*. Los Alamitos, CA: IEEE Computer Society Press.

Jones, C. (2010). *Software Engineering Best Practices*. New York: McGraw-Hill.

Kandt, R.K. (2006). *Software Engineering Quality Practices*. Boca Raton, FL: Auerbach.

Kasse, T. (2004). *Practical Insight into CMMI*. Norwood, MA: Artech House.

Kerzner, H. (2009). *Project Management A Systems Approach to Planning, Scheduling, and Controlling*, 10th ed. New York: John Wiley & Sons.

Keyes, J. (2003). *Software Engineering Handbook*. Boca Raton, FL: Auerbach.

Klipp, A. (2009). *The Software Engineer Job Description Handbook and Career Guide*. New York: Emereo. Kurble, K.E. (2008). *The Making of Information Systems Software Engineering and Management in a Globalized World*, 1st ed. Berlin: Springer.

Laplante P.A. (2011). *Encyclopedia of Software Engineering*, Volumes I & II. Boca Raton, FL: CRC Press.

Laporte, C.Y., Doucet, M., Bourque, P., and Belkébir, Y. (2007). Utilization of a set of software engineering roles for a multinational organization. In *Product-Focused Software Process Improvement 8th International conference PROFES 2007*. Berlin: Springer, pp. 35–50.

Maciaszek, L.A. (2001). *Requirements Analysis and System Design—Development Informatik Systems with UML*, Reading, MA: Addison-Wesley.

Mikkelsen, T. and Phirego, S. (1997). *Practical Software Configuration Management*. Upper Saddle River, NJ: Prentice Hall.

Neumann, R. (2013). *The Internet of Products*. Berlin: Springer.

Neumann, R., Georgieva, K., and Dumke, R. (2010a). Recruiting excellence for global players—How the most successful software company on earth sources talent. In CECMG/ DASMA, *Industrielle und gesellschaftliche Herausforderungen beim flexiblen Sourcing von IT-Projekten/-Dienstleistungen.* Aachen: Shaker, pp. 68–76,

Neumann, R., Georgieva K., and Dumke. R. (2010b). Down-top enterprise application development. In *5. Workshop Bewertungsaspekte serviceorientierter Architekturen (BSOA):* 101.112. Aachen: Shaker..

Neumann, R., Georgieva, K., Dumke, R., and Schmietendorf. A. (2011a). Reverse commerce—Adding information system support for customer-centric market coordination. In *Proceedings of the Fifth International Conference on Digital Society (ICDS 2011).* Gosier, Guadeloupe. IARIA, pp. 24–31.

Neumann, R., Georgieva, K., Dumke, R., and Schmietendorf, A. (2011b). Moving e-commerce towards e-commodity—a consequence of cloud computing. In *Proceedings of the Fifth International Conference on Digital Society (ICDS 2011),* Gosier, Guadeloupe. France: IARIA, pp. 32–38,

Palmer, S. (1998). People and Self Management—Team Leader Development Series. Oxford, UK: Butterworth-Heinemann.

Paul, D., Yeates, D., and Hindle, K. (2006). *Business Analysis,* London: British Computer Society.

Perry, W.E. (2006). *Effective Methods for Software Testing,* 3rd ed. New York: John Wiley & Sons.

Pfleeger, S.L. (1998). *Software Engineering—Theory and Practice.* Upper Saddle River, NJ: Prentice-Hall.

PMI. (2008). *A Guide to the Project Management Body of Knowledge,* 4th ed. Newtown Square, PA: Project Management Institute.

Rozanski, N. and Woods, E. (2005). *Software Systems Architecture: Working with Stakeholders Using Viewpoints and Perspectives.* Reading, MA: Addison-Wesley.

SEI. (2011). *SEI,* viewed 1 July 2014, http://www.sei.cmu.edu/architecture/research/ previousresearch/duties.cfm

Skyttner, L. (2005). *General Systems Theory—Problems, Perspectives, Practice.* Hackensack, NJ: World Scientific.

Sodhi, J. and Sodhi, P. (2001). *IT Project Management Handbook.* Washington, DC: Management Concepts.

Sommerville, I. (2008). *Software Engineering,* 8th ed. Reading, MA: Addison Wesley.

Wang, Y. and King, G. (2000). *Software Engineering Processes—Principles and Applications.* Boca Raton, FL: CRC Press.

Watkins, J. (2004). *Testing IT: An Off-The-Shelf Software Testing Process.* Cambridge, UK: Cambridge University Press.

Zuse, H. (1998). *A Framework of Software Measurement.* Berlin: de Gruyter.

Chapter 4

Discovery of IT Human Factors

Based on the specific personal competencies discovered in the previous chapter, here the goal is to analyze the responsibilities of each IT role in order to find the weak areas. We use a well-accepted method for failure analysis—the FMEA—as it affords the possibility of analyzing each process to find the weak points and the influencing factors behind them. These influencing factors are actually the IT human characteristics that we evaluate in Chapter 5 to find the personal productivity in the software development process.

4.1 Classical Failure Mode and Effect Analysis

Progress is the heart of failure mode and effect analysis (FMEA). The constant need for change and improvement is the engine keeping the FMEA process running. This idea may not be new, but it is performed in a systematic way to address problems and failures and to search for solutions.

FMEA is defined as a specific methodology for the estimation of system, design, process, or service failures such as errors, risks, and other concerns (Stamatis, 1995). When a failure is found, it is evaluated with occurrence, severity, and detection characteristics. Therefore, depending on the values of these marks, an action is taken, planned, or ignored. The idea is to decrease the likelihood of a problem or its consequences.

The main goal of FMEA is to predict problems before they occur, to make the product safer, or optimize the process, and lead the company during the production process in order to satisfy the customers' needs. Usually there are two main kinds of FMEA: (over an existing product) product FMEA and (over process development stages) process FMEA. When product and process FMEA are conducted together they significantly reduce the costs of manufacturing and developing. It is considered that process FMEA is more important because of the early stages where the failures can be detected and prevented, which gives a result of a more robust process and no need for after-the-fact corrective actions.

Nowadays, FMEA is part of every quality system, which means that collecting the right information and drawing conclusions is not the only part. In order to get the maximum, the company needs to implement the proposed improvements that are the results of the FMEA. The reasons for conducting an FMEA and the benefits are proven and more than clear:

- Improved quality, reliability, safety of the products or services.
- Improves the company's image and competitiveness.
- Increased customer satisfaction.
- Reduced product development time and costs.
- Helps determine the redundancy of the system.
- Helps define the corrective actions.
- Helps in identifying errors and their prevention.
- Helps decide the priority of the failures and associates the right preventive operations.
- Helps reduce the customer's complaints.
- Increases the productivity.
- Develops early criteria for development. (Stamatis, 1995, p. 126 ff.)

4.1.1 Concept of Failure Mode and Effect Analysis

After all, FMEA is an engineering method first used in aircraft building and car manufacturing, so it is described as a part of some industries, like a quality standard. When a particular organization succeeds in implementing these standards, it is capable of controlling the processes and determining the acceptability of its products or services.

Every FMEA method performed in the right way provides the company with useful information that can be used efficiently to reduce work, optimize processes, or prevent serious loss. Due to the consecutive and constructive method, the task can be performed more effectively. The early study of possible problems is of significant importance, and every failure is evaluated for its effects on the whole system, product, or process.

If the method is used in a corrective way, it shows the actions to prevent failures reaching the customer and raises the reliability and quality of the process or product. The process of conducting a FMEA looks like that shown in Figure 4.1, where we can see four main steps, which we discuss later (Stamatis, 1995).

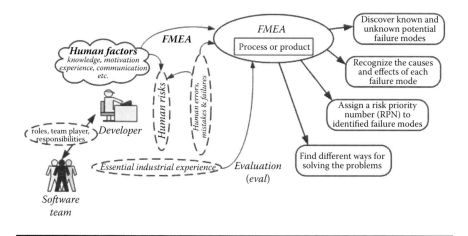

Figure 4.1 The FMEA process. (Reprinted from D. Stamatis, *Failure Mode and Effect Analysis*. Wisconsin: ASQC Quality Press. 1995. With permission.)

In another aspect FMEA is a method of bringing satisfaction to the customers. In the modern world we know that the most important thing in order to stay in the market is having quality products. The main key here is to achieve detection of quality concerns before the product reaches the hands of the users. That is why FMEA should start as soon as some information is provided, because the team conducting the FMEA will practically never have all the data. At the beginning, the technique should be executed over the design stage or concept, but for better results it can be used throughout the development process and the whole product life cycle to identify failures. Every product is expected to do something specific and to be in use for a long time. A product failure is when it does not function in the expected way. Even the simplest products can malfunction in some way.

FMEA includes everything that can be done in order to make the product work closer to 100%: this means even the problems that occur during the exploitation of the product. In those cases when the product malfunctions or fails to work, we talk about failure modes. Each failure mode should be described with the frequency with which it occurs and to what damages it's leading, and how the system is affected. The types of FMEA are described in the following (adapted from Stamatis (1995)):

System FMEA: It is applied over systems and their interaction. Its focus is the function failures in the system. The benefits that it brings are
  1. Identification of system alternatives
  2. Discover redundancy
  3. Potential for managing future problems
  4. Recognition of failures in the system's interaction

Design FMEA: Used for analysis of products ready for manufacturing. The profit from the design FMEA:
1. Prioritizing the design improvement actions
2. Information for product design validation and testing
3. Defines alternatives for design requirements
4. Mitigation of safety issues

Process FMEA: This is performed when the manufacturing and assembly process is being analyzed. The advantages of this FMEA are
1. Recognition of the process deficiencies
2. Proposing and prioritizing the corrective actions
3. Exposure of the manufacturing or assembly process
4. Track down the meaningful changes

Service FMEA: This FMEA analyzes services before they arrive at the customer. The gain from the performed service FMEA can be observed in the facts:
1. Helps to evaluate the job flow
2. Exposure of the system and process
3. Implementation of a control plan
4. Prioritizing improvement actions

4.1.2 Methodological Steps in FMEA

In order to achieve problem-solving results, FMEA needs to be conducted strictly, consecutively, and constructively, following eight main steps (see McDermott, Mikulak, and Beauregard (2009) and Stamatis (1995)):

Step 1. Gather a team and review the process or product.
Step 2. Brainstorm unknown risks.
Step 3. Assign different effects caused by the failures.
Step 4. Prioritize: assign severity, occurrence, and detection rankings for each failure mode.
Step 5. Calculate the RPN number.
Step 6. Collect data, analyze, and measure the failure modes for action.
Step 7. Apply methods to reduce high-priority/high-risk failures.
Step 8. After performing actions evaluate the performance of the system again.

The bottom-up approach of FMEA looks like that shown in Figure 4.2.

Step 1: Gather the team, review the process.
When gathering the team we must know that the proper people are going to take part. Everyone should know the field of the work. Prior to the start of the FMEA the team leader has to make available for everybody a detailed flowchart of the development process if they are conducting

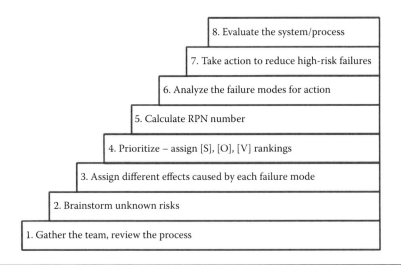

Figure 4.2   The bottom-up approach of FMEA.

a *process FMEA* or an engineering drawing of the product in the case of *product FMEA*. Sometimes it is recommended to have an expert in the group available for answering questions and giving useful hints.

Step 2: Brainstorm unknown risks.

Having a good overview of the process or product, the team is ready for brainstorming. The members try to brainstorm any kind of ideas and various suggestions about what could affect the process or the product quality and stability.

Because of the large variety of topics it is recommended to conduct several brainstorming series each focusing on different elements of the process FMEA: people, resources, equipment, and methods. This, of course, helps for deeper understanding and finding of failure modes.

Step 3: Assign different effects caused by each failure mode.

In computer programming we explain this step as an if {} then {} construction. The team should think: *if* a problem occurs, *then* what are the consequences. In some cases failures can cause several effects, but in others, only one. This step is very important because of the further assigning of severity and occurrence.

Step 4: Prioritize: assign severity, occurrence and detection rankings.

After examining every risk carefully the team puts every effect in a table, describes the influence, and assigns a rank from 1 to 10 for each of the three components (severity, occurrence, and detection). Every member should be able to understand the rankings: the more descriptive explanations there are for every ranking scale, the better the FMEA process is.

Step 5: Calculate RPN number.

This number most often serves as a guide and is not given serious importance because of the different effects of every failure mode. However, it can be used as an instrument for measuring; if it's under a defined value the team does not take any action. Calculation:

$$Risk\ Priority\ Number = Severity \times Occurrence \times Detection \qquad (4.1)$$

Step 6: Analyze the failure mode for action.

In this step each failure mode is analyzed by ranking and effects and is given a priority for action. The team decides which the highest risks are and where to put work.

Step 7: Take action to reduce high-risk failures.

Probably this is one of the most important steps where the team decides what actions to implement in order to reduce the severe problems as much as possible. The ideal case is when no future failure modes are observed but this is not always achievable. At the very least the team must aim at increasing the detection and mitigation of the failure.

Step 8: Evaluate the system/process performance.

After implementation of the methods for reducing failures the team continues to measure the performance of the process/system, confirms the results, and performs another FMEA. Recommendations should be made after answering the questions:

Is the process better than before?

Are the improvements enough to have good RPNs?

Is it urgent to conduct another FMEA?

Every organization, according to its resources and budget, makes its own decision as to how many FMEA analyses it should conduct. Nevertheless, the long-term goal is always to eliminate every risk and the short-term goal is to reduce the impact as much as possible. After all, we have to remember: FMEA is a continual method of improvement.

The FMEA parameters are described in the following. The project team analyzes every element of the process, working through the entire output which is to be delivered to the customer. At every step the team tries to brainstorm and find unknown and potential problems and offer solutions to already known risks. Every problem is estimated and has a different priority. It is very important to have a measurement scale so the team knows which risks are critical for the system. There are three indicators the team uses to define the priority of the failures:

- Severity—[S]
- Occurrence—[O]
- Detection—[D]

Severity: Shows what the impact of the failure is over the system or over processes and how serious the consequences are. After all, the main goal of the FMEA team is to take action and reduce the most important failures. The team uses a scale from 1 to 10 to express how serious one problem can be: 1 stands for "no danger" and 10 for "critical." These numbers help to prioritize the risk and help in focusing on the serious risks. Examples of failures are malfunction in UPS system which leads to data loss, or improper use of a variable in accounting software, which results in loss of accuracy. Another important reason why we use this rank is that we may face a failure which leads to another failure or component disability (Stamatis, 1995).

Occurrence: This measure shows us how often a failure occurs. The team also has to have in mind the severity number at this step. Some examples are how often we face program failures because of an erroneous algorithm or how often hardware experiences excessive voltage. Of essential importance here is that the team must find the cause of the failure. Again we use a ranking: occurrence ranking [O], from 1 to 10. If the rank is high (above 7), precocious mechanisms should be determined. But sometimes in a situation where occurrence is not high but the severity for the failure has a rank above 8 the team must also react. At this step it is always necessary to look for the severity rank with the combination of occurrence (Stamatis, 1995).

Detection: The chance or the capability of the team to detect the failure before it reaches the customer. The last two steps work in combination and every combination of them is marked with a detection number that shows the possibility that the failure will not be detected. A high number of detections means a higher chance that the failure will escape detection (Stamatis, 1995).

RPN Number: When the last three steps are completed, an *RPN* (risk priority number) has to be calculated. It shows us which of the process steps and parts are under high risk and have to be taken under control measures. The number is calculated by multiplying the severity, occurrence, and detection numbers:

$$RPN = S \times O \times D \qquad (4.2)$$

RPN numbers are calculated for every system/process and every subsystem/subprocess in order to find where the critical parts are. The subprocess with highest RPN number needs a corrective method to be applied and it is not always the severity numbers which define this; for instance, it could be failure which is hardly detectable and occurs quite often, but does not have a serious effect (Stamatis, 1995).

All the steps and entire FMEA process should be documented using a worksheet. There are different kinds of worksheets according to the types of FMEA. The form captures all the information in a clear and well-organized way. Everything is included: recommended measures and methods, implementations, and all the numbers for occurrence, severity, detection, and RPN. Once the team has all the information they have to deal with four main objectives:

- Reduce the impact of the failure mode.
- Minimize the severe effect as much as possible.
- Try to eliminate the occurrence or put the levels as low as it can.
- Improve the occurrence detection.

4.1.3 Software FMEA

Technical systems are used in a large variety of areas in industries worldwide. A considerable amount of software specialists and software code are used to move these industries forward. As a consequence, a great deal of attention is focused on the identification and avoidance of technical risks and failures. A very powerful tool for analysis, and preventing and predicting errors is the systematic and constructive method, FMEA, which is approved and accepted in many different fields of manufacturing, including cars, airplanes, computers, and so on. In most cases a bottom-up technique is used to identify failures and malfunctions in every component of the system or process (Mäckel, 2006).

The method was first used in the military, but those concepts and ideas are not compatible and do not apply in modern technologies. Therefore, companies nowadays have developed new sets of priorities, guidelines, rules, and standards for their own use. FMEA based on hardware and system levels is well understood, applicable, and working in a good way because of the known risks and failures of hardware behavior. But in present times the accent is on the software level; more systems and functionalities are based on the software process, which explains the need for software-based FMEA. "Software modules do not fail, they only display incorrect behavior" (Pentti and Atte, 2002).

Anyway our goal is not to focus on SFMEA but only to show that it has its application in the software industry and in this way to motivate our modification of the method over human actions during the software engineering process.

SFMEA is also a step-by-step systematic method for analyzing the software architecture, software design, or process while taking care of the technical risks of reliability, safety, stability, availability, and so on. A great advantage of the method is to use the information and documentation from every department taking part in the process of development—system, software, test, and service—so the FMEA team is able to have a clear and deeper insight of the problems. Figure 4.3 shows which are the critical moments in the software life cycle and where the FMEA should take part (Mäckel, 2006).

There is relatively little information published on the use of FMEA for software systems but we provide a short overview of the papers discussing the benefits introduced by the SFMEA. Banerjee has applied the method in the practice and observed an "improvement of the reliability of the software production process, resulting in higher product quality as well as in higher productivity" (Banerjee, 1995).

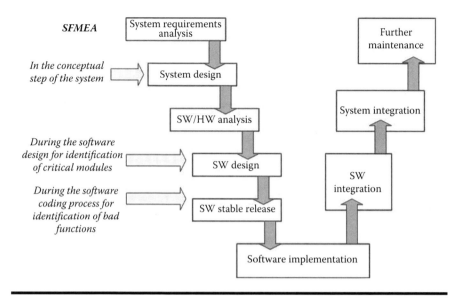

Figure 4.3 Application of the software FMEA. (Reprinted from O. Mäckel, *Software FMEA, Opportunities and benefits of FMEA in the development process of software-intensive technical systems,* **http://www.fmeainfocentre.com/papers/. 2006. With permission.)**

The statement that detailed SFMEA validates that the software has been planned and constructed to reach the correct and safe requirements from the beginning is also defended in the scientific work of Pentti and Atte (2002), Lauritsen and Stalhane (2005), Hartkopf (2004), Ozarin and Siracusa (2003), Bowles and Hanczaryk (2008), Nguyen (2001), and Goddard (2000). The authors point out that the use of FMEA in the software process brings early identification of potential software failure modes and is an excellent practice that supports the whole life cycle. At the same time each of them has demonstrated a concrete application of the FMEA method in the software development process. Motivated by this wide use of the FMEA method, due to its universal manner we have decided to apply it over the software development phases but pointed to the human roles and the actions that they perform.

4.2 Adopted FMEA for Software Personnel

We have already introduced the FMEA methodology. Its evaluation and failure detection were broadly explained. Considering the FMEA strong points in analysis and corrective recommendations, the decision to apply it first over the software development process (Georgieva, 2010d) and then over the software development roles and their responsibilities was logical and consecutive (Georgieva, Neumann, and Dumke, 2011a).

The price of the human errors that we all pay in everyday life can be very high when faced with software applications. Therefore detecting and decreasing their effect is a vital development step in each production process or system. With a software human factor FMEA could be made an evaluation over the human failure modes' severity and occurrence and in this way these errors can be ranked according to their criticality. The other analysis that can be done adopting the FMEA technique is to discover the human features behind these errors, problems, or failures. Nevertheless our goal is not only to find the possible risks but to find out why they occur and to try to resolve them. On this step the chosen method gives us a special benefit, as it delivers the information why a particular failure mode appears and what the employee's fault is and what his personal characteristics could be that led to this problem. We observe in the application of the adopted method the discovery of the human factors, or the specific human features behind the different failure modes on a particular software team.

4.2.1 Performing Software Human Factor FMEA

The form in which the FMEA analysis is performed could be changed in every company and could be adapted to particular goals and expected problems. We first show the possible entries in such analysis and then concentrate on the chosen fields that are important in our case. We focus on process FMEA as the activities that we want to analyze are actually the different software phases and the human actions inside, which are nothing but a number of processes.

The form presented in Table 4.1 lists the generally expected entries that should be managed when conducting a process FMEA. For our research we have adopted the method and added the column Human Factors that gives us the essential information for further research over the criticality of the personal features in the software process.

The first part between 1 and 9 is the introductory data. These are not mandatory fields; however, they have information that may be important in future examination. The main parts are numbers 10 to 23; these are mandatory items and are the essential part of the FMEA conduction. Additional to the form there are signatures, which may not be mandatory, but bring an authoritative look to it and can be a sign that the analysis is ready. The 23 items according to Stamatis (1995) are presented here:

1. *Process Identification:* The name of the process or a reference number is stated here, adding identity to the process that is manipulated.
2. *Manufacturing or Design Responsibility:* The prime responsibility is stated here: this may be the name of the activity, machine, or material.
3. *Involvement of Other Areas:* Mentions if other people or systems are connected to this part.
4. *Involvement of Suppliers or Other:* When additional persons are taking part in the design, manufacturing, or assembly of the part.

Table 4.1 Software Human Factor FMEA Template Form

		Prepared by: (7)	
Process name: (1)	Supplier involvement: (4)		
Part name: (2)	Model/product: (5)	FMEA date: (8)	
Involvement of others: (3)	Engineering release date: (6)	FMEA rev. Date: (9)	

Process function (10)	Potential failure mode (11)	Potential effect(s) of failure (12)	Severity (13)	Potential cause(s)/ mechanism(s) of failure (14)	Human factors (15)	Occurrence (16)
Detection method (17)	Detection (18)	RPN (19)	Recommended action(s) (20)	Responsibility and target completion date (21)	Action results (23)	

Action(s) taken and completion date (22)	Severity
	Occurrence
	Detection
	RPN

5. *Model or Product:* This is the place to specify the name of the model or product using the process.

6. *Engineering Release Date:* The planned date for release.

7. *Prepared By:* The FMEA analyst is stated here as well as some additional information such as address, telephone, or e-mail.

8. *FMEA Date—Original:* The starting date of the process.

9. *FMEA Dare—Revision:* The date of the last revision.

10. *Process Function:* "This is the process intent, purpose, goal or objective."

11. *Potential Failure Mode:* This is the possible problem, failure, or defect. This is where the person can go wrong. Each action provides the possibility for misunderstanding, omitting, incompletion, or falsely interpreting. Therefore, each process function may have several failure modes. Each one must be recorded for future analysis. The potential error should be stated briefly but clearly, in this way facilitating evaluation of the consequences.

12. *Potential Effect of the Failure:* This field is for the result of the wrongly fulfilled responsibilities. Potential problems must be foreseen and tracked down so their effect can be estimated and their occurrence removed. Here again more than one entry can be written. The impact can be observed from several sides, including the influence over the next part of the process and over other related parts of the development.

13. *Severity:* This is a value assigned for the importance of the effect of the failure. The values are in the area from 1 to 10, where 1 indicates that there is no effect on the process and 10 points catastrophic influence. The exact effect of the failure should be indicated so that an appropriate ranking can be performed.

14. *Potential Mechanism, Causes of Failure:* These are the reasons that cause the already described failure. Here the root cause of the failure must be identified. This is a key item in the analysis, because it directly exposes the human factors behind the potential problem.

15. *Human Factors:* The human factors that have the most significant impact on the failure are listed here when a team member performs her responsibilities. There are cases where more than one factor affects the situation as shown in Table 4.1.

16. *Occurrence:* This is a numeric value, indicating the frequency with which a failure happens. Again the scale is from 1 to 10, where 10 is constant occurrence. This element is important because it affects the entire priority value of the problem when calculating the RPN.

17. *Detection Methods:* These are the tools used to recognize the failure. For human errors this could be brainstorming, sample filing, daily reports, team meeting, or manager's observation.

18. *Detection:* This value shows the rate of detection of the particular failure. This rating is in the range from 1 to 10 and 10 means observing the problem every time. It must be noticed that this detection is for the likelihood of the error happening to be noticed and not for the particular human error.

19. *RPN (Risk Priority Number):* This is the product of the severity, occurrence, and detection. It is mostly used to prioritize the failures. The RPN has no other meaning apart from the ranking.
20. *Recommended Actions:* The activities that should be undertaken in order to mitigate the failure are listed here. In the HF FMEA the main object of observation is the human factor. Therefore these prescribed actions are mainly intended to correct the reasons of the failure behavior.
21. *Responsible Area or Person and Target Completion Date:* The person responsible for the recommended actions and the planned date on which they should be finished must be entered here.
22. *Action Taken and Completion Date:* This is one of the actions filled in the recommended actions list. It is desirable that this be a top activity in the list, guaranteeing maximum increase in human performance.
23. *Action Results:* After the recommenced corrective action is done, a severity, occurrence, and detection value is calculated again, determining a RPN grade. The new RPN should be better, indicating progress in the person's performance and recovery from the failure.

These 23 steps represent the adopted software human factor FMEA method, used for investigating the human factors behind the employees' performance. For our further investigation only the human factors behind the different failures or potential problems are important, and because of this we have taken only a part of the FMEA form, shown in the following tables.

We have conducted the FMEA in a strictly analytical way regarding the responsibilities of the software development team members, stated in the previous part. A logical consecutive analysis is conducted in order to define the human features responsible for the variety of mistakes. We have left the RPN and its components out of the analysis as our goal is to find all human factors and not to evaluate them at this step.

4.2.1.1 Software Human Factors FMEA of Project Manager Role

We have analyzed the responsibilities of the project manager, which were listed above. They are just slightly combined so that we have optimized the FMEA table. After obtaining the FMEA result we built Table 4.2 with all human factors that influence the performance of the project manager. We can express all needed personal characteristics for the project manager in the following manner (with the details in Table 4.3):

$$HF_{ProjectManager}^{FMEA} = \{Coordination,\ Self\text{-}management,\ Stress,\ Competence, \quad (4.3)$$

$$Knowledge,\ Effectiveness,\ Concentration,\ Communication,$$

$$Self\text{-}development,\ Liberalism,\ Control,\ Egoism,\ Confidence,\ Organization\}$$

Table 4.2　Human Factors for the PM

Human Factors for the Project Manager
Coordination
Self-management
Overload = Stress
Competence
Knowledge
Effectiveness
Concentration
Communication
Self-Development
Liberalism
Control delegation
Selfish = Egotism
Over self-confident
Self-organization

Source: Extracted from the SHF-FMEA Table 4.3.

Table 4.3 SHF-FMEA over the Project Manager Role

Process Function	Potential Failure Mode	Potential Effect(s) of Failure	Potential Cause(s)/ Mechanism(s) of Failure	Human Factors	Detection Method(s)	Recommended Action(s)
Ensures that the software development process works as intended	PM is not monitoring the development process closely enough	The development process may be running with hidden problems	Developers may issue problems that they do not report to PM and cope with them on their own, providing inferior solutions	**Coordination, management**	Reports, meetings, and cooperation between the employees	PM meets regularly with the team members and discusses progress and all accompanying problems
Responsible for leading the work process until the completion of the project	PM is not taking responsibility for the project, pointing finger at developers and team leader (TL)	Developers and TL are being distracted by new responsibilities or changes in the project	PM is not managing the project in the right manner; PM is not aware of his particular duties	**Overload, competence, knowledge, effectiveness**	Developers not spending all their time coding but rather organizing meetings, scheduling phases, and planning events	PM being aware of her duties, so developers can focus on developing code

continued

Table 4.3 (continued) SHF-FMEA over the Project Manager Role

Process Function	Potential Failure Mode	Potential Effect(s) of Failure	Potential Cause(s)/Mechanism(s) of Failure	Human Factors	Detection Method(s)	Recommended Action(s)
Coordination between the development team and the business stakeholders to ensure matching of goals and products in the expected time	PM is not communicating enough with the development team and clients and not monitoring the development process	Team may run over the deadline, due to too little control and motivation	PM is looking at future deals and neglects the current ones; PM has left all obligations to development team and believes they will manage alone	**Competence, concentration, coordination, management**	A deadline is crossed; project is not fitting all clients' expectations	PM should be constantly tracking the development process asking questions and making himself sure everything is as it should be
Working with the business stakeholders, who work closely with the functional analyst during the first stages	PM is omitting meetings with the business stakeholders and FA in the beginning	PM is losing time at a later phase for not being clear what the project is about and what has to be done	PM is busy performing other duties; PM believes that early talks do not concern her	**Overload, competence, coordination**	PM is not familiar with solutions specifications and time is needed so he can embrace them and direct them to TL	PM should be more disciplined, always attend predevelopment meetings

Responsible for status reports, that show urgency and demand concrete answers	PM is not insisting on getting constant status report	PM is not pointing urgency and action and is leaving the team to manage alone	PM believes these are TL responsibilities; PM is busy with other tasks	**Coordination, overload, communication**	Development team is not hardworking; this may lead to project not finished on time and requirements not fulfilled	PM should be more skilled in team motivation; PM should monitor and report the status in order to use this info at a later stage
PM coordinates several projects	PM is working on too many projects	PM mixes the people in different teams, tasks, and schedules	Too many projects confuse the PM; he is not examining the record with the team and their responsibilities	**Overload, competence, coordination**	PM may come unprepared to a meeting due to a mistake about the team and project	PM should prepare the documents well over the development assigned to the employees
Organizing the team responsibilities	PM is pushing the people to their limit	Team is always being pushed without sense of relief or acknowledgment	PM is demanding quick decisions and in this way pushing the team to work to their limit	**Development, communication, liberalism**	Team is stressed, always being pushed onward	PM should understand the team effort for solving problems; PM should build a good team atmosphere

continued

Table 4.3 (continued) SHF-FMEA over the Project Manager Role

Process Function	Potential Failure Mode	Potential Effect(s) of Failure	Potential Cause(s)/ Mechanism(s) of Failure	Human Factors	Detection Method(s)	Recommended Action(s)
Executing and controlling the work	PM is not regularly keeping an eye on specific issues	PM may lose track of a problem	PM has a lot of details to pay constant attention to; PM is not responsible for the small issues	**Competence, control delegation, coordination**	In the case of well-known problem the PM cannot profit from previous decisions and knowledge	PM should be more focused on the big problems that arise and not on each issue
Look at the big picture to evaluate risk, time, and costs	PM is not keeping an eye on development progress	PM cannot evaluate whether the project will be completed on time	PM is delegating this responsibility to TL; PM has too many projects	**Coordination, overload**	Comparing current progress with other projects	PM should take care of the project; estimating its properties and details
Communicating with the team to ensure that all problems are correctly understood	At meetings PM is always speaking on a topic without listening to make sure the members have understood it	PM is taking over meetings without letting anyone else say a word and not ensuring that the team has understood him	PM is feeling like a central figure and does not want to give the floor to someone else; PM thinks everyone understands her	**Selfish, overly self-confident, communication**	Problems may remain unclear; further meetings may be needed; PM may be not understood	PM should listen to his team members and assure himself that everything is clear

Makes sure that the process is going according to requirements	PM is not tracking the project closely	PM is not controlling the project and it can slip away	PM has too many obligations and is delegating obligations to the TL, who is not fulfilling them	**Overload, coordination**	Predicted results may not match the actual results	PM, even if delegating some task to TL, must keep an eye on it
Document, obtain approval, and track all changes in project parameters	PM is gathering all project details but not documenting them for current project's reference	There is no concrete record for the current project	PM is gathering documents but not organizing them in a useful manner	**Organization, skills, competence**	If someone is looking for details over a completed project	PM should be well organized working with tools supporting good documentation
Finalizing the project	PM is not fulfilling the guidelines and cannot finish the project as expected	Other team members are considered responsible	PM believes it is not her task to determine all rules and to give clear "orders"	**Coordination, competence**	TL coping with too many issues, rather than concentrating on major specific ones	PM should be aware what his duties are and should perform them strictly

4.2.1.2 Software Human Factors FMEA of Team Leader Role

Analogously to the project manager we have analyzed the responsibilities of the team leader, listed above. They are just slightly combined for optimization of the FMEA table. After obtaining the FMEA result we built Table 4.4 with all human factors that influence the performance of the team leader, shown below. We can show all needed personal characteristics for the team leader in the following manner (with the details in Table 4.5):

$$HF_{TeamLeader}^{FMEA} = \{Hardworking, Knowledge, Communication, Attention, \quad (4.4)$$

$$Conscientiousness, Leader\ skills, Mental\ overload, Fear,$$

$$Competence, Experience, Technical\ understanding, Planning\ skills,$$

$$Monitoring, Appreciation, Cooperation, Management\}$$

Table 4.4   Human Factors for the TL

Human Factors for the Team Leader
Hardworking
Knowledge
Communication
Attention
Conscientiousness
Leader skills
Mental overload
Stress
Competence
Experience
Technical understanding
Planning skills
Monitoring
Appreciation
Cooperation
Fear
Management

Source: Extracted from the SHM-FMEA Table 4.5.

Table 4.5 SHF-FMEA of Team Leader Role

Process Function	Potential Failure Mode	Potential Effect(s) of Failure	Potential Cause(s)/ Mechanism(s) of Failure	Human Factors	Detection Method(s)	Recommended Action(s)
Mediates between the solution architect and the developers	The work of the developers does not entirely match what the SA has chosen as an architecture	The architecture created from the developers cannot be matched to the one from the SA due to differences	TL is not familiar with the architecture of the SA; he has not observed the work of the developers and they have slipped from the requirements and design selected by the SA; TL does not approve the architecture selected by SA and has a better solution; TL has decided to change a small design pattern in one place, but has no global view and that causes inconsistency	**Hardworking, knowledge, communication, attention, conscientiousness**	When the implemented parts have to be connected; during SA, TL observation over the process	TL being familiar with the SA's selected architecture; TL not making solo decisions; better communication between developers, TL, and SA

continued

Table 4.5 (continued)   SHF-FMEA of Team Leader Role

Process Function	Potential Failure Mode	Potential Effect(s) of Failure	Potential Cause(s)/ Mechanism(s) of Failure	Human Factors	Detection Method(s)	Recommended Action(s)
Lead and mentor the developers when they have problems, which cannot be mitigated by themselves alone	TL is not providing the needed help to the developers	Developers lose time and effort in solving issues, which are TL obligations	TL has too much work and obligations to fulfill; developers are not informing TL on time; TL is stubborn and tries to make the work in her own way; TL is not a good leader	**Communication, knowledge, leader skills**	Developers make own decisions without communicating with the TL; They turn to SA for guidance and he is not adequately prepared for that; implementations that experience lack in performance and design	TL asking constantly for questions or foggy issues; TL being more open for developers' requests; TL having more time to personally observe the developers' work

Discussing all the details in the architecture that the SA didn't explain and in this way supporting the program specification	TL had not understood completely the proposed software architecture	TL cannot support a correct specification for the developers	TL does not have the qualities to understand the software architecture and specification	**Knowledge, skills**	The lack of accurate specification; lack of competent leadership from the TL	TL participating more when the architecture is being laid down by the SA; asking questions and paying attention
Refines the SA's vision and makes the practical concepts clear	TL has not understood the SA vision in depth	TL is not able to refine the concepts	TL had no time to perform an in-depth analysis of the SA's design and architecture; SA design is too complex	**Mental overload capacity, stress**	The analysis is poor and the TL design innovations don't amount to better performance	TL having more practice in designing solutions and applying patterns; TL communicating more with the SA

continued

Table 4.5 (continued)   SHF-FMEA of Team Leader Role

Process Function	Potential Failure Mode	Potential Effect(s) of Failure	Potential Cause(s)/ Mechanism(s) of Failure	Human Factors	Detection Method(s)	Recommended Action(s)
TL chooses the methodologies and techniques that will be used in a particular project	TL does not possess good technical knowledge	Developers have to manage problems on their own or turn to the SA	TL does not have enough practice; TL cannot solve problems due to lack of time; TL cannot choose proper methodology due to misleading factors or lack of experience	**Overload, competence, experience**	Developers are asking questions that cannot be answered	TL spending more time in problem solving and communication with colleagues
Continuous evaluation of the solution decisions	TL is not keeping constant track of the project	Constant evaluation is not performed	TL does not perform evaluations over the developers' work due to lack of time; TL is not able to see pattern problems due to lack of knowledge; TL is not well aware of the SA architecture	**Conscientiousness, competence, knowledge**	The proposed patterns are not correct and do not fulfill the specific project needs	TL keeps constant track of the project, observing his developers; asking questions; being curious

Mastery of developer skills but with conceptual vision	TL does not possess the conceptual vision to transform concepts into solutions	Concepts are not fully transformed, or are transformed improperly	TL is thinking like a developer; his view is not wide enough; he has not mastered all skills needed to be a good TL	**Technical understanding, competence**	Visible in the design decisions TL is making as well as the patterns TL is choosing for the solution	TL enriching her knowledge; TL trusting on guidance by SA and colleagues
Direct, motivate, and plan the team's work; create an open, creative, and friendly work environment	TL does not have qualities to motivate his team	Team members are working in a stressful atmosphere and are unsatisfied	TL is not skilled at leading the team; TL has not enough time to monitor team's work; TL does not appreciate team effort and creative thinking	**Planning skills, attention, monitoring, appreciation**	Easily seen that team is not feeling good and members are not well motivated	TL attending team management courses; TL paying more attention to his developers; TL having more practice in project planning

continued

Table 4.5 (continued) SHF-FMEA of Team Leader Role

Process Function	Potential Failure Mode	Potential Effect(s) of Failure	Potential Cause(s)/Mechanism(s) of Failure	Human Factors	Detection Method(s)	Recommended Action(s)
Take responsibility for the progress of the team's work	TL is not aware of the problems in the team	TL is not taking responsibility for progress and team	TL is not constantly speaking with the team members; TL is not keeping track over the project progress; TL is not making a proper use of all team resources	**Communication, cooperation, competence**	Seen at meetings; Easy to notice when big problems arise	TL having time for her team members; TL making a proper planning of the resources; TL able to motivate her team
Manage, train, and help to the development team; conflict solving	TL is not helping the team members	Team members are having problems and this is observed in their work	TL does not have leader qualities; does not provide proper help and training due to lack of time or ideas and knowledge how to perform that; TL is not aware of all the problems	**Management, leader skills**	Can be seen that the employees are not satisfied with their work	TL paying more attention to developers; TL having better management qualities; TL being there to protect and mentor his developers

				Fear, overload, competence		
Provide status reports of the team activities against the program plan; keep the project manager informed of task accomplishment	TL is not providing reports periodically	PM is not informed of project progress, project issues, and success	TL has too many obligations; TL is afraid of giving bad news; TL has omitted her duties of reporting; TL is not reporting status due to lack of progress		PM is not satisfied with TL's work; TL is not present at meetings or has no report	TL paying more attention to all his duties; TL not being late at giving bad news; TL always talking to PM; TL keeping track of project progress, plan, and schedule

4.2.1.3 Software Human Factors FMEA of Business Analyst Role

Analogously to the previous role here are the analysis of the business analyst role and of course Table 4.6 with the human factors. We can summarize the needed personal characteristics for the business analyst in the following manner (with the details in Table 4.7):

$$HF^{FMEA}_{BusinessAnalyst} = \{Intelligence, Knowledge, Work\ overload, Concentration, \quad (4.5)$$

$$Analysis\ skills, Competence, Communication, Planning, Openness\}$$

Table 4.6 Human Factors for the BA

Human Factors for the Business Analyst
Intelligence
Knowledge
Work overload
Concentration
Analysis skills
Competence
Communication
Planning
Openness

Source: Extracted from the SHF-FMEA Table 4.7.

Table 4.7 SHF-FMEA of Business Analyst Role

Process Function	Potential Failure Mode	Potential Effect(s) of Failure	Potential Cause(s)/ Mechanism(s) of Failure	Human Factors	Detection Method(s)	Recommended Action(s)
Provide technical expertise (Typically in information technology applications)	BA is not providing technical expertise	Absence of expert judgment over client requirements	BA is not skilled enough to perform the needed expertise; BA has no knowledge in the researched area; BA has too many other obligations	**Intelligence, knowledge, work overload**	Poor or no technical report; not helping the TL and PM, searching for skilled and experienced colleagues	BA being supported by other skilled colleges in case of need; BA increasing his knowledge when coming across new topic of development; attending refresher courses

continued

Table 4.7 (continued)   SHF-FMEA of Business Analyst Role

Process Function	Potential Failure Mode	Potential Effect(s) of Failure	Potential Cause(s)/ Mechanism(s) of Failure	Human Factors	Detection Method(s)	Recommended Action(s)
Understand user and other stakeholder needs and conduct requirements analysis	Incorrectly understood the clients' needs; unsuccessful requirements analysis	An analysis that does not satisfy clients' requests; incomplete or partly useful analysis	The client is not explaining his desires directly; BA is distracted and not following the stakeholder's idea; not all requirements are gathered and the analysis is not complete; BA has not the skills to perform good analysis	**Concentration, knowledge, analysis skills**	Analysis being examined by stakeholder, other BA, manager	BA attending courses for additional technical knowledge; BA paying more attention to stakeholders' requirements; having more time for a proper analysis to be created; client/BA being well prepared for the meeting

| Identify application solution alternatives | Associate wrong alternative; incorrect identification of a solution as an alternative | Colleagues being misled when reading/examining the proposed alternative solutions | Not enough knowledge to recognize the correct alternative; unfamiliar with the project details | **Knowledge, intelligence** | During further work from the architect, colleagues, manager | BA becoming more experienced in the researched area; BA becoming familiar with the requirements; better understanding of the proposed strategies and analysis |
| Analyze existing logic with the idea to redesign or automate | Wrong identification of an existing system | Confusion in future work; misleading of colleagues | Unfamiliar with project details | **Knowledge, competence** | Analysis being examined, other employees | BA being familiar with the requirements and good understanding of the existing system |

continued

Table 4.7 (continued) SHF-FMEA of Business Analyst Role

Process Function	Potential Failure Mode	Potential Effect(s) of Failure	Potential Cause(s)/ Mechanism(s) of Failure	Human Factors	Detection Method(s)	Recommended Action(s)
Recommend implementation strategies	Incorrect strategies being recommended	Wasting time for refactoring; misled in the following choice of frameworks and architectures	Unfamiliar with the strategy as well as with the project	**Knowledge, competence**	Problems in the future work, when the incompatibilities surface	Better knowledge of the strategies, requirements, and impact of the proposed solution
Document recommendations to enable estimation of project scope, quality, time, cost, and risks	Not all requirements are documented	Requirements analysis is not complete, further calculations of budget and time are not correctly performed	BA is not familiar with all requirements	**Knowledge, competence**	Noticed during requirements discussion by colleagues or manager inspection	BA being aware of requirements and details; having experience in budget and time scheduling

Conduct root-cause analysis of the problems	Not understanding the potential problems	Project cost and budget are badly calculated, time is incorrectly scheduled; problems are overlooked or ignored	BA has no full and entire overview of the project and its properties	**Knowledge, competence, communication**	Noticed during later planning, management, checks, budget and schedule examinations	Practice at project analysis and scheduling; attending courses; presentations
Develop, maintain, and monitor related policies, procedures, instructions	Policies and procedures are not developed	Omitted procedures/policies	BA has no time to perform all his duties; BA has no experience in producing policies or procedures; BA is not well versed in the project and cannot propose new initiatives	**Planning, knowledge, competence**	Discovered during manager's check	BA having more time for his obligations; BA gathering knowledge about new practices; BA being familiar with all parts of the project

continued

Table 4.7 (continued)   SHF-FMEA of Business Analyst Role

Process Function	Potential Failure Mode	Potential Effect(s) of Failure	Potential Cause(s)/ Mechanism(s) of Failure	Human Factors	Detection Method(s)	Recommended Action(s)
Reports about research findings or new business solutions	Missing such reports, which means no innovativeness	Missing of new ideas, new trends and solutions	BA has no time to do this research; BA is not innovative enough and not open for new ideas	**Knowledge, openness**	Noticed when being inspected from the PM, or in discussions	BA having more time; attending conferences and workshops; BA observing other perspectives

4.2.1.4 Software Human Factors FMEA of Software Architect Role

Analogously to the previous roles here are the analysis of the software architect role and Table 4.8 with the human factors. We can summarize the needed personal characteristics for the software architect in the following manner (with the details in Table 4.9):

$$HF_{SoftwareArchitect}^{FMEA} = \{Knowledge, \, Hardworking, \, Intelligence, \quad (4.6)$$

$$Communication, \, Competence, \, Creativity, \, Cooperation,$$

$$Emotional \, stability, \, Mental \, overload, \, Attention, \, Judgment,$$

$$Experience, \, Problem \, solving, \, Leader \, thinking, \, Perception, \, Professionalism\}$$

Table 4.8   Human Factors for the SA

Human Factors for the Software Architect
Knowledge
Hardworking
Intelligence
Communication
Competence
Creativity
Cooperation
Emotional stability
Mental overload
Attention
Judgment
Experience
Problem solving
Leader thinking
Perception
Professionalism

Source: Extracted from the SHF-FMEA Table 4.9.

Table 4.9   SHF-FMEA of the Software Architect Role

Process Function	Potential Failure Mode	Potential Effect(s) of Failure	Potential Cause(s)/ Mechanism(s) of Failure	Human Factors	Detection Method(s)	Recommended Action(s)
Defining the software architecture	Problems/ failures in the architecture	The project is not developed as planned	SA is not completely aware of all project requirements; SA is not very familiar with the architecture; SA is not an expert in the field (does not have enough experience, knowledge)	**Knowledge, hardworking, intelligence, communication, competence, creativity, cooperation, emotionally stable**	Detached during implementation; observation by TL or colleague SA; noticed when the selected architecture is not correctly fitted during implementation	SA being familiar with department policies, guidelines, instructions related to software development; being familiar with the organization's software architectural style

Derive the requirements for the software architecture	Wrong requirements or no full and comprehensive list of them	Improper architecture is designed	SA is not familiar with the requirements; SA is not aware of the architecture details	**Knowledge, competence, communication**	Detected during examination by the TL, colleagues, SA during discussions	Training in principles and techniques for software development; ensure all the project's technological requirements are correctly gathered, understood, and properly translated for production
Match the software and derived requirements to the chosen architecture components and interfaces	Incorrect matching; impossibility of matching the components	Requirements are not satisfied	SA is not familiar with all requirements; SA chooses an architecture that cannot correspond to the requirements	**Knowledge, competence, communication**	Discovered during implementation; during further design and scheduling by SA or TL	SA having more time to perform the selection; SA being helped by the BA; SA spending more time with the documentation

continued

Table 4.9 (continued)   SHF-FMEA of the Software Architect Role

Process Function	Potential Failure Mode	Potential Effect(s) of Failure	Potential Cause(s)/ Mechanism(s) of Failure	Human Factors	Detection Method(s)	Recommended Action(s)
Identify the key design issues for a successful development	Improper issue is selected (identified) as a key design issue	The most important issue is not resolved	SA cannot spot the main issue correctly	**Knowledge, competence, overload**	SA is not entirely familiar with the project; SA has too many projects to manage	SA spending more time on the particular project
Generate alternatives and constraints for the architecture	Alternative, constraints are not generated	Wrong architecture, or no possibility for variability	SA cannot find alternatives because she is not experienced with the software technologies, standards, and regulations	**Knowledge, competence, attention, judgment, experience**	When alternative is needed, in case the selected architecture turns out to be ineffective	SA having experience with more architectures so she can propose solutions

| Identify the requirements that are connected with the effectiveness and cost | Effectiveness and cost are incorrectly calculated | Wrong selection of the architecture; project runs out of budget; not good performance | SA is not experienced in cost and time calculations; SA cannot manage and coordinate the technological services and staff | **Problem solving, leader thinking, intelligence, knowledge** | Noticed when project is being examined by manager or the selected architecture is being checked by other SA or TL | SA having more practice in budget planning, as well as in other parts of the software development such as testing and training |
| Document, approve, and track all technological changes | Documenting is omitted | Not all changes are recorded | SA has no time to track every single detail; not all changes have been reported; changes happen without SA approval | **Overload, communication, perception, communication** | Noticed later in the development process when certain changes are missing from the documentation | SA or colleagues keeping track of the changes; no changing without SA approval and documentation |

continued

Table 4.9 (continued) SHF-FMEA of the Software Architect Role

Process Function	Potential Failure Mode	Potential Effect(s) of Failure	Potential Cause(s)/ Mechanism(s) of Failure	Human Factors	Detection Method(s)	Recommended Action(s)
Preparing risk mitigation strategies	SA has left the risk strategies to his colleagues	Risk evaluation and mitigation is not performed	SA has not enough time; SA decides to delegate issue to TL, who is not properly informed/ prepared for that	**Overload, problem solving, communication**	Records about the risk evaluation and mitigation	SA should be performing his obligations himself; in the case of delegation a special plan how to act should be made
Be familiar with the organization's software architectural style	SA is not familiar with the organization style	SA is implying decisions that are not following the architectural style	SA has not taken enough time to make herself familiar with the organizations' style and rules; SA is neglecting rules and proposing new ones	**Knowledge, hardworking, professionalism**	SA's work style can be observed by the TL and manager	SA should be working as a part of the team and the organization and not making solo decisions

4.2.1.5 Software Human Factors FMEA of Software Developer Role

Here are the analysis of the software developer and Table 4.10 with the human factors. The summarized personal characteristics for the software developer look like the following (with the details in Table 4.11):

$$HF_{SoftwareDeveloper}^{FMEA} = \{Hardworking, Knowledge, Persistence, Concentration, \quad (4.7)$$

Intelligence, Attention, Competence, Personal overload, Dutifulness,

Communication, Cooperation, Motivation, Achievement, Responsibility,

Talkativeness, Coordination, Personal organization}

Table 4.10 Human Factors for the SD

Human Factors for the Software Developer
Hardworking
Knowledge
Persistence
Concentration
Intelligence
Attention
Competence
Personal overload
Dutifulness
Communication
Cooperation
Motivation
Achievement
Responsibility
Talkativeness
Coordination
Personal organization

Source: Extracted from the FMEA Table 4.11.

Table 4.11 SHF-FMEA of the Software Developer Role

Process Function	Potential Failure Mode	Potential Effect(s) of Failure	Potential Cause(s)/ Mechanism(s) of Failure	Human Factors	Detection Method(s)	Recommended Action(s)
Designs different software components	The designed elements are incorrect or do not follow the requirements	The produced code is not fully operational	SD is not familiar with all requirements; SD has not tested; SD is not asking questions in case of problems; SD is not skilled in programming language and logic	**Hardworking, knowledge, persistence**	Can be seen in the code, bugs or other problems; lack of fulfilled requirements will show at later phase: testing; quality control	SD having good programming skills; SD sharing problems with colleagues; SD being familiar with the requirements and paying attention to debugging
Approve software only if sure that it is safe, meets the specifications, has passed appropriate tests, and is not a threat to life or the environment	Neglect obligations such as inspecting the code or checking if all requirements are met	Software is stated as approved and according to the specification although it isn't	SD is distracted by something; SD omits debugging; SD has too much work or too little time; SD is not concentrating; SD is not skilled in programming and testing	**Concentration, knowledge, intelligence**	Bugs and problems can be seen in the code; problems are spotted by testers, QA	SD paying more attentions to his work and requirements; SD having more time to look things up

| Strive to fully understand the specifications for software on which they work | Not attempting to understand all requirements | Requirements are not all understood and specification is not familiar to SD | SD is not paying attention to requirements and specification with the idea that TL will tell them what to do; SD is omitting readying and understanding the specification; SD has no time to read the specification | **Attention, concentration, competence, overload** | Obvious in meetings with TL; obvious in case SD has to think of a decision on a question | SD paying more attention to his obligations; SD having time to perform an in-depth analysis |
| Ensure adequate testing, debugging, and review of software and related documents | Proper testing and debugging is missing; paper work is skipped | Documents are not created and the proper testing and review of software is not performed | SD has too many obligations and no time to perform this one; SD is bored with doing paperwork | **Overload** | Obvious that the documents are not written; code is not well tested | SD having more time for all tasks; SD being motivated to do her paperwork and review of code |

continued

Table 4.11 (continued)   SHF-FMEA of the Software Developer Role

Process Function	Potential Failure Mode	Potential Effect(s) of Failure	Potential Cause(s)/ Mechanism(s) of Failure	Human Factors	Detection Method(s)	Recommended Action(s)
Maintain the integrity of data, being sensitive to outdated or flawed occurrences	Not paying great attention to data management	Integrity of data may be lost	SD is not skilled at data management; SD omits duties to manage data; SD is careless about outdated or flawed occurrences	**Skills, knowledge**	Lost integrity of data is hard to spot but when found difficult to fix	SD being careful and experienced at data management
Take responsibility for detecting, correcting, and reporting errors in software and associated documents	Neglecting obligations such as bug detecting and tracking	Errors and bugs are not corrected and not documented	SD is bored and not motivated to search for errors; SD has no time to document each error; SD is pointing finger at the tester for looking for and documenting the errors	**Concentration, overload, dutifulness**	Not taking responsibility in front of TL; lack of errors report	SD having more time for his responsibilities; SD being motivated in bug searching, fixing, and documenting

Integrating software modules into software components and units	Not correctly integrating all parts	Components are put together correctly but are not fully operational	SD is not skilled at the specific programming language; SD has not made sure his code will work with those of his colleagues	**Competence, knowledge, communication**	Visible when trying to put all parts together	SD talking more to colleagues; SD paying attention to others' code
Assigned full or part time to participate in project team activities	Not participating in team activities	SD is left outside of the team and is not sharing the team spirit	SD is not social; SD has too much work; SD is not interested in communicating with others	**Communication, cooperation,**	SD is not attending team meetings; team-building	SD trying to be more social; SD attending team activities
Responsible for contributing to overall project objectives and specific team deliverables	Not contributing to project activities	Specific deliverables are not performed	SD is careless in her work; does not perform her duties; SD is not motivated	**Motivation, concentration**	Easy to spot that SD is not effective and motivated in his work	SD being more careful in his work; TL can find different ways to stimulate the SD to give his best

continued

Table 4.11 (continued) SHF-FMEA of the Software Developer Role

Process Function	Potential Failure Mode	Potential Effect(s) of Failure	Potential Cause(s)/ Mechanism(s) of Failure	Human Factors	Detection Method(s)	Recommended Action(s)
Participates with TL in application documentation	Does not cooperate with the TL	TL is left alone to do all the documentation	SD has no time for this responsibility; SD is not willing to do paperwork; SD has no good style at making such documents	**Overload, achievement, competence**	TL is doing all the work himself; TL is not receiving help from SD	SD cooperating with the TL; SD being motivated to work together with the TL
Designs, codes, and builds the application	Designing and coding are not performed on high level	The code is full of errors; bad performance; not following the requirements	SD is not a skilled developer; SD is not familiar with the requirements; SD does not consult with colleagues or TL and works alone	**Knowledge, competence, intelligence, communication**	Bad code can be easily discovered by inspection; not meeting the requirements is also obvious in later checks	SD being more experienced; SD working better with colleagues; SD paying more attention to his work

Participates in code reviews and testing	Not performing his duties by testing and reviewing	QA is left out to test by himself and with no help from SD	SD has no time for helping colleagues; SD is not willing to help; SD has too many other obligations	**Cooperation, communication**	Lack of desire to help is easy to spot and difficult to tolerate	SD working better with colleagues and eager to help
Fixes bugs, defects, and shortcomings	Omits testing and bug fixing	Code is left without fixing	SD does not have time; throwing responsibility to QA; SD is not good at bug detecting and fixing	**Cooperation, responsibility, knowledge, competence**	Bugs in the code are found during QA testing	SD being more precise in his work; SD paying more attentions to bug fixing
Work with colleagues within the designated project guidelines	Not being friendly and cooperative	SD is not easy to work with and is not a good team player	SD is not friendly; prefers working alone; does not socialize with colleagues	**Social contact, communication, talkativeness**	It is obvious in his lack of communication and cooperation	SD trying to socialize; perform better in team work in order to fulfill project needs

continued

Table 4.11 (continued)   SHF-FMEA of the Software Developer Role

Process Function	Potential Failure Mode	Potential Effect(s) of Failure	Potential Cause(s)/ Mechanism(s) of Failure	Human Factors	Detection Method(s)	Recommended Action(s)
Notify the TL of any expected difficulties or issues arising	Trying to resolve problems on her own	TL is not notified of the problems that have occurred; SD is making decisions that may not be within his competency	SD believes it is in his authority to answer such questions; SD does not want to bother TL; SD feels proud and independent managing issues on his own, neglecting team's procedure of informing	**Competence, coordination, organization**	Difficult to spot, may be seen later, when the problem becomes really big and eventually SD has to inform his TL	SD should know her place in the team and always inform TL in case of a major issue

4.2.1.6 Software Human Factors FMEA of Software Tester Role

Here are the analysis of the software tester and Table 4.12 with the human factors. The summarized personal characteristics for the software tester look like the following (with the details in Table 4.13):

$$HF^{FMEA}_{SoftwareTester} = \{Competence, Knowledge, Communication, \qquad (4.8)$$

$$Personal\ attitude,\ Motivation,\ Overload,\ Concentration,$$

$$Understanding,\ Coordination,\ Self\text{-}confidence,\ Creativity,$$

$$Imagination,\ Open\ minded,\ Self\text{-}organization\}$$

Table 4.12 Human Factors for the ST
Human Factors for the Software Tester
Competence
Knowledge
Communication
Personal attitude
Motivation
Overload
Concentration
Understanding
Coordination
Too high self-confidence
Creativity
Imagination
Open minded
Self-organization

Source: Extracted from the SHF-FMEA Table 4.13.

Table 4.13 SHF-FMEA of the Software Tester Role

Process Function	Potential Failure Mode	Potential Effect(s) of Failure	Potential Cause(s)/ Mechanism(s) of Failure	Human Factors	Detection Method(s)	Recommended Action(s)
Work with the QA to build a test strategy and test plans	Missing tests and wrong test strategy	Undiscovered problems, which at later step will be very expensive to mitigate	Lack of communication between tester and QA; unable to agree on the needed strategy; lack of knowledge about the needed testing	**Competence, knowledge, communication, personal attitude**	In meetings where the testing strategy is discussed	More communication between the team members that have this obligation; teaching seminars in order to get new knowledge in the area
Designing and implementing test scripts and test cases	False test scripts and test cases	Inefficient testing that ends with undiscovered problems	Lack of knowledge which leads to incomplete and inefficient testing; lack of time for full testing; lack of motivation	**Competence, knowledge, personal attitude, motivation**	Discussions about the test scripts and cases; inspections from the TL; later when the application is not working as expected	Discussions with the TL; enough time for testing; seminars and motivation from the TL

| Functional analysis of the software application in the actual environment | Some steps in this functional analysis are not identified correctly or omitted during testing | There are steps in the functional analysis left untested and this may lead to some wrong functionality or errors | ST has no time to test everything; ST has not prepared a functional testing strategy | **Overload, competence, concentration** | Detected when the software is not working as expected in the real environment | Being careful and performing test on each functional part in the concrete environment; the ST expanding her view to predict what may go wrong and perform the necessary testing steps |
| Design, specification, and implementation of the test environment and the test data | Wrong specified test environment and test data | The software cannot be correctly tested; not all problems are discovered and mitigated | Not enough knowledge and experience with the needed techniques; wrong identified test data; little time | **Overload, competence, knowledge** | Detected later on when problems occur; it is possible that some errors stay undiscovered | Paying more attention and more time for designing the environment and the datasets; additional learning |

continued

Table 4.13 (continued) SHF-FMEA of the Software Tester Role

Process Function	Potential Failure Mode	Potential Effect(s) of Failure	Potential Cause(s)/ Mechanism(s) of Failure	Human Factors	Detection Method(s)	Recommended Action(s)
Understanding of the software development process, the operating system, and network infrastructure used for deployment of the software	ST does not understand in depth the development process or the complete architecture of the network used	In readying for installation program some limitations implied by the network or by some software design specifics may not be considered	The ST does not have a good understanding of software development; may be not attending team meetings; be unfamiliar with network architecture; be unfamiliar with the architecture on which the software is built	**Knowledge, understanding, coordination**	Observed when the software is not proceeding properly and cannot be deployed	Paying great attention to development details as well as to the network infrastructure

				Knowledge, overload, motivation		
Execute the tests, document the results and maintain the records	Wrong tests, wrong results, and lack of documentation of the whole process	Undiscovered failures in the software; lack of documentation that could be used in the next testing process	Not enough knowledge how to build the tests; lack of time and desire to write documentation		Detected in meetings when discussing testing progress and documentation; detected later on when evaluating the results	ST must pay more attention in the testing and documenting process; has to put more effort into achieving the software goals
Being familiar with similar type of software, its complexity and typical functionality	ST is not very familiar with other software products of the type	ST cannot use experience from similar projects and it is possible that he overlooks some problems	ST has no time to search for other similar solutions with ready testing process and prefers to build it on his own, but conducts failures	**Overload, too high self-confidence**	Difficult to discover, but the problems occur at a later step when evaluating the testing process	Analysis of common systems in the field that can be used as basis for the current testing process

continued

Table 4.13 (continued) SHF-FMEA of the Software Tester Role

Process Function	Potential Failure Mode	Potential Effect(s) of Failure	Potential Cause(s)/ Mechanism(s) of Failure	Human Factors	Detection Method(s)	Recommended Action(s)
Being familiar with the latest standards, tools, and methods that can be used in the testing process	ST is not constantly enriching his knowledge in the area	New standards or methods may be new for her	ST is not learning new techniques due to being old-fashioned or unmotivated; ST is missing new items and tools that will make his work easier	**Creative, imagination, open minded**	Can be discovered only when other colleagues criticize his work	ST should be constantly looking for new information and new ideas in order to use the most trendy solutions
Perform defect tracking, status reporting, and auditing	ST is not continuously tracking the current software system	Threats, defects, may remain undetected or untraced in the documentation reporting	ST does not have time to perform new defects search; ST postpones tasks for tracking and reporting due to not being motivated	**Overload, organization, motivation**	Lack of written reports, defect tracking, and auditing is obvious	More control over the ST's obligations so that she performs defect tracking and status reporting
Retesting after fixing problems	ST is not performing retesting, or only partly	New failures	ST does not have time to perform the retesting or he does not have the desire to do that	**Overload, motivation**	Observed with the occurrence of new problems in the software	Control and motivation over the testing team

4.2.1.7 Software Human Factors FMEA of Software Quality Engineer Role

Here is the analysis of the software quality engineer and Table 4.14 with the human factors. The summarized personal characteristics for the software quality engineer look like the following (with the details in Table 4.15):

$$HF^{FMEA}_{SoftwareQualityEngineer} = \{Overload,\ Coordination,\ Communication, \qquad (4.9)$$

Competence, Knowledge, Self-confidence, Planning,

Attention, Intelligence, Understanding, Patience,

Friendliness, Concentration, Professionalism, Cooperation}

Table 4.14 Human Factors for the SQE

Human Factors for the Software Quality Engineer
Overload
Coordination
Communication
Competence
Knowledge
Over–self-confidence
Planning
Attention
Intelligence
Understanding
Patience
Friendliness
Concentration
Professionalism
Cooperation

Source: Extracted from SHF-FMEA Table 4.15.

Table 4.15 SHF-FMEA of the Software Quality Engineer Role

Process Function	Potential Failure Mode	Potential Effect(s) of Failure	Potential Cause(s)/ Mechanism(s) of Failure	Human Factors	Detection Method(s)	Recommended Action(s)
Planning and implementing a product testing regime during the development and construction process	Planning and implementation of the testing scenarios are not performed	The test regime is being developed after the code has been written and this affects the whole development process	QE is having too much obligations; QE is not being helped by ST and Architect for the project requirements; QE does not have enough experience	**Overload, coordination, communication, competence, knowledge**	Lack of performed test cases is obvious in the number of bugs	QE having more time for his duties; QE being helped and monitored by SA or TL; QE being skilled in planning and implementing of testing regimes
Responsible for guaranteeing a quality level for the end client	Not taking responsibility and pointing finger at the development team	Bad atmosphere in the team due to QE's desire not to take responsibility	QE not admitting his mistakes; QE not familiar with all his obligations; QE not able to plan all needed actions	**Self-confidence, competence, planning**	Can be seen at team meetings	QE being able to admit being wrong and taking responsibility for his work

Understand the requirements of the project's technological scope, its required functionality and quality grade	Not all requirements (functionality and quality) are met	Not all requirements are checked, tested and inspected, resulting in product being not fully operational like specified	QE is not familiar with requirements due to not attending team meetings; not reading specification; not checking what is written and interpreting it on his own; not getting proper explanations	**Coordination, attention, intelligence, knowledge, understanding**	Can be seen at a later phase by testers or even users	QE making effort to be familiar with requirements; paying attention when being explained about details, value of project
Assuring the needed level of quality in the completed objectives	Time is pressing the team so some tests are omitted	Parts of the development are left not inspected in depth, hidden bugs may have remained	QE is really pressed by the time; QE is not being patient to perform each test again and again; the code is not well introduced by SDs	**Overloaded, patience, coordination**	Lack of proper quality level is visible in testing as well as on a later phase by the user/client	Better schedule of all properties; all team members working according it; better control by the TL

continued

Table 4.15 (continued) SHF-FMEA of the Software Quality Engineer Role

Process Function	Potential Failure Mode	Potential Effect(s) of Failure	Potential Cause(s)/ Mechanism(s) of Failure	Human Factors	Detection Method(s)	Recommended Action(s)
Works with the Business Analyst and the Software Architect to convert the requirements and design documents into a set of testing cases and scripts	Not good communication with BA and SA; requirements are not good transformed into test cases and scripts	The produced tests are not useful and do not meet project level and details; the project is not correctly tested and not all client needs are satisfied	QE is not social and is not communicating with colleagues; QE is pretending to know all and makes tests and analyses on his own; QE not being familiar with the requirements	**Friendliness, coordination, communication, competence**	Can be seen when the project is not meeting the client requirements; the communication level in the team is not good and the atmosphere is not productive	QE being more social and providing better work atmosphere in team; QE carefully reading and examining requirements when transforming them to test cases
Performs random testing of all components to check again for errors in the system	Not performing random testing and relying only on the testers	A random bug may not be found	QE does not have time for this testing; QE does not know how to perform this random testing	**Overload, knowledge, competence**	Can be discovered or not, depending on how random the bug is	QE making all diversity of tests so he can spot the bug or at least the situation in which it may show up

| Measurement and quantification of the completed solution performance | Not making performance tests | The performance of the solution is not measured and could be quite low | QE has no time to measure quality due to bad schedule; QE may not be familiar with the tests for performance | **Overload, knowledge, competence** | Bad performance can be seen later, when the solution is brought to the clients | QE having time and skills for performance testing |
| Be familiar with the organization's software architectural style, departmental testing policies, criteria, strategy and procedures | QE is not familiar with organization testing policies and software strategies | QE's way of testing and documenting does not meet the organization's expectation | QE is not introduced to the specific working style; QE has problems to work according to the organization's politics | **Coordination, knowledge, competence** | Can be seen if he is not keeping the organization's rules or practices and is making decisions on his own | QE should be given time to become familiar with the organization's testing practices and development style |

continued

Table 4.15 (continued)   SHF-FMEA of the Software Quality Engineer Role

Process Function	Potential Failure Mode	Potential Effect(s) of Failure	Potential Cause(s)/ Mechanism(s) of Failure	Human Factors	Detection Method(s)	Recommended Action(s)
Being familiar with the latest standards	Not familiar with the needed standards and testing technologies	The work of QE is not compliant with standards and technologies; does not follow organization's politics	QE is not paying attention to the latest standards and technologies due to the fact that he is not familiar with them or he does not agree with them and has other point of view	**Concentration, professionalism**	Obvious in his work; can be observed his way of making things and taking decisions	QE should follow project and organization's politics for making decisions, should be familiar with new designs and standards, associated to the project
Provide advice and guidance on quality issues when and where needed	QE is not providing proper help when asked	Those looking for QE's help are left with questions	QE does not have time for such questions; QE is not a helpful person and is avoiding communicating with colleagues	**Overload, character, communication, cooperation**	Can be observed in the everyday communication and cooperation process	QE should be ready to discuss and help his colleagues; Team building

4.3 Summary of Software Human Factors FMEA

We conducted the innovative adoption of the FMEA as software human factor FMEA in a strictly analytical way of the responsibilities of the software development team members, explained in Chapter 3, and were able to uncover many different human features behind different failures or potential problems in the software development process. Here we show once again all the factors for the different roles and after this put them together in order to gain the full list of human factors that are critical for the software engineering process.

$$HF_{ProjectManager}^{FMEA} = \{Coordination, Self\text{-}management, Stress, \quad (4.10)$$

$$Knowledge, Effectiveness, Concentration, Communication, Self\text{-}development,$$

$$Liberalism, Control, Egoism, Confidence, Competence, Organization\}$$

$$HF_{TeamLeader}^{FMEA} = \{Hardworking, Knowledge, Communication, Attention,$$

$$Conscientiousness, Leader skills, Mental overload, Competence, Experience,$$

$$Technical understanding, Planning skills, Monitoring, Appreciation,$$

$$Cooperation, Fear, Management\}$$

$$HF_{BusinessAnalyst}^{FMEA} = \{Intelligence, Knowledge, Work overload, Concentration,$$

$$Analysis skills, Competence, Communication, Planning, Openness\}$$

$$HF_{SoftwareArchitect}^{FMEA} = \{Knowledge, Hardworking, Intelligence, Communication,$$

$$Competence, Creativity, Cooperation, Emotional stability,$$

$$Mental overload, Attention, Judgment, Experience, Problem solving,$$

$$Leader thinking, Perception, Professionalism\}$$

$$HF_{SoftwareDeveloper}^{FMEA} = \{Hardworking, Knowledge, Persistence, Concentration,$$

$$Intelligence, Attention, Competence, Personal overload, Dutifulness,$$

$$Communication, Cooperation, Motivation, Achievement,$$

$$Responsibility, Talkativeness, Coordination, Personal organization\}$$

$$HF\,^{FMEA}_{SoftwareTester} = \{Competence,\ Knowledge,\ Communication,\ Personal\ attitude,$$

$$Motivation,\ Overload,\ Concentration,\ Understanding,\ Coordination,$$

$$Self\text{-}confidence,\ Creativity,\ Imagination,\ Open\ minded,\ Self\text{-}organization\}$$

$$HF\,^{FMEA}_{SoftwareQualityEngineer} = \{Overload,\ Coordination,\ Communication,\ Competence,$$

$$Knowledge,\ Self\text{-}confidence,\ Planning,\ Attention,\ Intelligence,\ Understanding,$$

$$Patience,\ Friendliness,\ Concentration,\ Professionalism,\ Cooperation\}$$

Summarizing these factors into one with the help of the following formula:

$$HF\,^{FMEA}_{Software\,Process} = \{HF\,^{FMEA}_{ProjectManager},\ HF\,^{FMEA}_{TeamLeader},\ HF\,^{FMEA}_{BusinessAnalyst}, \qquad (4.11)$$

$$HF\,^{FMEA}_{SoftwareArchitect},\ HF\,^{FMEA}_{SoftwareDeveloper},\ HF\,^{FMEA}_{SoftwareTester},\ HF\,^{FMEA}_{SoftwareQualityEngineer}\}$$

and after merging them and taking out the repeated ones we have Table 4.16 with human factors or characteristics that influence the software development performance.

Having all the critical human factors for the software process we were faced with a new problem. How can we measure these traits and how can we examine a person in order to be able to understand which features he or she possesses and to what extent so we can find out how they influence work performance.

We manage this challenge in the next two chapters. First we adopt a well-known psychological method in order to measure personal features and then a special statistical method in order to find out how they influence the individual's performance.

Table 4.16 Summary of Performance-Related Human Factors

1. Coordination	13. Over-self-confident	25. Cooperation	37. Persistence
2. Self-management	14. Self-organization	26. Fear	38. Dutifulness
3. Mental overload = stress	15. Hardworking	27. Management skills	39. Motivation
4. Competence	16. Attention	28. Intelligence	40. Achievement
5. Knowledge	17. Conscientiousness	29. Analysis skills	41. Responsibility
6. Effectiveness	18. Leader skills	30. Openness	42. Talkativeness
7. Concentration	19. Experience	31. Creativity	43. Personal attitude (satisfaction)
8. Communication	20. Personal growth	32. Emotional stability	44. Technical understanding
9. Self-development	21. Understanding ability	33. Judgment	45. Imagination
10. Liberalism	22. Planning skills	34. Problem-solving ability	46. Patience
11. Control delegation	23. Observing ability	35. Perception	47. Friendliness
12. Selfish = egotism	24. Appreciation	36. Professionalism	

References

Banerjee, N. (1995). Utilization of FMEA concept in software lifecycle management. *Transactions on Information and Communications Technologies*, 11(6): 219–230.

Bowles, J. and Hanczaryk, W. (2008). Threat effects analysis: Applying FMEA to model computer system threats. In *Annual Reliability and Maintainability Symposium*, Las Vegas, January, pp. 6–12.

Georgieva, K. (2010d). Conducting FMEA over the software development process. *Software Engineering Notes*, 35(3): 35.

Georgieva, K., Neumann, R., and Dumke, R. (2011a). Failure mode and effect analysis for the software team capabilities. In *MetriKon 2011—Praxis der Software-Messung*. Aachen: Shaker, pp. 55–66.

Goddard, P. (2000). Software FMEA techniques. In *Reliability and Maintainability Symposium*, Los Angeles: IEEE, pp. 118–123.

Hartkopf, S. (2004). From a single discipline risk management approach to an interdisciplinary one: Adaptation of FMEA to software needs. In *Eleventh Annual International Workshop on Software Technology and Engineering Practice (STEP'04)*. Los Alamitos, CA: IEEE Computer Society Press.

Lauritsen, T. and Stalhane, T. (2005). Safety methods in software process improvement. In *Software Process Improvement 12th European Conference, EuroSPI 2005*. Berlin: Springer, pp. 95–105,

Mäckel, O. (2006). *Software FMEA, opportunities and benefits of FMEA in the development process of software-intensive technical systems*. Viewed 15 February 2014, http://www.fmeainfocentre.com/papers/

McDermott, R., Mikulak, R., and Beauregard, M. (2009). *The Basics of FMEA*. Boca Raton, FL: CRC Press.

Nguyen, D. (2001). Failure modes and effects analysis for software reliability. In *Reliability and Maintainability Symposium*, Philadelphia: IEEE. pp. 219–222.

Ozarin, N. and Siracusa, M. (2003). A process for failure modes and effects analysis of computer software. In *Reliability and Maintainability Symposium*. Los Alamitos, CA: IEEE Computer Society Press, pp. 365–370.

Pentti, H. and Atte, H. (2002). *Failure Mode and Effects Anlysis of Software-Based Automation Systems*. Helsinki: VTT Industrial Systems.

Stamatis, D. (1995). *Failure Mode and Effect Analysis*. Wisconsin: ASQC Quality Press.

Chapter 5

Definition and Evaluation of IT Human Factors

The previous chapter introduced many human factors of software development team members generated by the adopted FMEA (failure mode and effect analysis) analytical approach. Here we had the challenge to find out how we can measure these human factors in such a way as to find the connection between the factors and individual performance. After much research we decided to adopt the "Big Five" theory, widely used in the recruitment and personnel selection process, in order to be able to evaluate all these factors and to find the connection with individual performance. Adopting this method for our needs we were able to measure specific personal traits and personal productivity and use this information in the next chapter to discover the dependence between human characteristics and productivity. The next steps in our approach are shown in Figure 5.1.

5.1 Five Personal Features

The Big Five model is a comprehensive, data-driven approach that evaluates five different compound personal traits in order to build a complete psychological profile. The five factors were discovered and formulated by several independent researchers and had a long maturing process, summarized by Digman (1990).

The first idea about analyzing the human personality came in the beginning of the twentieth century from McDougall (1932), but the first version of the model was proposed by Ernest Tupes and Raymond Cristal (1961). This proposal reached the academic audience 20 years later and by this time there were already other

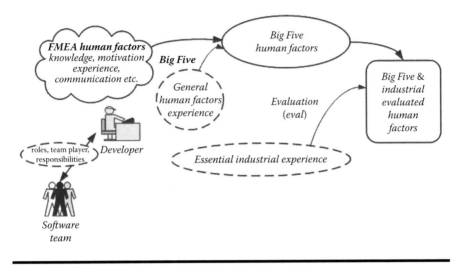

Figure 5.1 Refinement of the human factors approach.

scientific papers proposing similar ideas. In 1990 Digman developed the Five-Factor model and a few years later Goldberg (1993) refined it to the highest level. The interesting point in the history of the Big Five is that the personal features were discovered by different scientists to be the same and, that although there are some differences, all came to the decision that these five features in particular with their facets (John, Robins, and Pervin, 2008) describe human behavior in the best way. The Big Five traits are also referred to as the "Five Factor Model" or FFM (Costa and McCrae, 1992) and as the global factors of personality (Russell and Karol, 1994). The Big Five factors are openness, conscientiousness, extroversion, agreeableness, and neuroticism (OCEAN). Sometimes the neuroticism element is called emotional stability and the openness factor is called intellect. Here we give a short explanation of these traits.

Openness to Experience/Intelligence (Inventive/Curious vs. Cautious/Conservative): Openness, in some places also called intelligence, is the ability of people to accept and to search for new ideas, knowledge, experience, and so on. It describes the originality and complexity of an individual and distinguishes the imaginative from down-to-earth people (John et al., 2008). Such persons are ready for new experiences, intellectually searching, and impressed by art. People with low levels of openness are traditional and have conventional understandings.

Conscientiousness (Efficient/Organized vs. Easygoing/Careless): This is a feature that expresses self-discipline and determination and desire for achievement. It expresses an intention to behave in a planned matter, goal-directed and thinking before acting. Such people follow norms and rules; they are always on time, study hard, and give their best to the job. They are not impulsive and show high values of thoughtfulness (John et al., 2008). Low levels of conscientiousness are displayed by disorganized people who don't really care how they are performing in their job and don't feel responsible for their actions.

Extroversion (Outgoing/Energetic vs. Shy/Withdrawn): Extroversion can be described by positive emotions, the desire to seek stimulation and the company of others. It is an energetic and positive attitude to the world and is described with features including sociability, activity, assertiveness, and positive emotionality. For these people it is easy to approach strangers, to introduce themselves, to be the leader, and the center of a company (John et al., 2008). When being around people they like to talk, put themselves forward, and be the center of attention. Introverts lack the social cheerfulness and activity levels of the extroverts. They tend to be quiet and less interested in the social world.

Agreeableness (Friendly/Compassionate vs. Competitive/Outspoken): This feature is expressed in compassionate and cooperative behavior. It shows a prosocial and communal orientation toward others and can be described with traits such as altruism, tender-mindedness, trust, and modesty (John et al., 2008). This characteristic is very important for social harmony and understanding. Such people are generous, kind, friendly, caring, cooperative, and ready to compromise their own interests. People with a low level of agreeableness put their own interest first and exhibit traits such as suspicion, unfriendliness, and uncooperativeness.

Neuroticism (Sensitive/Nervous vs. Control/Confident): Neuroticism is characterized with the propensity to negative emotions such as anger, nervousness, and depression. It contrasts with emotional stability and is expressed with emotions including feeling anxious, nervous, sad, and tense (John et al., 2008). People with a high score of neuroticism tend to accept ordinary situations as threatening and small obstacles as hopelessly difficult. They are in negative emotional states for long times and this influences their working process. Persons with low neuroticism are not so easily disturbed and are emotionally stable.

The defining facets for the Big Five trait domains are shown in Table 5.1. The table shows three different approaches for the Big Five and their facets, summarized by Oliver John and his colleagues in their book, *Handbook of Personality: Theory and Research* (John et al., 2008). These facets give additional understanding for the Big Five traits and help us on the next step when matching the discovered software human factors to the Big Five.

"Some facets (e.g., CPI Adventurousness) are listed once under their primary Big Five domain (e.g., Openness) and again in brackets under another Big Five domain if their best-matching facet appears there (e.g., next to NEO Excitement-Seeking, which is an Extraversion facet on the NEO-PI-R but also has a substantial

Table 5.1 Defining Facets for Big Five Trait Domains

Lexical Facets (Saucier and Ostendorf, 1999)	NEO-PI-R Facets (Costa and McCrae, 1992)	CPI-Big Five Facets (Soto and John, 2008)
Extroversion (E) Facets		
E Sociability	E Gregariousness	E Gregariousness
E Assertiveness	E Assertiveness	E Assertiveness/ Leadership
E Activity/ Adventurousness	E Activity	[O Adventurousness]
E Unrestrained	E Excitement-Seeking	E Social Confidence vs. Anxiety
[A Warmth/Affection]	E Positive emotions	
	E Warmth	
Agreeableness (A) Facets		
A Warmth/Affection	[E Warmth]	A Modesty vs. Narcissism
A Modesty/Humility	A Modesty	A Trust vs. Suspicion
A Generosity	A Trust	A Empathy/Sympathy
A Gentleness	A Tender-Mindedness	A Altruism
	A Compliance	
	A Straightforwardness	
Conscientiousness (C) Facets		
C Orderliness	C Order	C Orderliness
C Industriousness	C Achievement Striving	C Industriousness
C Reliability	C Dutifulness	C Self-Discipline
C Decisiveness	C Self-Discipline	
[O Perceptiveness]	C Competence	
	C Deliberation	
Neuroticism (N) Facets		
N Insecurity	N Anxiety	N Anxiety
N Emotionality	N Angry Hostility	N Irritability
N Irritability	N Depression	N Depression
	N Self-Consciousness	N Rumination– Compulsiveness
	N Vulnerability	[E Social Confidence vs. Anxiety]
	N Impulsiveness	

Table 5.1 (continued)   Defining Facets for Big Five Trait Domains

Lexical Facets (Saucier and Ostendorf, 1999)	NEO-PI-R Facets (Costa and McCrae, 1992)	CPI-Big Five Facets (Soto and John, 2008)
Openness (O) Facets		
O Intellect	O Ideas	O Intellectualism
O Imagination/Creativity	O Aesthetics	O Idealism
O Perceptiveness	O Fantasy	O Adventurousness
	O Actions	
	O Feelings	
	O Values	

Source: O.P. John, R.W. Robins, and L.A. Pervin, *Handbook of Personality: Theory and Research.* New York: Guilford Press, 2008. With permission.

secondary correlation with Openness)" (John et al., 2008). Table 4.4 in John et al. (2008) shows another detailed list with the central trait adjectives for the Five Factors.

5.2 Matching Big Five Traits with IT Human Factors

The Big Five trait domain that we are adopting in our method is the NEO-PI-R; with its 30 facets it is the most comprehensive. Based on the analysis from Chapters 2 through 4 we have found the personal competencies and special human factors that influence the individual's performance. Having these critical human factors for the software process we were faced with the problem of how to measure them. For this purpose we used the following matching between critical human factors and the Big Five psychological traits. This matching helps us to evaluate the human traits and in this way to observe the dependence between them and performance. In the following we show the matching between the human factors that we have found and the Big Five traits (see Table 5.2).

After the matching process was over we found a few additional features that didn't pass into the Big Five traits and we decided to include them as additional factors. These are experience and motivation. Under experience we have the following subtraits: competence, knowledge, and technical understanding. Inasmuch as the values for the Big Five are in percentages, we decided to use percentages for the additional factors also. In order to estimate the value of motivation we used special questions, shown in Table 5.5 and evaluated them in the same manner as the Big Five test. For evaluation of experience we took a 20-year basis for 100% and calculated the values based on that.

Table 5.2   Matching between Big Five Traits and Software Human Factors

NEO-PI-R Facets (Costa and McCrae, 1992)	Human Factors Important for Software Development Process
Extroversion (E) Facets	Communication
E Gregariousness	Selfish = egoism
E Assertiveness	Over–Self-Confident
E Activity	Leadership Skills
E Excitement-Seeking	Management Skills
E Positive Emotions	Talkativeness
E Warmth	Judgment
Agreeableness (A) Facets	Liberalism
A Modesty	Appreciation
A Trust	Cooperation
A Tender-Mindedness	Problem Solving
A Compliance	Perception
A Straightforwardness	Persistence (by low A)
	Friendliness
Conscientiousness (C) Facets	Coordination
C Order	Self-Management/Organization
C Achievement Striving	Control Delegation
C Dutifulness	Effectiveness
C Self-Discipline	Hardworking
C Competence	Attention
C Deliberation	Planning Skills
	Professionalism
	Dutifulness
	Achievement
	Responsibility
Neuroticism (N) Facets	Mental Overload; Stress
N Anxiety	Concentration
N Angry Hostility	Fear
N Depression	Emotional Stability
N Self-Consciousness	Personal Attitude
N Vulnerability	Patience
N Impulsiveness	

Table 5.2 (continued)   Matching between Big Five Traits and Software Human Factors

NEO-PI-R Facets (Costa and McCrae, 1992)	Human Factors Important for Software Development Process
Openness (O) Facets	Self-Development
O Ideas	Personal Growth
O Aesthetics	Understanding Ability
O Fantasy	Observing Ability
O Actions	Intelligence
O Feelings	Analysis Skills
O Values	Creativity
	Imagination

The last and the most important factor we evaluated was performance. In order to evaluate it we again used several sources: first self-evaluation, then the supervising personnel/manager, and last but not least the evaluation of colleagues. In this manner we were able to calculate the value of the performance/productivity also in percentage of the managed work per month. Thus we can summarize the seven factors that we decided to investigate in connection with individual performance:

1. Openness
2. Conscientiousness
3. Extroversion
4. Agreeableness
5. Neuroticism
6. Experience
7. Motivation

5.3 Evaluation Test

To measure the seven personal characteristics listed above we adopted the Big Five questions and added additional ones to evaluate the other two factors and also the approximate performance. First we look over the standard questions, shown in Table 5.3, and then we take a look at the additional ones. The table shows all positive and negative questions for the Big Five traits. The questions are taken from an online pool for scientific collaboration, *International Personality Item Pool* (1997).

We have 10 questions per factor and they can be categorized into positive or negative. Every question has five options for an answer: Very Inaccurate,

Table 5.3 Big Five Questions

Positive Questions	Negative Questions
Extroversion	
I am the life of the party.	Don't talk a lot.
Feel comfortable around people.	Keep in the background.
Start conversations.	Have little to say.
Talk to a lot of different people at parties.	Don't like to draw attention to myself.
Don't mind being the center of attention.	I am quiet around strangers.
Agreeableness	
I am interested in people.	I am not really interested in others.
Sympathize with others' feelings.	Insult people.
Have a soft heart.	I am not interested in other people's problems.
Take time out for others.	Feel little concern for others.
Feel others' emotions.	
Make people feel at ease.	
Conscientiousness	
I am always prepared.	Leave my belongings around.
Pay attention to details.	Make a mess of things.
Get chores done right away.	Often forget to put things back in their proper place.
Like order.	Shirk my duties.
Follow a schedule.	
I am exacting in my work.	

Table 5.3 (continued)   Big Five Questions

Positive Questions	Negative Questions
Emotional Stability	
Am relaxed most of the time.	Get stressed out easily.
Seldom feel blue.	Worry about things.
	I am easily disturbed.
	Get upset easily.
	Change my mood a lot.
	Have frequent mood swings.
	Get irritated easily.
	Often feel blue.
Openness/Intelligence	
Have a rich vocabulary.	Have difficulty understanding abstract ideas.
Have a vivid imagination.	I am not interested in abstract ideas.
Have excellent ideas.	Do not have a good imagination.
I am quick to understand things.	
Use difficult words.	
Spend time reflecting on things.	
I am full of ideas.	

Source: International Personality Item Pool, 1997. With permission.

Moderately Inaccurate, Neither Inaccurate nor Accurate, Moderately Accurate, or Very Accurate. Depending on the question type—positive or negative—from one to five points are given. The evaluation in Table 5.4 shows this point of view.

The additional questions are listed in Table 5.5 and are taken from a position paper about behavior-based assessment (Smolders et al., 2009) and help us to evaluate motivation and experience factors. The additional questions about motivation are answered like the previous ones, as shown in Table 5.4, and the questions regarding experience are answered in plain explanatory text. The questions in their

Table 5.4   Points for Different Answers

	Points for Statement	
Answer	*Positive*	*Negative*
Very inaccurate	1	5
Moderately inaccurate	2	4
Neither inaccurate nor accurate	3	3
Moderately accurate	4	2
Very accurate	5	1

Table 5.5   Additional Questions for Experience and Motivation

Questions for Experience and Motivation Factors	
Motivation	*Experience*
You feel the goals you are supposed to achieve are realistic and attainable?	What is your current working position?
Feedback from your manager/supervisor is clear and directed at improving your performance?	What is your age?
Your job is both interesting and challenging?	How many years have you worked at your current position?
You feel that your current salary motivates you to perform?	
The advancement and growth opportunity within the organization motivates you to perform better?	
You receive recognition for your achievements from your manager/supervisor?	
You receive ongoing training to improve your ability and skills?	
Your manager/supervisor lets you take responsibility for the tasks you perform?	
Your current performance appraisal system motivates you to achieve your goals and improve your performance?	

Source: Smolders et al. *Unpublished manuscript.* 2009. With permission.

actual form in the test were randomized, and this is because if answered one after the other from a particular type, they tend to seem the same and a person can simply copy the previous statement without thinking about the current one.

One more very important question was included in the test: "With what percentage would you estimate your everyday performance?" As already said in order to measure this, we used the personal evaluation and those from the supervising head and from colleagues for each examined person. In addition to the self-estimation we asked supervisors/managers and colleagues separately how they would evaluate the work of the examined person in successful amount of work per month. Having all these questions we were able to build our test and to distribute it around different software companies. We used an online platform (Zoho Challenge, 2010), so that it was easy to access, fill in, and evaluate.

We distributed the questionnaire to five companies, and from 200 participants we gained 73 usefully completed tests. Then we summarized the data (many tests had identical results) and presented it in Table 5.6. The people that answered the test were between 26 and 55 years old with different experience on their current position (20 years = 100%). The numbers of the people according to their positions are as follows:

Project Manager—6
Business Analyst—10
Software Architect—10
Team Leader—10
Software Developer—15
Quality Engineer—10
Software Tester—12

Having the complete data we were able to do a correlation analysis with the main goal of finding the connection between performance and the seven personal traits (Georgieva, Neumann, and Dumke, 2010e). This analysis can be seen in Table 5.7. We use these results to choose the factors for building our predictive mathematical model in the next chapter.

5.4 Summary of Definition and Evaluation of IT Human Factors

We introduced the well-known Big Five theory in order to match the already discovered software/IT human factors to the five factors and to measure them in this way. Adding two new traits to the basic ones gave us the possibility of covering the

Table 5.6 Summarized Test-Results Data

Performance [%]	Motivation [%]	Conscientiousness [%]	Openness [%]	Agreeableness [%]	Experience [%]	Extroversion [%]	Emotional Stability [%]
46	30	36	58	40	20	46	78
47	34	36	60	42	7.5	50	64
49	40	38	66	44	15	44	68
53	50	40	68	100	5	60	88
58	46	46	68	46	35	60	66
61	56	42	98	48	100	86	66
62	58	48	70	98	10	90	94
64	52	44	72	50	10	58	66
64	54	90	96	96	5	54	76
66	55	44	72	52	25	58	84
69	60	50	96	54	50	60	88
70	60	50	94	94	5	74	64
72	61	52	74	56	12.5	78	60
73	62	88	74	92	10	54	72
76	66	54	94	58	10	56	68

78	64	56	78	60	5	58	78
79	68	86	78	62	15	28	52
80	78	84	92	64	40	42	82
81	75	58	80	90	15	50	70
83	70	60	82	66	25	56	66
84	80	62	82	88	7.5	60	68
85	72	82	92	68	50	64	78
87	82	64	88	86	35	72	84
89	85	66	82	70	10	76	86
90	90	68	90	84	20	84	60
91	95	70	86	72	40	88	66
92	88	72	86	74	12.5	52	82
93	93	74	84	76	35	72	68
93	98	76	90	82	50	56	86
94	99	78	88	80	50	60	80
95	100	80	84	78	65	60	98

Table 5.7 Correlation Analysis

	Motivation	Conscientiousness	Openness	Agreeableness
Performance	0.968941	0.721512	0.598376	0.416717

	Experience	Extroversion	Emotional Stability	
Performance	0.251489	0.194627	0.12840	

complexity of critical human factors for the software process and to evaluate them. The factors that we examined are listed below:

1. Openness
2. Conscientiousness
3. Extroversion
4. Agreeableness
5. Neuroticism
6. Experience
7. Motivation

and we can summarize

$$^{BigFive}HF^{FMEA}_{Software\ Process} : BigFive\ (HF^{FMEA}_{Software\ Process}) \tag{5.1}$$

$$= \{Openness,\ Conscientiousness,\ Extroversion,\ Agreeableness,$$

$$Neuroticism,\ Experience,\ Motivation\}$$

This transformation of role-based human factors to a list of seven characteristics is visualized in Figure 5.2. Having the test ready we used an online platform to distribute it to different software companies and after this to evaluate the results. Analyzing them we have found the correlation between performance and the other seven factors and we were able to observe that the biggest correlation values are for the traits: motivation, conscientiousness, openness, and agreeableness.

These could be summarized as follows:

$$^{eval\ (BigFive)}HF^{FMEA}_{Software\ Process} = \{Motivation,\ Conscientiousness, \tag{5.2}$$

$$Openness,\ Agreeableness\}$$

These four personal characteristics play the main role in the model development process for IT human resources performance prediction.

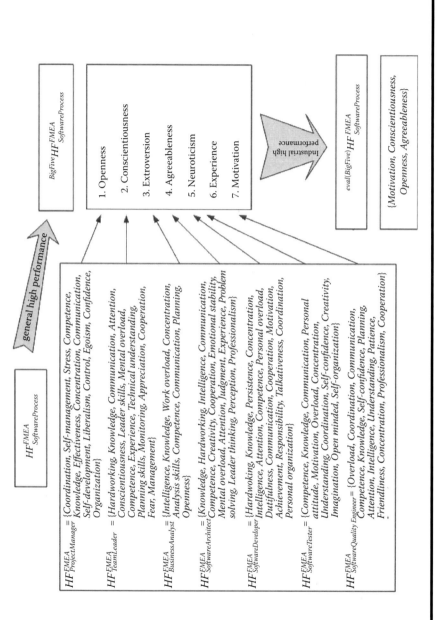

Figure 5.2   Mapping of role-based human factors to Big Five and their industrial evaluation.

References

Costa, P.T. and McCrae, R.R. (1992). *Revised NEO Personality Inventory (NEO-PI-R) and NEO Five-Factor Inventory (NEO-FFI). Professional Manual.* Odessa, FL: Psychological Assessment Resources.

Digman, J. (1990). Personality structure: Emergence of the five-factor model. *Annual Review of Psychology* 41: 417–440.

Georgieva, K., Neumann, R., and Dumke, R. (2010e). Psychological-based measurement of personnel performance. In *Proceedings of the 2010 International Conference on Software Engineering Research & Practice, WORLDCOMP 2010 (SERP 2010).* Las Vegas: CSREA Press, pp. 543–546.

Goldberg, L.R. (1993). The structure of phenotypic personality traits. *American Psychologist,* 1(48): 26–34.

International Personality Item Pool. (1997). viewed 7 March 2014, http://ipip.ori.org/New_IPIP-50-item-scale.htm

John, O.P., Robins, R.W., and Pervin, L.A. (2008). *Handbook of Personality: Theory and Research.* New York: Guilford Press.

McDougall, W. (1932). Of the words character and personality. *Character Personality,* I: 3–16.

Russell, M. and Karol, D. (1994). *16PF Fifth Edition Administrator's Manual.* Champaign, IL: Institute for Personality & Ability Testing.

Saucier, G. and Ostendorf, F. (1999). Hierarchical subcomponents of the Big Five personality factors: A cross-language replication. *Journal of Personality and Social Psychology,* 76(4): 613–627.

Smolders, K.C., de Kort, Y.Y., Kaiser, F.G., and Tenner. A. D. (2009). Need for recovery in offices: Behavior-based assessment. Unpublished manuscript.

Soto, C.J. and John, O.P. (2008). *Measuring Big Five domains and 16 facets using the California Psychological Inventory.* Unpublished manuscript.

Tupes, E. and Cristal, R. (1961). Recurrent personality factors based on trait ratings. *Technical Report ASD-TR-61-97, TX:* Personnel Laboratory, Lackland Air Force Base.

Zoho Challenge. (2010). Viewed 6 January 2014, https://challenge.zoho.com/dellly

Chapter 6

Model Development for IT Human Performance Prediction

The objective in this book is to present a model that is able to evaluate and prognosticate employee performance. In order to achieve this we needed first to look for possible solutions (Chapter 2) and to analyze the software process itself and its organization in the form of software teams (Chapter 3) with special roles. We had to analyze these roles (Chapter 4) in order to find the most important human features that influence the software process and to find a method that can describe the relationship between the already discovered software human factors and the way that they influence the employees' productivity (Chapter 5).

As consequence we needed a method with a defined number of trials, and using the data gained from the previous chapters will give us the maximum information about the mathematical dependence we are looking for, a method that can prove that this dependence is correct and can describe it with a mathematical model. In this chapter we describe the development of the model for IT human performance prediction and end with the desired mathematical model that describes the connection between the special psychological traits and performance (see the principles in Figure 6.1). Later, in Chapter 7 we experimentally prove its effectiveness and accuracy.

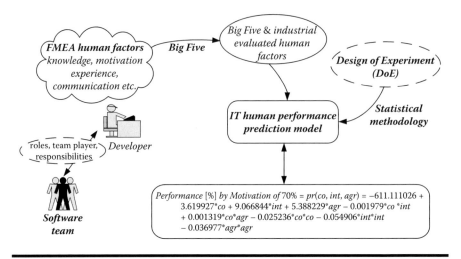

Figure 6.1 Prediction model.

6.1 Experimental Design and Analysis

Looking for a method that can be applied for the development of the desired mathematical model we had some restrictions:

- We had a limited amount of data gained from IT personnel.
- We had to develop the model with a minimum of experiments (because of the limited data).
- We had to find the connection between the selected personal features and software productivity.

Having this in mind we chose to adopt the design of experiment (DoE) because of the following advantages (Shivhare and McCreath, 2010):

- Gain maximum information from a specified number of experiments.
- Study effects individually by varying all operating parameters simultaneously.
- Take account of variability in experiments or processes themselves.
- Characterize acceptable ranges of key and critical process parameters contributing to identification of a design space, which helps to provide an "assurance of quality."

We focus on experiments run in the laboratory or on paper aimed at quantifying the effect of one or more variables over a certain end effect or end parameter. Thus we apply the techniques of experimental design and analysis (founded over 80 years ago by Sir Ronald Fisher). The experiments supported by this technique aim to quantify the effect of qualitative variables over one particular end variable/product/effect that can be separately quantitatively measured.

We can visualize the process as a combination of different factors (controllable or not) that transform the input into some output with special characteristics. Here is a short explanation of the steps in the chosen method (Montgomery, 2008).

I. Recognition of and Statement of Problem

First we have to formulate the problem that we want to resolve; we have to understand its nature, and find all the different factors that influence it. A clear statement of the problem often contributes substantially to better understanding of the phenomenon being studied and the final solution.

II. Preplanning of Experiment

1. *Choice of factors, levels, and range*: We have to choose the input factors that we are going to analyze later, that are important for our experiment. There are different types of factors: potential design factors, held-constant factors, allowed-to-vary factors, and so on, but we do not discuss them because they are not concerned with our particular experiment. When we are ready with the selection of the input factors, we have to decide how these factors will change, in what range, and the specific levels at which runs will be made.

2. *Selection of response variable*: In selecting the response variable, we should be certain that this variable really provides useful information about the process under study. In our case we do not have any doubts which is the response variable as we have a special type of passive experiment, which we explain later, and because of this we know which is our response variable and what exactly we want to observe about it.

3. *Choice of experimental design*: When we have the pre-experimental planning and we are ready with our factors and response variable we have to make the next decision about the particular design. We have to consider the number of replicates, the selection of a suitable run order for the experimental trials, and the determination of whether blocking or other randomization restrictions are involved. Also we have to decide what type of design we are going to use for our modeling process. In our work we have chosen the central composite rotatable design, introduced by Box, Draper, and Hunter (Box and Draper, 2007; Box and Hunter, 1957) because it is the best design to build an invariant response surface. We discuss it later.

III. Performing Experiment and Analysis of Gained Results

4. *Conducting the experiment*: It is vital to monitor the process carefully and to ensure that everything is being done according to the plan. Errors in experimental procedure will destroy the experimental validity.

5. *Statistical analysis of the data*: Statistical methods are used to analyze the data so that the results will be clear mathematical conclusions and not observations or judgments. Hypothesis testing and model adequacy checking are important analysis techniques. We discuss the whole process of validity check on our designed experiment later.

6.2 Algorithm for Conducting Experimental Design

6.2.1 Recognition and Statement of Problem

In the present research the task is to obtain a predictive mathematical model for the effectiveness of software personnel, based on individual psychometric qualities. Obtaining such a model is based on experimental studies conducted according to the methodology of the planned experiment and statistical analysis for its adequacy. The experiment is a set of targeted actions that reveal the principle of operation of the studied object (Montgomery, 2008). Depending on the nature of the organization and methods for obtaining the results, the experimental studies are active and passive.

The active experiment is applicable only for controllable experimentation objects. The investigator sets the levels of factors and maintains their values at a certain stage of the experiment (Fang, Li, and Sudjianto, 2006). The *passive experiment* is represented by a passive registration of output parameter values, obtained at a given combination of input parameters (factors). In this case the investigated object is observed without interfering with the researcher in its operation (Fang et al., 2006).

In our case—when investigating the effectiveness of software personnel—depending on the individual psychometric qualities, we use this special type of passive experiment. Types and evaluation of the psychometric qualities (characteristics) of personnel and the related efficiency of the company are determined through the collection and processing of questionnaire data. There we observe the current state of the firm based on a fixed set of uncontrolled factors.

This method is used for research work regarding manufacturing production and other types of companies; for processing the experimental results regression analysis is used (Mason, Gunst, and Hess, 2003). The mathematical model, obtained as a result of the experiment, is presented by a geometrical response surface and can have the following form, for example, for a two-factor experiment (see Figure 6.2; Myers, Montgomery, and Cook, 2009; Box and Draper, 2007).

If we have k factors, then the factorial space has dimension of $(k + 1)$. When we have limited information about the objects that we are investigating, the analytical type of the response surface is unknown. Then we can assume that the surface can be represented as a Taylor order part in the field of experimental points of the factorial space (Atkinson and Donev, 1992) and it looks like the following:

$$y = b_0 + \sum_{i=1}^{k} b_i x_i + \sum_{\substack{i=1 \\ i<j}}^{k} b_{ij} x_i x_j + \sum_{\substack{i=1 \\ i<j<g}}^{k} b_{ijg} x_i x_j x_g + \ldots + \sum_{i=1}^{k} b_{ii} x_i^2 + \ldots \quad (6.1)$$

where y is evaluation of the parameter of optimization and x_i, x_j, ..., x_k are coded values of the factors. b_i, b_{ij}, b_{ijg}, ... b_{ii} are estimates of the regression coefficients.

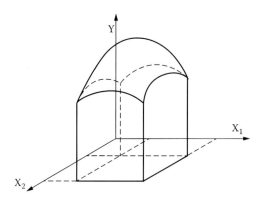

Figure 6.2   Response surface for two-factor model.

Usually in industrial practice the most commonly used models are second-degree polynomials, as the practice shows that in almost 100% of the cases they are adequate (Montgomery, 2008). Because of this we can reason our choice for the mathematical model of second-order Taylor and we can continue with the preplanning of the experiment.

6.2.2 Preplanning the Experiment

The experiment preplanning includes all preparation actions for conducting the planned experiment. They are as follows:

- Collection, compilation, and analysis of the *a priori* information and conducting of preliminary single-factor experiments
- Analysis and selection of the parameter(s) of optimization; choosing the one that most fully and accurately characterizes the object of study
- Analysis and selection of the factors affecting the optimization parameter
- Analysis of the factorial space; choice of domain of a function and local domain of change of the factors; determining the zero point (beginning) of the matrix of the planned experiment, the intervals of variation of the factors, and the coordinates of all matrix points of the planned experiment.

6.2.2.1 Parameters of Optimization and Their Requirements

Optimization parameters are quantitative characteristics of the object of study, which allow establishment of the existing relations between input and output parameters of the system. From a mathematical point of view, the searching of such relations is possible only in the presence of a single parameter of optimization.

The optimization parameters can vary depending on the type of object and purpose of the work. Conditionally we can divide them into economical, technoeconomical, technological, and statistical. They must meet the following requirements (Montgomery, 2008):

- It must characterize the object of study clearly, effectively, and completely.
- It must be quantitative and assigned a certain value.
- It must conform to the requirement of uniqueness in the statistical sense, that is, a set of factor values corresponds to a single value of the optimization parameter.
- To conform to the universality criterion, it must comprehensively characterize the object.
- It should have a clear physical sense, should be understandable for the researcher, and easy to measure.

6.2.2.2 Input Factors Requirements

The number of factors in industrial research is very large. The researcher seeks to include in the study all the relevant factors that determine the functioning of the object. There are a number of requirements to the input factors (Montgomery, 2008):

- Be manageable: To accept values that are kept constant throughout the experiment, or change in some predictable way.
- Be unique: Not be a function of other factors.
- Be consistent: All combinations are feasible and safe.
- Be independent: There is no correlation between the factors. This is particularly important in passive experiments because one factor is difficult to manage if it is a function of another.
- Have a quantitative assessment and a high degree of correlation with the parameter of optimization.

Each factor has its own function domain. The boundaries of this domain are usually set with rigid restrictions that no one can corrupt in the process of experimentation. The domain boundaries give the factor space in which to obtain an adequate mathematical model (see Figure 6.3).

After selecting the function domain we should find the local area for conducting the experiment. In that local area the factors change their values in the process of implementation of the planned experiment. The local area is smaller than the whole domain of the function. In general, the factors are size variables; their dimensionality can be different and also their numerical values can be of a different type. Because of this usually the experiment is not done in the original dimensions but in a coded one, which is a linear translational conversion of the factorial space.

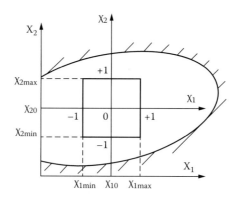

Figure 6.3   Domain of a function for two-factor experiment.

Coding is preceded by selecting the position of the center of the new coordinate system (0 or X_0) and choice of the variation interval determining the location of the upper and lower limits of each factor during the experiment Xi_{max} and Xi_{min} (see Figure 6.3). Coding is performed by mathematical translation of the coordinate system in the new one with zero point with coordinates $X_{10}, X_{20}, ..., X_{k0}$ (point 0 in Figure 6.3).

The 0 point is called the center of the planned experiment in coded values. In the new coded space the maximum (upper) level of the factor corresponds to 1 and the minimum (lowest) to –1. The formulas for the transition (Brownlee, 1965; Cox, 1957; Davies 1967) from natural in encoded values and vice versa are given below:

$$x_i = \frac{Xi - Xi_0}{\Delta Xi} \tag{6.2}$$

$$Xi = Xi_0 + \Delta Xi$$

where

$$\Delta Xi = \frac{Xi_{max} - Xi_{min}}{2}$$

is called the interval of variation (sometimes semi-interval) and Xi is the coded value of the ith factor.

Having the zero point determined from the min and max values of a factor, we should choose the variance intervals (±1) in a way that the values of the star points (in our case ±1.682) are inside the factor space; otherwise our experiment will not be correct as we won't be able to cover all needed points. The particular calculations of these values are shown in Section 6.3.3 in Figure 6.13.

6.2.2.3 Select Type of Planned Experiment

We choose to use the central composite rotatable plan from the type 2^k because of its advantages, explained in the following section. Then we have to choose the function domain and the local domain for each of the factors, and we have to pay special attention when choosing the center of the experiment as it is the starting point in the planning process. For zero point is taken this point of the factorial space in which single-factor experiments have previously been held, which give information that there is expected to be a localized region closest to the response optimum. The domain area must cover all points of the planned experiment, including the star points (explained in Section 6.5).

The determination of the size of the domain area is done by conducting preliminary single-factor experiments with each of the factors. The single-factor experiments indicate the type of interaction of each factor with the parameter of optimization (linear or second degree). They also show the correlation degree between each factor and the optimization parameter. The correlation degree is taken as an indicator showing which of the factors has greater (or less) influence on the optimization parameter. This is used to sort out the factors according to their influence degree, which reflects the choice of the type of planned experiment (how many factors and how they will be included in the matrix of the experiment). Conducting preliminary single-factor experiments provides information about the size and range of variation for each factor and consequently about the zero point of the plan and the value of the variance interval. It describes the size of the hypercube side (when working with coded values) in the planned experiment.

The next stage of the experimental research is to decide which of the factors will be included in the experiment plan. Factors by which the optimization parameter has extreme values and the correlation coefficient is high are included with priority in the matrix of the planned experiment.

6.2.3 Performing Experiment and Analysis of Results

6.2.3.1 Planning the Experiment

Planning the experiment includes: determining the plan of the experiment, determining the necessary and sufficient number of experiments and observations with the already chosen model of design, establishing the matrix of the experiments, and randomization of the trials.

The plan of this experiment is a set of data specifying the number, conditions, and sequence of implementation of necessary and sufficient trials in order to solve the task with the needed accuracy. It is presented in the form of a design matrix (rectangular table), the rows of which satisfy the tests and their position in the factor space, and the columns, the coded values of the factors, and the parameter of optimization (Table 6.2).

Analysis of the results gained includes the calculation and statistical estimation of the coefficients of the model, writing the gained mathematical model in coded and natural values, and examining its adequacy. The type of mathematical model, whose coefficients we will determine (calculate) is as already explained chosen to be second degree and it determines the structure of the planned experiment. It will also be of second degree; this means that it will consist of experimental points at the endpoints of the cube (hypercube); it can have two, three, or more changeable factors. It will have duplicated experimental points in the center of the plan and two star points (explained in Section 6.5) for each axis of the factorial space.

There are many options to determine the matrix of the planned experiment (central composite orthogonal design; central composite rotatable design; "D"-optimal plans, plans of Hartly, etc.) but we choose to work with the central composite rotatable design for its advantages. This method was proposed by Box and Hunter (1957) and Cohran and Cox (1957) and later examined by Myers (1971). It offers the following advantages (Khuri and Cornell, 1996; Myers, Montgomery, and Cook 2009):

- Ensures the invariance of the plan and of the parameter of optimization by rotating the coordinate system around its center.
- The model obtained by the rotatable plan describes the response surface with equal accuracy (equal variance) in all directions of the coordinate axes.
- Surface lines of the same value of variance are concentric circles or hyperspheres with a center coinciding with the beginning of the coordinate system.
- The variances of the mathematical model are the same for all points that are equidistant from the design center and have the minimum values.

The central composite rotatable plan is built (Montgomery, 2008) using the following common construction rules:

- Build a full factorial experiment with a number of experiments $N_1 = 2^k$.
- To the experimental points of the full factorial experiment are added experiments in $2k$ star points located at a distance of $\pm \alpha$ (star arm) from the center of the plan; the values of α are calculated according to formula (6.3).
- To all these experimental points are added N_0 observations in the center of the plan ($x_i = 0$).
- k is the number of the changing factors.

The difference between central composite rotatable and central composite orthogonal plans lies in the manner of selecting the size values of the star arm α and the number of observations in the center of the plan. The size of the star arm by the central composite rotatable plan is calculated based on the invariance condition of the plan. This formula calculation is as follows:

$$\alpha = \sqrt[4]{N_1} = 2^{\frac{k}{4}} \qquad (6.3)$$

The number of the duplicate observations N_0 in the center of the plan is chosen so as to achieve uniformity. This means that we should obtain almost identical values of dispersion (variance) of the optimization parameter in the factor space and the number of observations should also be sufficient for statistical analysis of the results.

The planning, where through suitable choice of the number of observations in the center of the plan almost equal distribution of the variance in the whole area can be achieved, and the variance has the same value for all points equidistant from the center, is called *rotatable-uniform planning*.

To provide uniformity of the plan, N_0 is determined by the relationship (Dean and Voss, 1999):

$$N_0 = \lambda\left(N_1 + 4\sqrt{N_1 + 4}\right) - N_1 - 2k \qquad (6.4)$$

where λ = 0.7844, 0.8385, 0.8705, 0.8918, 0.907, 0.9185, and k = 2,3,4,5,6,7 (Dean and Voss, 1999).

To ensure an orthogonal rotatable plan, N_0 is determined by the relationship (Dean and Voss, 1999):

$$N_0 = 4\sqrt{N_1} - 2k + 4 \qquad (6.5)$$

The necessary data to build a central composite rotatable plan can be seen in Table 6.1, and Table 6.2 shows the data for a central composite rotatable plan with

Table 6.1 Experimental Points and Size of Star Arm by Rotatable Plans with Different Numbers of Factors

k	N_1	N_α	N_0	N	α
2	2^2	4	5	13	1,414
3	2^3	6	6	20	1,682
4	2^4	8	7	31	2,000
5	2^5	10	10	52	2,378
6	2^6	12	15	91	2,828
7	2^7	14	21	163	3,333

Source: A. Dean and D. Voss, *Design and Analysis of Experiments.* Berlin: Springer, 1999. With permission.

Table 6.2 Matrix for Rotatable Plan of Second Level—Type 2^3 [a]

	Experiment No.	X_1	X_2	X_3	y
Full factorial experiment 2^3	1	−1	−1	−1	y_1
	2	+1	−1	−1	y_2
	3	−1	+1	−1	y_3
	4	+1	+1	−1	y_4
	5	−1	−1	+1	y_5
	6	+1	−1	+1	y_6
	7	−1	+1	+1	y_7
	8	+1	+1	+1	y_8
Star points	9	−1,682	0	0	y_9
	10	+1,682	0	0	y_{10}
	11	0	−1,682	0	y_{11}
	12	0	+1,682	0	y_{12}
	13	0	0	−1,682	y_{13}
	14	0	0	+1,682	y_{14}
Experiments in the center of the plan	15	0	0	0	y_{15}
	16	0	0	0	y_{16}
	17	0	0	0	y_{17}
	18	0	0	0	y_{18}
	19	0	0	0	y_{19}
	20	0	0	0	y_{20}

[a] Factors are in coded form.

$k = 3$. By an equal number of observations in the experimental points, the estimates of the coefficients in the regression equation are determined by the dependencies (Dean and Voss, 1999):

$$b_0 = a_1 \sum_{l=1}^{N} y_l - a_2 \sum_{i=1}^{k} \sum_{l=1}^{N} x_{il}^2 y_l \tag{6.6}$$

$$b_i = a_3 \sum_{l=1}^{N} x_{il} y_l$$

$$b_{ij} = a_4 \sum_{l=1}^{N} x_{il} x_{jl} y_l$$

$$b_{ii} = a_5 \sum_{l=1}^{N} x_{il}^2 y_l + a_6 \sum_{i=1}^{k} \sum_{l=1}^{N} x_{il}^2 y_l - a_2 \sum_{l=1}^{N} y_l$$

where $a_1, a_2, a_3, a_4, a_5, a_6$ are defined from Table 6.3 depending on the number of factors and the type of plan. Values of the coefficients a are used to calculate the estimates of the coefficients b in the regression equations obtained with the central composite orthogonal plan or central composite rotatable plan (see Table 6.3).

The estimates of the variances of all the regression coefficients are calculated by the formulas (Dean and Voss, 1999):

$$s^2[b_0] = a_1 s^2[y] \tag{6.7}$$

$$s^2[b_i] = a_3 s^2[y]$$

$$s^2[b_{ij}] = a_4 s^2[y]$$

$$s^2[b_{ii}] = a_7 s^2[y]$$

Table 6.3   Values of the Coefficients α

k	N_1	a_1	a_2	a_3	a_4	a_5	a_6	a_7
		\multicolumn{7}{c}{*Central Composite Rotatable Plan*}						
2	2^2	0.2000	0.1000	0.1250	0.2500	0.1250	0.0187	0.1000
3	2^3	0.1663	0.0568	0.0732	0.1250	0.0625	0.0069	0.0568
4	2^4	0.1429	0.0357	0.0417	0.0625	0.0312	0.0037	0.0357

Source: A. Dean and D. Voss, *Design and Analysis of Experiments*, Berlin: Springer, 1999. With permission.

where

$$s^2_{repro}[y] = \frac{1}{N_0 - 1} \sum_{u=1}^{N_0} (y_{0u} - y_{0mean})^2 \qquad (6.8)$$

is dispersion of reproducibility, N_0 is the number of experiments in the 0 point, y_{0u} are the real values of y in the 0 point, and y_{0mean} is their mean value.

6.2.3.2 Statistical Analysis

If $|b_{0,i,ij,ii}| > s[b_{b,i,ij,ii}]\, t_{Student}$, where $t_{Student}$ is the coefficient of *Student*—a table value (Dean and Voss, 1999)—then the corresponding coefficient is significant. This means that the coefficient is important for the regression equation and will take part in it. The conditions of importance for all regression coefficients are checked in this manner. The validation for adequacy of the whole mathematical model is done by the Fisher's criterion (Fisher and Yates, 1973; Dean and Voss, 1999):

$$F_{calculated} = \frac{s^2_{adequacy}}{s^2_{reproducibility}} \qquad (6.9)$$

where the dispersion (variance) of adequacy is determined by the dependence (Dean and Voss, 1999):

$$s^2_{adequacy} = \frac{\displaystyle\sum_{l=1}^{N=20} (y_{measured} - y_{calculated})^2}{N - k' - (N_0 - 1)} \qquad (6.10)$$

N is the number of the experiments, N_0 is the number of experiments in the 0 point, and k' is the number of significant coefficients in the obtained mathematical model. If $F_{calculated} \leq F_{table}$ the model is adequate; this means that it is true and gives exact results, but if $F_{calculated} > F_{table}$ the model is not adequate and we cannot use it because it does not describe the experiment in a useful manner. The values of F_{table} are taken from Dean and Voss (1999).

6.2.3.3 Interpretation of Results

The planning of experiment from second-order finishes with finding an adequate quadratic equation (mathematical model) of the form (Dean and Voss, 1999):

$$y = b_0 + \sum_{i=1}^{k} b_i x_i + \sum_{\substack{i=1 \\ i<j}}^{k} b_{ij} x_i x_j + \sum_{\substack{i=1 \\ i<j<g}}^{k} b_{ijg} x_i x_j x_g + \ldots + \sum_{i=1}^{k} b_{ii} x_i^2 + \ldots \qquad (6.11)$$

The model obtained must be analyzed in order to find the nature of the response surface in the examined area and also if there is a maximum point (extremum) for this surface; if so, then the coordinates of this point have to be found.

This analysis begins with the transformation of the above equation into canonical form. The canonical transformation is presented by the choice of a new coordinate system, which greatly facilitates the geometric analysis of the equation. This transformation is expressed in determining the center of the response surface (if it exists), then relocating the original coordinate center into the new-found one (by this relocation the linear members $b_i x_i$ are dropped out) and after this rotating the coordinate axes (by this rotation the members $b_i x_i x_j$ are dropped out too). Having all these changes, the quadratic equation of the response surface in canonical form looks like this (Dean and Voss, 1999):

$$y = y_s + \theta_{11} z_1^2 + \theta_{22} z_2^2 + \ldots + \theta_{mm} z_m^2 \qquad (6.12)$$

where y_s is the value of the response surface in the center of the new coordinate system, z_i are the new coordinate axes rotated in the factor space with a special angle to the old ones Xi, and θ_{ii} are the canonical coefficients.

The procedure for the canonical transformation of the model contains the following steps (Myers, Montgomery, and Cook, 2009):

1. Determine the coordinates of the center of the response surface $(x_{1s}, x_{2s}, \ldots, x_{is}, \ldots, x_{ms})$ by solving the system of linear equations, obtained after aligning to zero the first derivative of y for each X_i;

$$\frac{\partial y}{\partial x_i} = 0, i = 1, \ldots, k \qquad (6.13)$$

If the determinant of system (6.13) is not equal to zero, the response surface has a center, but if it is equal to zero then the surface does not have a center within the factorial space. In this case the center is accepted to be either in the beginning of the old coordinate system or in a point that holds the "best" response value.

2. Calculating the surface response value in the new center, y_s (or finding the free member of the canonical equation). This is done as the already calculated coordinates x_{is} from (6.13) are substituted in Equation (6.11).

3. Determination of the canonical coefficients θ_{ii}. For this purpose we build the characteristic equation:

$$f(\theta) = \begin{vmatrix} b_{11} - \theta & 0{,}5b_{12} & ... & 0{,}5b_{1i} & ... & 0{,}5b_{1m} \\ 0{,}5b_{21} & b_{22-\theta} & ... & 0{,}5b_{2i} & ... & 0{,}5b_{2m} \\ ... & ... & ... & ... & ... & ... \\ 0{,}5b_{i1} & 0{,}5b_{i2} & ... & b_{ii} - \theta & ... & 0{,}5b_{im} \\ ... & ... & ... & ... & ... & ... \\ 0{,}5b_{m1} & 0{,}5b_{m2} & ... & 0{,}5b_{mi} & ... & b_{mm} - \theta \end{vmatrix} = 0 \qquad (6.14)$$

where $b_{ij} = b_{ji}$. The canonical coefficients are roots of Equation (6.14). The checkup for correctness of the calculations is done by the formula:

$$\sum_{i=1}^{m} b_{ii} = \sum_{i=1}^{m} \theta_{ii} \qquad (6.15)$$

4. Writing Equation (6.11) in canonical form

$$y = y_s + \theta_{11}z_1^2 + \theta_{22}z_2^2 + ... + \theta_{mm}z_m^2 \qquad (6.16)$$

and determining the type (as geometrical figure) of the response surface.
5. Obtaining a system of equations that links the new coordinate axes with the old ones:

$$z_1 = \cos\alpha_1(x_1 - x_{1s}) + \cos\beta_1(x_2 - x_{2s}) + ... + \cos v_1(x_i - x_{is}) + ... + \cos\omega_1(x_m - x_{ms})$$

$$\cdots\cdots\cdots\cdots\cdots\cdots\cdots\cdots\cdots\cdots\cdots\cdots\cdots\cdots\cdots\cdots\cdots\cdots\cdots\cdots\cdots\cdots\cdots$$

$$z_m = \cos\alpha_m(x_1 - x_{1s}) + \cos\beta_m(x_2 - x_{2s}) + ... + \cos v_m(x_i - x_{is}) + ... + \cos\omega_m(x_m - x_{ms})$$
$$(6.17)$$

Using special formulas that we are not further examining here (Dean and Voss, 1999) we can find the connection between the old and the new coordinate systems.

According to the θ_{ii} values obtained there exist different possibilities for the response surface (Myers, et al., 2009). This is done automatically later in the software we use. Because of this no other details are given here about the response surfaces. The explanation of our particular design of experiment and of the obtained results follows in the next section.

6.3 Development of the IT Human Performance Prediction Model

6.3.1 Recognition and Statement of Problem

The question that we have to answer, as already explained in the beginning of this chapter, is how and which human factors influence individual performance in a software company during the software development process.

In our case, when investigating the effectiveness of a software company, depending on individual psychometric qualities of the personnel, we use this special type of passive experiment (already explained above). Types and evaluation of the psychometric qualities (characteristics) of personnel and the related efficiency of the company are determined through the collection and processing of questionnaire data. There we observe the current state of the firm based on a fixed set of uncontrolled factors.

In Chapters 3 through 5, we conducted a full examination of the software development process with all stages and with the corresponding different roles and their responsibilities. We adopted the FMEA method to make this analysis in order to find the most important human characteristics, and then by adopting the Big Five theory we were able to conduct an evaluation of the data.

After summarizing the data we analyzed how each of the factors influences productivity and we calculated the necessary correlation values. These correlation values are actually our analysis, the factors that are the most important for productivity. From the data shown in the figures we can also see the min and max for each of the factors, which is very important when we want to find the factor space of our experiment. This information is shown here once again for better understanding (see Table 6.4). We can see the correlation values for the factors:

Correlation (Motivation, Performance) = 0.96
Correlation (Conscientiousness, Performance) = 0.72
Correlation (Openness, Performance) = 0.59
Correlation (Agreeableness, Performance) = 0.41
Correlation (Experience, Performance) = 0.25
Correlation (Extroversion, Performance) = 0.19
Correlation (Emotional Stability, Performance) = 0.128

Led by these results and the knowledge that correlation values between 0.3 and 0.5 have medium importance and more than 0.5 have great importance (Cohen, 1988), it was easy to decide that we would consider the first four factors.

Table 6.4 Correlation Analysis Between Personal Features and Performance

	Motivation	Conscient.	Openness	Agreeab.	Experience	Extrovert.	Emot.stab.
Performance	0.968941	0.721512	0.598376	0.416717	0.251489	0.194627	0.128402

Refer to Figures 6.4 to 6.10 to get a clear idea of exactly how these features influence performance. In Figures 6.4 to 6.7 (as Series 1) are the real points and Poly. (Series 1) are the polynomial functions that are maximal near the real values. In Figures 6.5 to 6.7 we see parabola-like graphics and maximum performance values for some mean to high values of the factors. This analysis is seen in more detail in the next part of the experiment as these connections between the factors and productivity are actually our goal.

We can see that the graphic in Figure 6.4 is different from the others. It is very near to a line and up to 85% (where the maximum is) it is growing; after

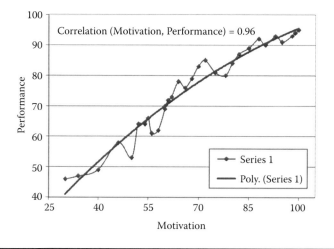

Figure 6.4   Correlation between motivation and performance.

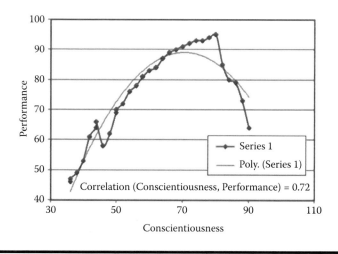

Figure 6.5   Correlation between conscientiousness and performance.

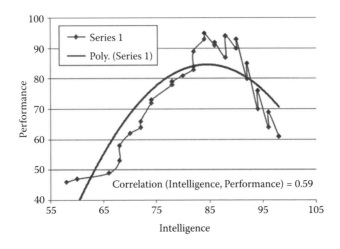

Figure 6.6   Correlation between intelligence and performance.

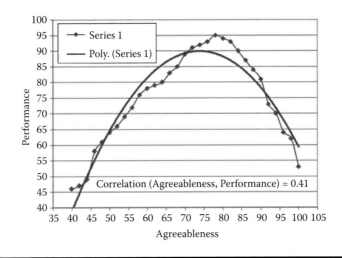

Figure 6.7   Correlation between agreeableness and performance.

this we have a slow reduction in the values. This can be explained with a complex subjective-psychological dependence: the growth of motivation up to 85% is connected with growth of the desire to give the best possible productivity at work and at higher values than 85% this desire is decreasing. This is explained because people with 100% motivation find it difficult to have a perspective on development as they have already reached the maximum; this is a kind of de-motivation and results in lower performance levels.

To make our experiment more comprehensive, we decided to perform three experiments for three crucial values of the motivation: 55%, 70%, and 85%. By these motivation levels we can see a significant change in performance values. Conducting these three experiments we can show how productivity changes through different values of motivation and make a comparison between them.

Processing the gathered data we have also built the correlation graphics between the other three factors (experience, extroversion, and emotional stability) and performance: Figures 6.8 to 6.10. We have also calculated the correlation values and as shown in Table 6.4, they have significantly low values. This shows that we cannot use them as predictors of human productivity because the connection is not clear enough and thus these factors are no longer of interest. This means that we have found the four most important human traits (motivation, conscientiousness, openness, and agreeableness) that influence performance and we continue our research

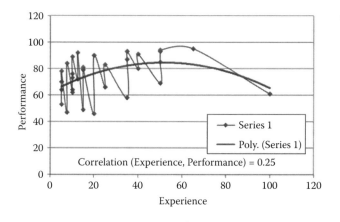

Figure 6.8   Correlation between experience and performance.

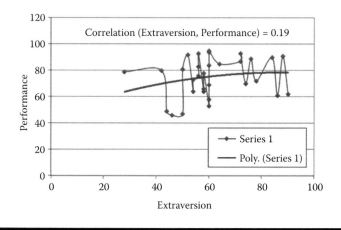

Figure 6.9   Correlation between extroversion and performance.

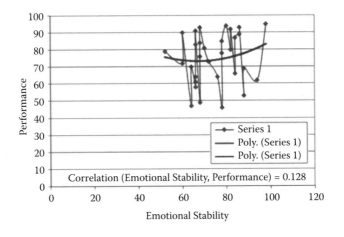

Figure 6.10   Correlation between emotional stability and performance.

work with them. From the figures we see the min and max values, which are important for determination of the factor space, and they are

Conscientiousness from 38% to 90%
Intelligence from 58% to 98%
Agreeableness from 40% to 100%

6.3.2 *Preplanning Experiment*

6.3.2.1 *Choice of Factors, Levels, and Range*

Having the analysis from the previous point and the theoretical background that explains how we select our input factors we can say that we have already found the factors that we will analyze and they are as follows: motivation, conscientiousness, intelligence, and agreeableness. In industrial practice the most commonly used models are second-degree polynomials. Because of this we can reason our choice for Taylor's second-order mathematical model.

The range or the factor space in our case is determined from the values of the factors, measured during the test. They vary in the following manner:

Conscientiousness from 38% to 90%
Intelligence from 58% to 98%
Agreeableness from 40% to 100%

As we have already explained, we conduct three experiments by motivation of 85%, 70%, and 55% and this means we have three factors that we observe in connection with the performance. We design an experiment for three factors at two levels, from the type 2^3 in the already mentioned ranges but we design three different experiments for every special value of the motivation factor.

6.3.2.2 Selection of Response Variable

In our research the examined response variable is the human performance in software development in connection with the special personal traits (motivation, conscientiousness, intelligence, and agreeableness). In order to measure this performance we decided to use the mean value between three different evaluations: the first is the employee's personal work evaluation, the second is the evaluation from colleagues, and the third is the supervisor's evaluation. In this way we have received a comprehensive value that we can use in our further experiment.

The formulas for these evaluations can be seen in Chapter 3, but we show them here once again (see (3.47) and (3.48)).

$$humanPerformance = \{HF_{IT} \times softwareDevelopmentProcess\} \qquad (6.18)$$

$$humanPerformanceEvaluation = \{personalAssessment,$$

$$supervisorAssessment, colleagueAssessment\}$$

$$r_{SR}^{(personalAssessment)} \in R_{SR}: personIT \times assessment \times workingProcess$$

$$\rightarrow personalAssessment$$

$$r_{SR}^{(supervisorAssessment)} \in R_{SR}: personIT \times supervisor \times assessment$$

$$\times workingProcess \rightarrow supervisorAssessment$$

$$r_{SR}^{(colleagueAssessment)} \in R_{SR}: personIT \times colleague \times assessment$$

$$\times workingProcess \rightarrow colleagueAssessment$$

$$person_{IT} = \{analyst, designer, developer, acquisitor, reviewer,$$

$$programmer, tester, administrator, qualityEngineer,$$

$$project\ leader, systemProgrammer, chiefProgrammer\}$$

Furthermore, our experiment leads to

$$HF_{IT} \rightarrow {}^{eval\,(BigFive)}_{DoE}\, HF\, {}^{FMEA}_{Software\,Process} \tag{6.19}$$

where *DoE* stands for the applied statistical method as the so-called design of experiment.

6.3.2.3 Choice of Experimental Design

There are many possibilities to determine the matrix of the planned experiment (central composite orthogonal design, central composite rotatable design, "D"-optimal plans, plans of Hartly, etc.) but we chose to work with the central composite rotatable design for its advantages. This method was proposed by Box and Hunter (1957) and Cohran and Cox (1957) and later examined by Myers (1971). It offers the following advantages (Khuri and Cornell, 1996; Myers et al., 2009):

- Guarantees the invariance of the plan and of the parameter of optimization.
- The model obtained by the rotatable plan describes the response surface with equal accuracy (equal variance) in all directions of the coordinate axes.
- In the whole factors space, the parameter of optimization has the same variance. This ensures that the calculation accuracy of the optimization parameter is independent of the place where we are going to build the experiment.
- The variance of the optimization parameter does not change by rotation and translation of its coordination system. This allows us to conduct the canonical experiment (rotation and translation of the coordination system) with the goal of finding the geometrical figure of the designed experiment.
- The fact that by rotatable experiments the variance does not change ensures the correctness of the statistical analysis of the gained mathematical model.

6.3.3 Realization and Analysis of Experiment

For conducting our experiments we worked in cooperation with the Technical University of Varna, Bulgaria, and used their kindly provided software tool to conduct all calculations needed for our design. In the following section we explain in detail the software used and the results that it provides in every step. The software was developed in the Bulgarian language and because of this the text in the windows is in Bulgarian, but the English explanation ensures understanding. The summarized results of all experiments can be found in the paper by Georgieva, Dumke, and Fiegler (2011b).

Of course it is also possible to use other software but we have two very fundamental reasons to choose this one:

1. Choosing to model our experiment with the central composite rotatable design it was impossible for us to find well-known software that supports us exactly with the desired steps for conducting the experiment.
2. Because of our cooperative work with the Technical University of Varna we did not have to pay for the software (whereas we would have incurred the expense of utiziling any other software) and gained exactly the appropriate tool for our goal.

Here we explain the steps in conducting the experiment and we visualized the whole process in the following screenshots. The software tool is specially developed for central composite rotatable plans and all calculations and statistical verifications are included. This makes the planning of our experiment much easier and supplies us at the end with the desired mathematical model and the response surface graphics.

The first step is to choose the number of factors (see Figure 6.11) that we are going to include in our experiment and as already explained we have decided to explore three factors, thus here we choose the second option which is the "three factors experiment."

In the next step (see Figure 6.12) we choose names for the factors. For convenience in the software product we decided to use the following abbreviations: *co* = conscientiousness; *int* = intelligence; *agr* = agreeableness, and *pr* = performance. The dimensions for the factors according to our methodology (test data) are in percentages. Figure 6.13 visualizes the different values of a factor that are important for the correct design of the experiment.

The first important point from the realization of the experiment is the determination of the zero point of the coordinate system. The plan of the experiment is built around it symmetrically. The zero point determination is made using the

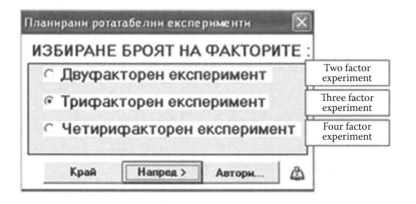

Figure 6.11   Choosing the number of the factors.

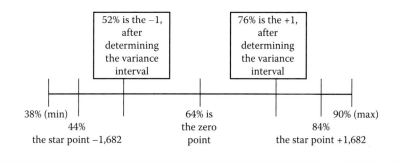

Figure 6.12   Selecting names and dimensions for the factors.

	52% is the −1, after determining the variance interval	76% is the +1, after determining the variance interval	

38% (min)		64% is	90% (max)
	44%	the zero	84%
	the star point −1,682	point	the star point +1,682

Figure 6.13   Determining the input information for conscientiousness.

values of the other factors, which can be seen in Figures 6.4 to 6.6, where the correlations between the factors and the performance are shown. Usually this one is chosen for zero point that is in the middle of the factor space, determined by the values of the input factors.

We next explain how we determine the zero levels and the variance intervals for every factor. For the first factor, conscientiousness, the factor space is between 38% and 90%; this means that the middle is 64% and this will be the zero point for cons. The variance intervals (±1) should be chosen in such a way that the values of the star points are inside the factor space; otherwise our experiment will not be correct as we won't be able to cover all needed points. The star points are usually chosen to be at a distance from the end of the factor space no larger than 15% of the distance between the two star points. This is done with a few experiments on the trial-and-error principle until the best values are found. For conscientiousness we have the following values (see Figure 6.13). We choose the values of the star points to make sure that they stay in the factor space after designing the experiment and these are 44% for −1.682 and 84% for +1.682. Based on them we calculate the values of +1 and −1 (52%, 76%). This means that for conscientiousness the variance interval will be ±12. Analogously we make the same calculations for the other two factors and gain the values:

Intelligence from 58% to 98%: This means that the zero point will be 78%; the star points will be approximately −1.682 = 62% and +1.682 = 94%. Then we can calculate the variance interval which will be: ±10 and −1 = 68% and +1 = 88%.

Agreeableness from 40% to 100%: This means that the zero point will be 70%; the star points will be approximately −1.682 = 45% and +1.682 = 95%. Then we can calculate the variance interval which will be: ±15 and −1 = 55% and +1 = 85%.

From the explanations above it follows that we can now write in our program (see the Figure 6.14) the input values for the experiment.

The first experiment that we conduct is by motivation of 55%. The screen in Figure 6.15 shows us the entire table of the experiment (already explained in the previous part of this chapter). We have altogether 20 experiments (all of them displayed with their coded and natural values): eight of them are in the eight possible combinations of the three factors; six are in the star points and the other six are in the zero point. We see the factors X_1, X_2, and X_3 first in their coded view and after this with their real experiment values and in the last column we add the value for the observed/resultant factor: the performance. We insert the measured performance values and on the next step check if they match with those calculated from the program. The software carries out all the needed calculations and delivers the information visualized on the screen in Figure 6.16.

We first see all coefficients b in the regression equation, calculated according to formulas (6.6) and after this we see $s^2[b]$ or Δb, the estimates of the variances of the regression coefficients according to formulas (6.7). Having these data we can

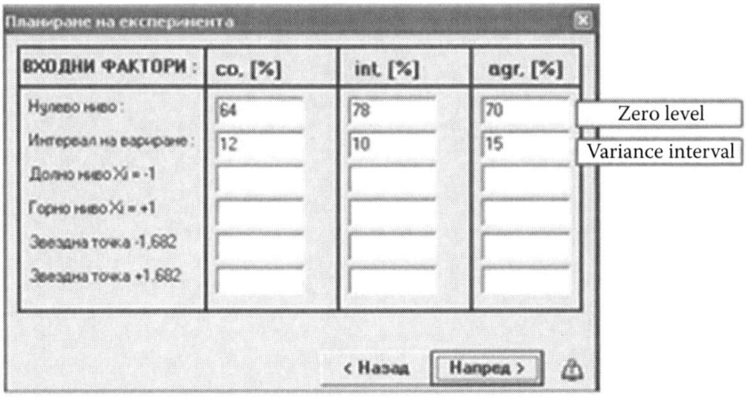

Figure 6.14   Input values for the factors.

План на експеримента и резултати от експер.

No (експер.)	Кодирани фактори			План на експеримента			Данни от експеримента
	X1	X2	X3	co.[%]	int.[%]	egr.[%]	pr.[%]
1	-1	-1	-1	52.000	68.000	55.000	44.29
2	1	-1	-1	76.000	68.000	55.000	51
3	-1	1	-1	52.000	88.000	55.000	52
4	1	1	-1	76.000	88.000	55.000	56.9
5	-1	-1	1	52.000	68.000	85.000	51.44
6	1	-1	1	76.000	68.000	85.000	58.83
7	-1	1	1	52.000	88.000	85.000	58.25
8	1	1	1	76.000	88.000	85.000	64.88
9	-1.682	0	0	43.816	78.000	70.000	55
10	1.682	0	0	84.184	78.000	70.000	66.15
11	0	-1.682	0	64.000	61.180	70.000	51
12	0	1.682	0	64.000	94.820	70.000	61.35
13	0	0	-1.682	64.000	78.000	44.770	43.29
14	0	0	1.682	64.000	78.000	95.230	55.64
15	0	0	0	64.000	78.000	70.000	69.5
16	0	0	0	64.000	78.000	70.000	69.9
17	0	0	0	64.000	78.000	70.000	69.6
18	0	0	0	64.000	78.000	70.000	69.2
19	0	0	0	64.000	78.000	70.000	69.8
20	0	0	0	64.000	78.000	70.000	69.1

Measured performance · Plan of the experiment

< Назад
В Clipboard
Запис
Напред >

Figure 6.15 Plan and results of the experiment (motivation = 55%).

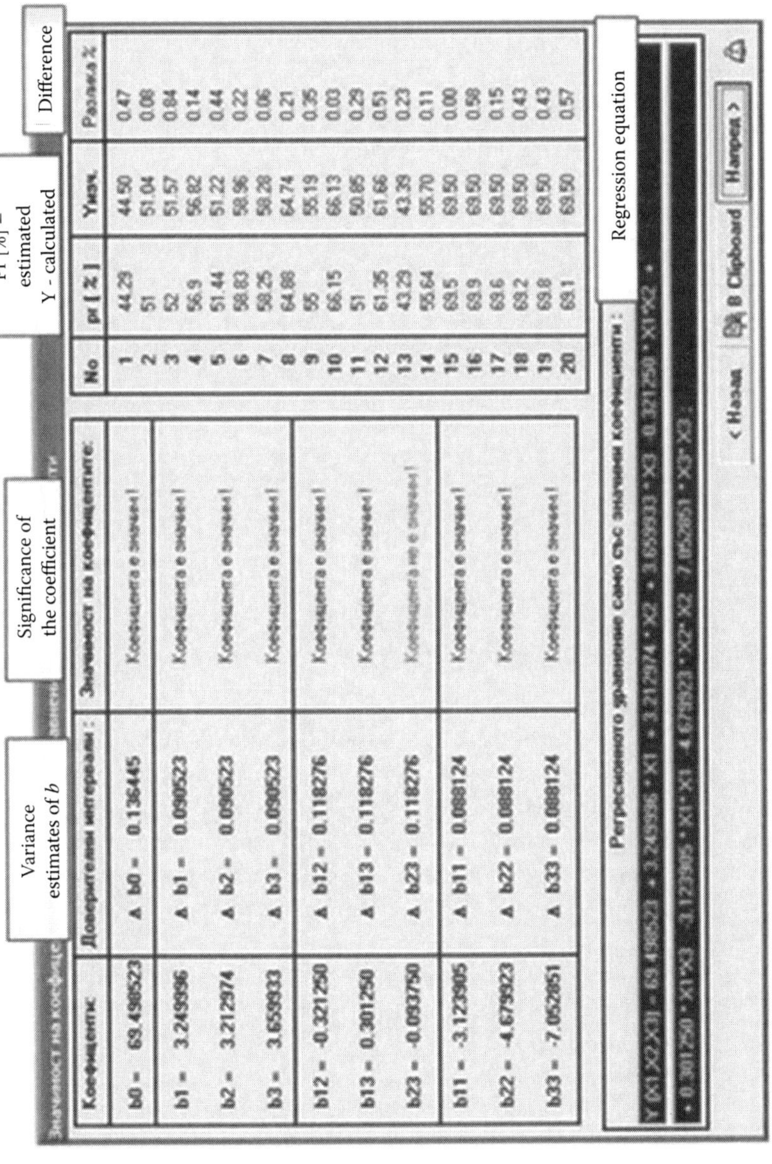

Figure content (screen capture, rotated):

Variance estimates of b — Доверительни интервали :

Коефициенти:	Доверителни интервали :
b0 = 69.498523	Δ b0 = 0.136445
b1 = 3.249996	Δ b1 = 0.090523
b2 = 3.212974	Δ b2 = 0.090523
b3 = 3.659933	Δ b3 = 0.090523
b12 = -0.321250	Δ b12 = 0.118276
b13 = 0.301250	Δ b13 = 0.118276
b23 = -0.093750	Δ b23 = 0.118276
b11 = -3.123905	Δ b11 = 0.088124
b22 = -4.679923	Δ b22 = 0.088124
b33 = -7.052951	Δ b33 = 0.088124

Significance of the coefficient — Значимост на коефициенти:

b0	Коефициента е значим!
b1	Коефициента е значим!
b2	Коефициента е значим!
b3	Коефициента е значим!
b12	Коефициента е значим!
b13	Коефициента е значим!
b23	Коефициента не е значим!
b11	Коефициента е значим!
b22	Коефициента е значим!
b33	Коефициента е значим!

Pr [%] – estimated / **Y – calculated** / **Difference**

No	pr [%]	Умн.	Разлика %
1	44.29	44.50	0.47
2	51	51.04	0.08
3	52	51.57	0.84
4	56.9	56.82	0.14
5	51.44	51.22	0.44
6	58.83	58.96	0.22
7	58.25	58.28	0.06
8	64.88	64.74	0.21
9	55	55.19	0.35
10	66.15	66.13	0.03
11	51	50.85	0.29
12	61.35	61.66	0.51
13	43.29	43.39	0.23
14	55.64	55.70	0.11
15	69.5	69.50	0.00
16	69.9	69.50	0.58
17	69.6	69.50	0.15
18	69.2	69.50	0.43
19	69.8	69.50	0.43
20	69.1	69.50	0.57

Regression equation — Регресионото уравнение само със значими коефициенти :

Y (X1) (X2) (X3) = 69.498523 + 3.249996 *X1 + 3.212974 *X2 + 3.659933 *X3 + 0.321250 *X1*X2 + 0.301250 *X1*X3 - 3.123905 *X1*X1 - 4.679923 *X2*X2 - 7.052951 *X3*X3

[< Назад] [В Clipboard] [Напред >]

Figure 6.16 Coefficients and the regression equation in coded form.

find out which of the coefficients are significant. We see that we have only the b_{23} that is not statistically significant and because of this the X value connected with it will not be included in the end equation. The next part of the screen is occupied with the data for the output factor: the performance. We have our estimated values; after this follow the calculated values from the program and then the difference between the two in percentage. This difference shows how near the calculated values are compared to the experimental ones. If the proposed data are very near the experimental ones this means that the possibility of obtaining an adequate model is very high. And vice versa: if the difference is high, then the possibility for an adequate model is low. The bottom of the screenshot shows the mathematical equation in coded form only with significant coefficients:

$$Y(X_1, X_2, X_3) = 69.498523 + 3.249996{}^*X_1 + 3.212947{}^*X_2 + 3.659933{}^*X_3$$

$$- 0.321250{}^*X_1{}^*X_2 + 0.301250{}^*X_1{}^*X_3 - 3.123905{}^*X_1{}^*X_1$$

$$- 4.679923{}^* X_2{}^*X_2 - 7.052851{}^* X_3{}^*X_3 \qquad (6.19)$$

On the next screenshot, Figure 6.17, there is a lot of information, thus we start with the first rows. There we see the variance of adequacy, according to formulas (6.8) and (6.10) and the Fisher criterion

$$F = \frac{s^2{}_{adequacy}}{s^2{}_{reproducibility}}$$

The Fisher criterion is $F = 0.98972 < F_{table} = 6.09$ (Dean and Voss, 1999) and this means that the resultant mathematical model is adequate and statistically correct.

Subsequently we have the regression equation in natural form that describes the model for which we searched. Having this equation we can predict the performance of every employee based only on her psychological features (motivation, conscientiousness, intelligence, and agreeableness). The model looks like:

Performance [%] *by Motivation* of 55% = $pr(co, int, agr) = -523.021607 + 3.139297{}^*co$

$$+ 7.793311{}^*int + 4.525325{}^*agr - 0.002677{}^*co{}^*int + 0.001674{}^*co{}^*agr$$

$$- 0.021694{}^*co{}^*co - 0.046799{}^*int{}^*int - 0.031346{}^*agr{}^*agr \qquad (6.20)$$

After we obtain the mathematical model we have to find the figure of the response surface and its central point. For this we use $D = -822.5758$ (D is the matrix discriminant of the coefficients of the model) which gives us the information that the response surface has a center. After this the program gives us the

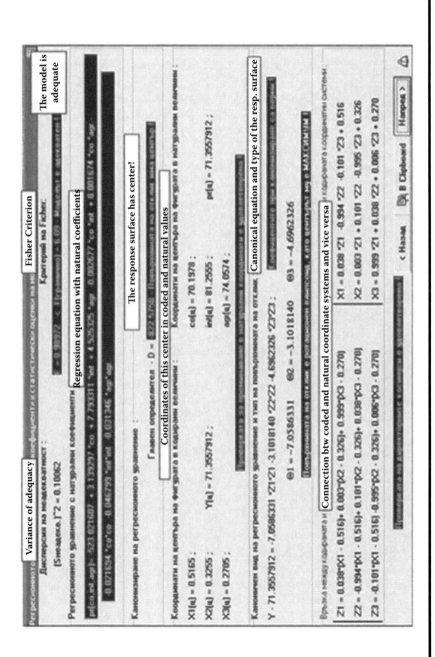

Figure 6.17 Regression equation in natural form and statistical analysis of the model.

calculated coded and natural values for this central point. Later on we obtain the canonical form of the regression equation and check if it is correct; this canonization gives us the information that the response surface has the form of a rotational ellipsoid and that the center is its maximum. Finally we have the equations that give us the connection between coded and natural coordinate systems and vice versa and a check that proves that the canonical transformation is correct.

On Figure 6.18 we see the two-dimensional intersections for all the possibilities (–1, 0, 1) for each of the input factors (X_1, X_2, X_3). For every cut we have a 3D graphic in MATLAB® on which we can see exactly what the response surface looks like and exactly where the maximum is.

For example, in Figure 6.19 we see the intersection for agreeableness and openness/intelligence where the other two factors (motivation = 55% and conscientiousness = 52%) are fixed because otherwise we cannot display the graphic on a 3D figure. Now we explain the first three graphics for the two-dimensional cut for agreeableness and intelligence, which we gain from the yellow equations in Figure 6.16. X_1 is the conscientiousness and the values of –1, 0, and +1 are actually the natural values of 52%, 64%, and 76%.

In Figure 6.19a we can see the performance response surface as a function of agreeableness and intelligence, where agreeableness changes between 40% and 100% and intelligence between 60% and 100%. The maximum point of the surface is approximately 75% of agreeableness and 80% of intelligence and is exactly 64%.

With 60% of intelligence, the connection between agreeableness and performance is an ellipse. The minimum performance values of 7% are due to agreeableness of 40%; when agreeableness grows to 75% we gain the maximum performance values of 42%; with agreeableness of 80% the performance is 40.7%. The further growth of agreeableness to 100% leads to a decrease of the performance values up to 20%. This can be explained with the specific influence of this psychometric characteristic over personal performance: the growing values of agreeableness up to 75% are characterized with performance growth because the employee is able to communicate and cooperate with his colleagues; he is able to accept others' ideas and to follow instructions. After these values the person loses his own judgment and cannot resolve any problem alone. The software engineer agrees with everyone and is no longer able to make decisions which leads to low performance values. Values around 40% mean that he is not able to cooperate and has difficulty working with other people; this of course also means low productivity.

The next observations are about the influence of intelligence over the performance. In Figure 6.19a with fixed agreeableness of 40% we can see that by intelligence of 60% the performance is only 7% and with growth of the intelligence values up to 80% we reach a performance of around 29%. The further growth of intelligence leads to a decrease of the performance values up to 13.3%. The observations have shown that with the increase of the intelligence after a specific point (around 80%), the observed software team members start to make very complex decisions and don't choose the optimal algorithm for resolving a problem. This

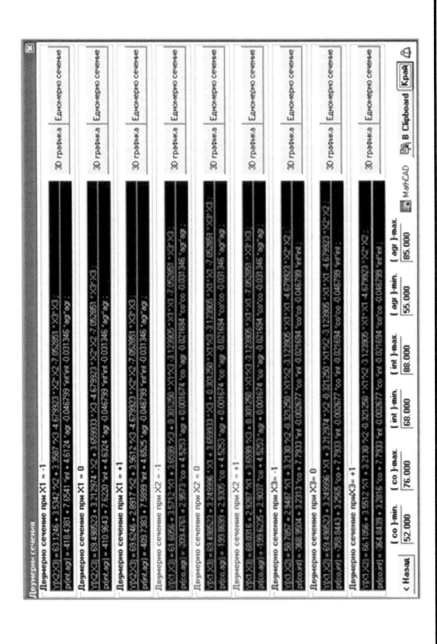

Figure 6.18 Two-dimensional intersections.

motiv = 55%; consc = 52%

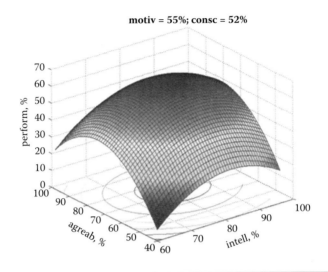

Figure 6.19(a) **Response surface by (motivation = 55% and conscientiousness = 52%).**

motiv = 55%; consc = 64%

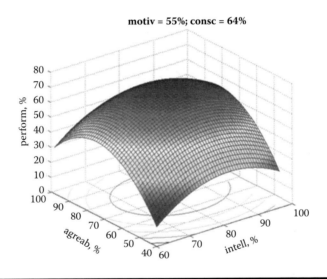

Figure 6.19(b) **Response surface by (motivation = 55% and conscientiousness = 64%).**

leads to complications and more mistakes in the work process; the employees need more time; and the solutions are not optimal. Because of this it is logical to observe the decrease in performance (productivity). With low values, even with 60% openness we have very low productivity, which shows that we need employees with above-average intelligence in order to manage the software engineering process.

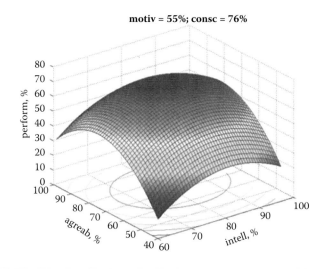

motiv = 55%; consc = 76%

Figure 6.19(c) Response surface by (motivation = 55% and conscientiousness = 76%).

The same experimental dependencies can be observed in Figures 6.19b and 6.19c, which can be analogously explained. Because of this we give only the specific points from the response surface. For example, in Figure 6.19c which is with conscientiousness of 76% we have that with intelligence of 60% and agreeableness of 40% the performance is only 13%. The performance maximum is with agreeableness of 80% and is 49%. The further growth of agreeableness to 100% leads to a reduction in the productivity value to 29%. When observing the intelligence values we can see that with 60% the performance is only 13% and by increasing the values up to 83% we gain the maximum point of around 34% productivity. The next increase of intelligence up to 100% results in 17% performance. Moving in intersection with the conscientiousness values of 76%, agreeableness of 75%, and of intelligence 83%, we can find the maximum performance value shown on Figure 6.19c and it is 70%.

Having these explanations we observed the influence of intelligence and agreeableness over performance, when the values for conscientiousness and motivation are fixed. Actually we observed the one-dimensional intersections of the corresponding dependencies for better understanding of the changing values.

In order also to describe the influence of conscientiousness over productivity we use the next figures (the origin is the second gray group of formulas in Figure 6.18) where intelligence takes values of 68%, 78%, and 88% and the motivation is fixed at 55%.

Figures 6.20a to 6.20c show the influence of agreeableness and conscientiousness on performance, where agreeableness changes between 40% and 100% and conscientiousness between 40% and 90%. The maximum point of the surface is approximately 75% of agreeableness and 70% of conscientiousness and is exactly 63%. The motivation is fixed at 55% and intelligence takes three particular values.

We explain only the connection between conscientiousness and performance and, as we see, it is again an ellipse with the following important points (see Figure 6.20a): with agreeableness of 40% we have values for conscientiousness between 40% and 90%. With conscientiousness between 40% to 55% we have very low performance of about 8% to 22%. When the conscientiousness values grow to 70% we have the maximum performance values of 27% and after this with conscientiousness of 80% we have 24.4% performance and with conscientiousness of 90% we have 18% performance. This can be explained with the specifics of this psychological characteristic: by growing to 70% it means that the software specialist is trying to do his best and to manage his work as well as possible. On the other hand this characteristic hinders the process of ignoring the unimportant details in everyday work, and this exactly leads to decreasing performance, when conscientiousness is higher than 70%. The employee loses too much time in checking details and spending time on unimportant problems that take more time, resulting in lower productivity. When the values are low, to 55%, we have very low performance and this is because such employees are not doing their job with the necessary respect and caution.

Figures 6.20b and 6.20c display the same experimental dependences and therefore we give only some values. For example in 45 (Figure 6.20c) which is with intelligence of 88% we have that with conscientiousness of 40% and agreeableness of 40% the performance is only 15.3%. The performance maximum has conscientiousness of 68% and is 33%. The further growth of conscientiousness to 90% leads to a reduction in the productivity value to 29%. Moving in intersection with the

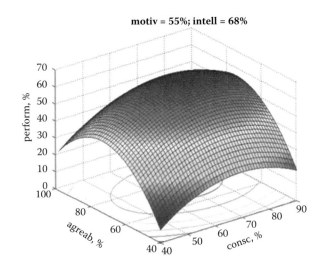

Figure 6.20(a)   Response surface by (motivation = 55% and intelligence = 68%).

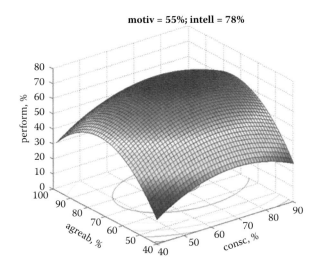

motiv = 55%; intell = 78%

Figure 6.20(b)   Response surface by (motivation = 55% and intelligence = 78%).

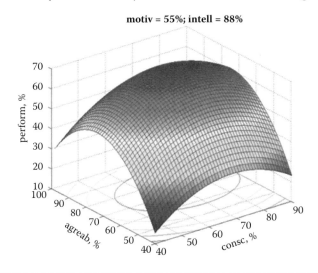

motiv = 55%; intell = 88%

Figure 6.20(c)   Response surface by (motivation = 55% and intelligence = 88%).

intelligence values of 88%, conscientiousness 68%, and agreeableness 75%, we can find the maximum performance value shown in Figure 6.20c and it is 69%.

The remaining three figures (6.21a,b,c) originate from the bottom three equations (Figure 6.18) and are absolutely analogous to the previous ones. The only difference is that here the dependence between intelligence, conscientiousness, and performance is visualized where the other factors motivation = 55% and agreeableness = 55%, 70%, and 85% are fixed. We do not explain the dependencies once

motiv = 55%; agreab = 55%

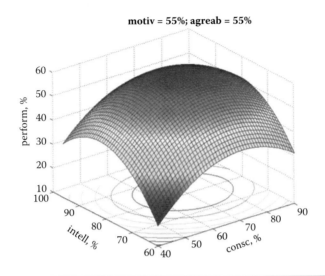

Figure 6.21(a) **Response surface by (motivation = 55% and agreeableness = 55%).**

motiv = 55%; agreab = 70%

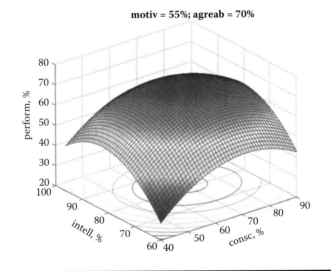

Figure 6.21(b) **Response surface by (motivation = 55% and agreeableness = 70%).**

again as we have already said they are the same as in the other figures. We give the figures just for better understanding.

The second experiment is with motivation of 70%. We do not explain again the first three screenshots from the program that are about the input data because they are the same every time. We continue with Figure 6.22, where we can see the plan

motiv = 55%; agreab = 85%

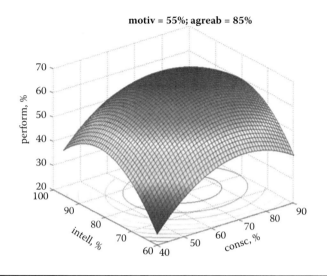

Figure 6.21(c)   Response surface by (motivation = 55% and agreeableness = 85%).

of the experiment with the 20 experiments (as already explained, eight of them are in the eight possible combinations of the three factors; six are in the star points and the remaining six are in the zero point). We see the factors X_1, X_2, and X_3 with their coded and real values, and in the last column we add the value for the observed/resultant factor, performance, but this time with motivation of 70%.

If we compare the performance values we see a significant difference: here we have performance values of 82.8% and in the previous experiment we had 69.9%. Thus we can make the first observation that by enhancing motivation, performance also grows significantly.

In Figure 6.23 we see all coefficients b in the regression equation and the Δb, the estimates of the variances of the regression coefficients. Having these data we can observe which of the coefficients are significant and which are not. We see that again only one coefficient b_{23} is not significant. The next part of the screen is occupied with the data for the output factor, the performance. We have our estimated values and after this follow the calculated values from the program and then the difference between them in percentage. We can see that again as in the first experiment the difference is very small and we can end with the following regression equation in coded form with significant coefficients:

$$Y(X_1,X_2,X_3) = 82.384068 + 3.932305^*X_1 + 3.748234^*X_2 + 4.439234^*X_3$$

$$- 0.237500^*X_1^*X_2 + 0.237500^*X_1^*X_3 - 3.633999^*X_1^*X_1$$

$$- 5.490612^* X_2^*X_2 - 8.319736^* X_3^*X_3 \qquad (6.21)$$

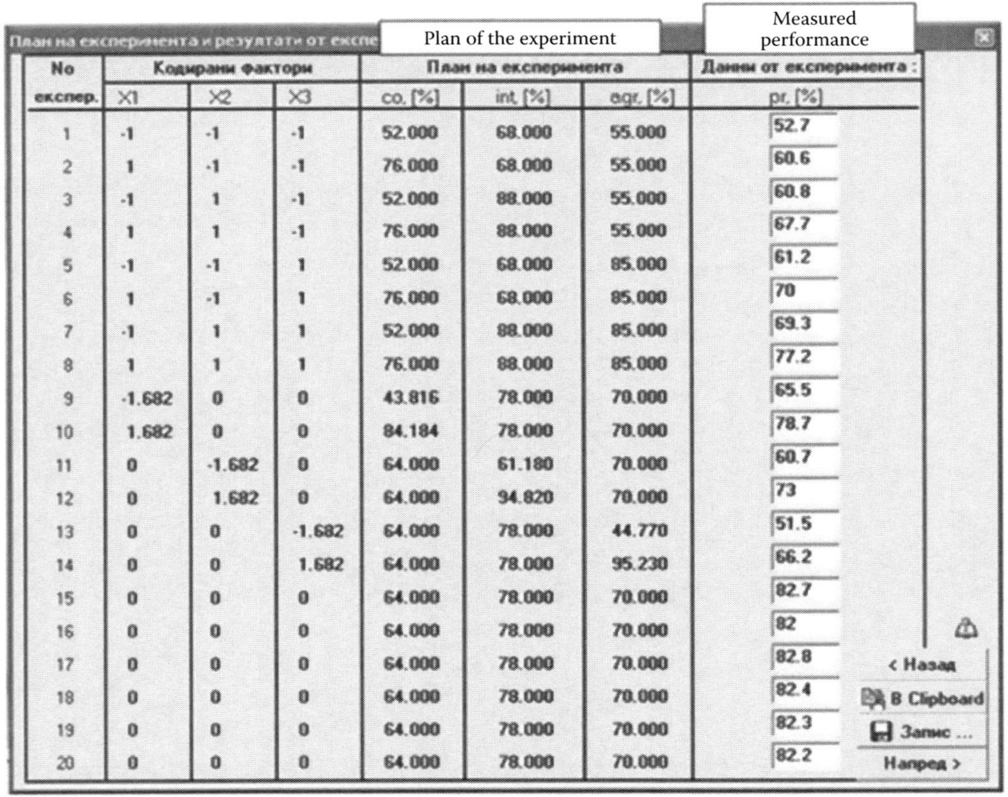

No експер.	Кодирани фактори X1	X2	X3	План на експеримента co.[%]	int.[%]	ogr.[%]	Данни от експеримента pr.[%]
1	-1	-1	-1	52.000	68.000	55.000	52.7
2	1	-1	-1	76.000	68.000	55.000	60.6
3	-1	1	-1	52.000	88.000	55.000	60.8
4	1	1	-1	76.000	88.000	55.000	67.7
5	-1	-1	1	52.000	68.000	85.000	61.2
6	1	-1	1	76.000	68.000	85.000	70
7	-1	1	1	52.000	88.000	85.000	69.3
8	1	1	1	76.000	88.000	85.000	77.2
9	-1.682	0	0	43.816	78.000	70.000	65.5
10	1.682	0	0	84.184	78.000	70.000	78.7
11	0	-1.682	0	64.000	61.180	70.000	60.7
12	0	1.682	0	64.000	94.820	70.000	73
13	0	0	-1.682	64.000	78.000	44.770	51.5
14	0	0	1.682	64.000	78.000	95.230	66.2
15	0	0	0	64.000	78.000	70.000	82.7
16	0	0	0	64.000	78.000	70.000	82
17	0	0	0	64.000	78.000	70.000	82.8
18	0	0	0	64.000	78.000	70.000	82.4
19	0	0	0	64.000	78.000	70.000	82.3
20	0	0	0	64.000	78.000	70.000	82.2

Measured performance — Plan of the experiment

< Назад · В Clipboard · Запис … · Напред >

Figure 6.22 Plan and results of the experiment (motivation = 70%).

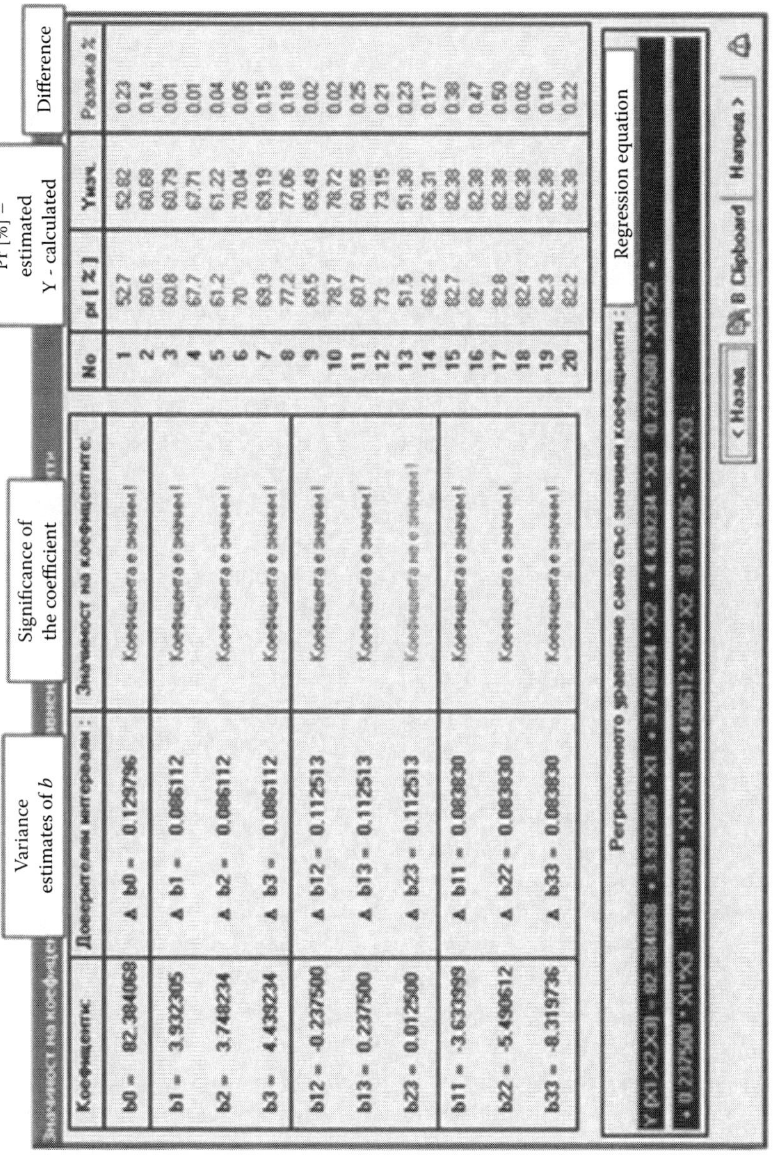

Figure 6.23 Coefficients and the regression equation in coded form.

On the next screenshot, Figure 6.24, we see the variance of adequacy, then the Fisher criterion. This statistical analysis shows that the gained model is correct and adequate and we have the regression equation in natural form that describes the performance of employees based only on their psychological features.

$$\textit{Performance [\%] by Motivation of } 70\% = pr(co, int, agr) = -611.111026 +$$

$$3.619927^*co + 9.066844^*int + 5.388229^*agr - 0.001979^*co^*int$$

$$+ 0.001319^*co^*agr - 0.025236^*co^*co - 0.054906^*int^*int$$

$$- 0.036977^*agr^*agr \tag{6.22}$$

The analysis for the response surface follows on the next part of the screenshot: if it has a center, and if so, the coordinates. They are displayed in coded and natural form. Later are shown the canonical equations and the proof that the translation between the different coordinate systems is correct. This canonization gives us the information that the response surface has the form of a rotational ellipsoid and that the center point is its maximum.

In Figure 6.25 we see the two-dimensional intersections for all the possibilities $(-1, 0, 1)$ for each of the input factors (X_1, X_2, X_3). For every cut we have a 3D graphic in MATLAB on which we can see exactly what the response surface looks like and exactly where the maximum is. As we explained these nine graphics for the previous experiment in detail, here we show only Table 6.5 with the corresponding values for the current case. Any further explanations would just be repetition of everything said before. For the interested reader we have shown all the graphics by motivation of 70% and 85% (see also the one-dimensional intersections in Richter (2012)).

The comparison between performance values with motivations of 55% and of 70%, made on the outer limits of the factor space, takes values that can be seen from Figures 6.19 through 6.21 (see also further evaluations in Richter (2012)). We can clearly see in the table that we have a significant increase in performance values with motivation of 70%, but the dependencies of the different characteristics and the productivity stay the same as already explained for the previous experiment.

The third experiment is with motivation of 85%. We start here directly with the explanation of the plan of the experiment shown in Figure 6.26 as the other steps are the same as for the other two experiments. We can see the plan of the experiment in Figure 6.26, with the 20 experiments (as already explained eight of them are in the eight possible combinations of the three factors; six are in the star points and the remaining six are in the zero point). We see the factors X_1, X_2, and X_3 with their coded and real values and in the last column we add the value for the observed/resultant factor, performance, but this time with motivation of 85%.

If we compare the performance values with the other two experiments we see the difference: in the first case we had performance of 69.9%, in the second 82.8%,

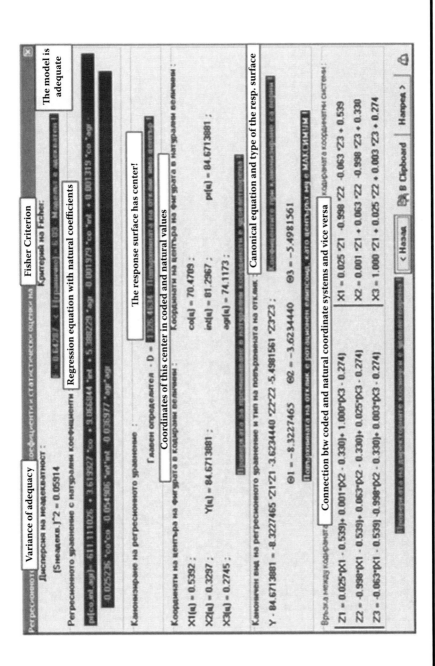

Figure 6.24   Regression equation in natural form and statistical analysis of the model.

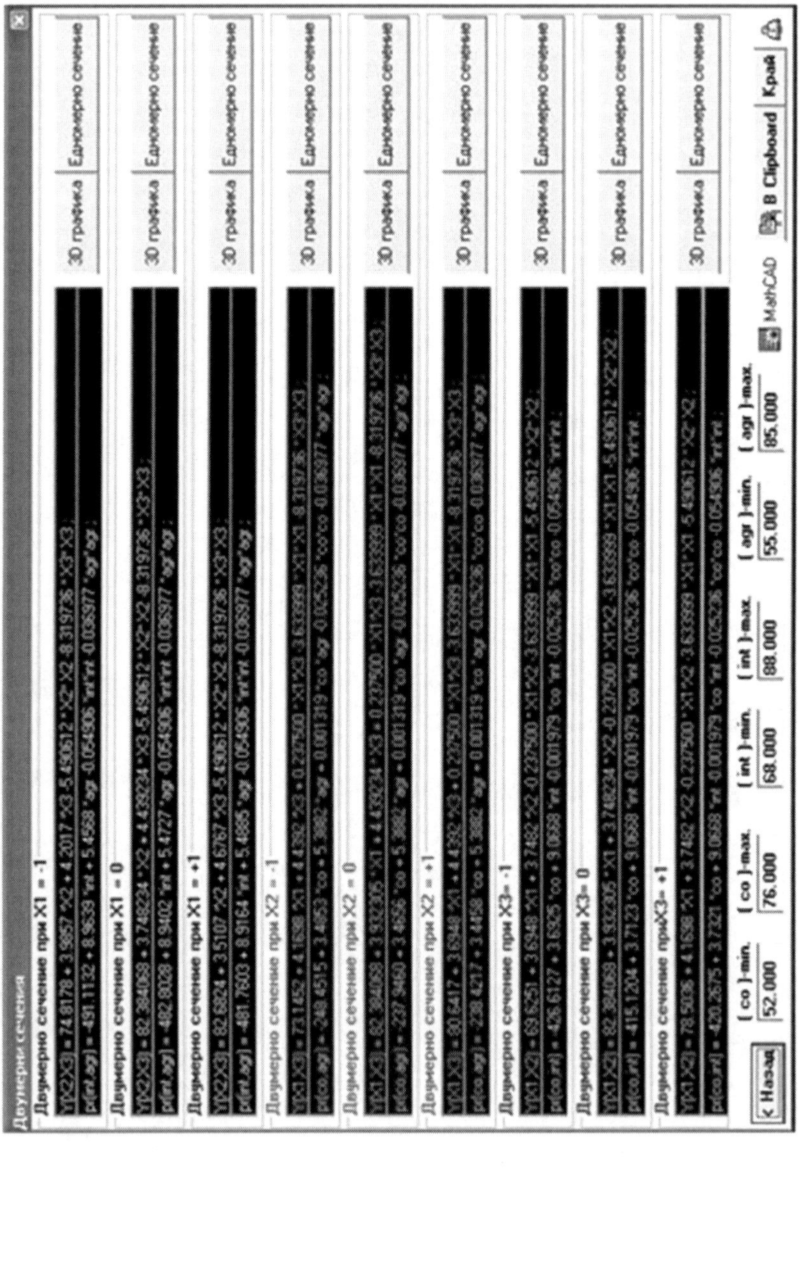

Figure 6.25 Two-dimensional intersections.

Table 6.5 Performance Value Comparison with Motivation of 55% and of 70%[a]

Conscientiousness [%]	Intelligence [%]	Agreeableness [%]	Motivation 55% Performance	Motivation 70% Performance
52	60	40	7	8.2
		75	42	50.3
		80	40.7	49
		100	20	25
52	60	40	7	8.2
	80		29	33.7
	100		13.3	15.3
76	60	40	13	16
		80	49	58
		100	29	34.6
76	60	40	13	16
	83		34	40.4
	100		17	21.2
40	68	40	8	9
55			22	26
70			27	32
80			24.4	29.4
90			18	22
40	88	40	15.3	17.5
68			33	39
90			23	28.4

[a] Measured on factor space outlines.

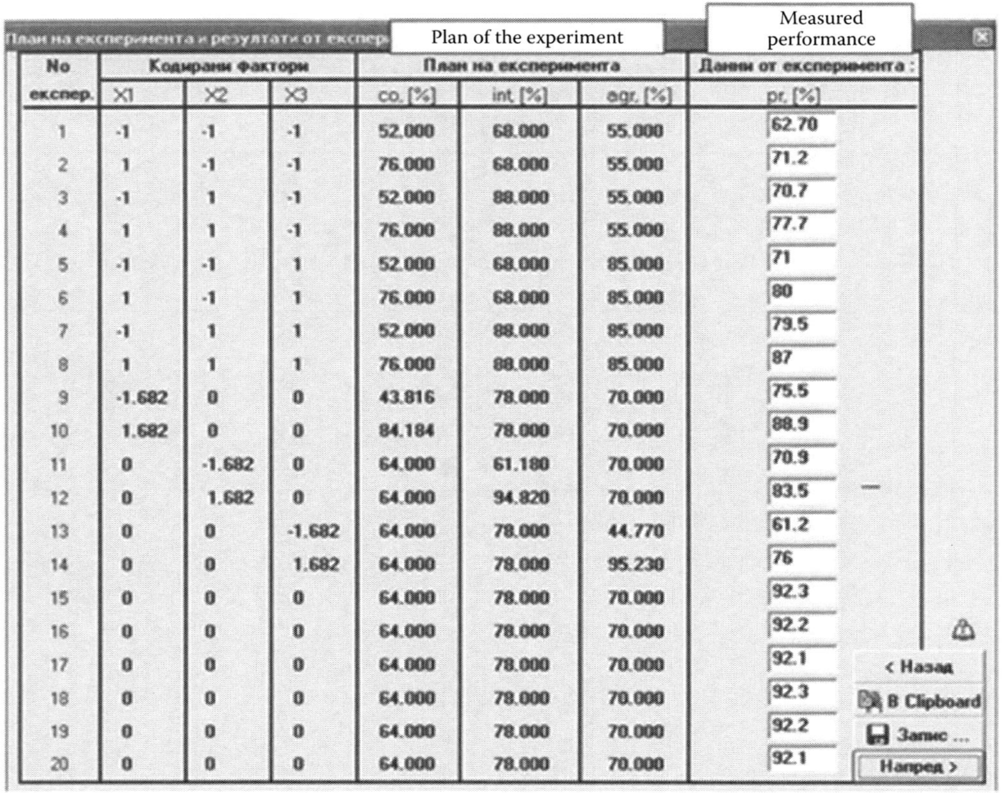

No экспер.	X1	X2	X3	co. [%]	int. [%]	egr. [%]	pr. [%]
1	-1	-1	-1	52.000	68.000	55.000	62.70
2	1	-1	-1	76.000	68.000	55.000	71.2
3	-1	1	-1	52.000	88.000	55.000	70.7
4	1	1	-1	76.000	88.000	55.000	77.7
5	-1	-1	1	52.000	68.000	85.000	71
6	1	-1	1	76.000	68.000	85.000	80
7	-1	1	1	52.000	88.000	85.000	79.5
8	1	1	1	76.000	88.000	85.000	87
9	-1.682	0	0	43.816	78.000	70.000	75.5
10	1.682	0	0	84.184	78.000	70.000	88.9
11	0	-1.682	0	64.000	61.180	70.000	70.9
12	0	1.682	0	64.000	94.820	70.000	83.5
13	0	0	-1.682	64.000	78.000	44.770	61.2
14	0	0	1.682	64.000	78.000	95.230	76
15	0	0	0	64.000	78.000	70.000	92.3
16	0	0	0	64.000	78.000	70.000	92.2
17	0	0	0	64.000	78.000	70.000	92.1
18	0	0	0	64.000	78.000	70.000	92.3
19	0	0	0	64.000	78.000	70.000	92.2
20	0	0	0	64.000	78.000	70.000	92.1

Figure 6.26 Plan and results of the experiment (motivation = 85%).

and here we have values of 92.3%. This confirms our previous observation that by enhancing the motivation, performance also grows significantly.

In Figure 6.27 we see the coefficients b of the regression equation and their estimation of variance, Δb. Having these data we can observe which of the coefficients are significant and which are not. We see that here all coefficients are significant. The next part of the screen is occupied with the performance data: we have the estimated values, the calculated ones, and then the difference between them. We can see that again as in the other two experiments the difference is very small and we can end with the following regression equation in coded form with significant coefficients:

$$Y(X_1,X_2,X_3) = 92.183152 + 3.993549^*X_1 + 3.748571^*X_2 + 4.400294^*X_3$$

$$- 0.375000^*X_1^*X_2 + 0.125000^*X_1^*X_3 + 0.125000^*X_2^*X_3$$

$$- 3.536538^*X_1^*X_1 - 5.304741^* X_2^*X_2 - 8.346049^* X_3^*X_3 \qquad (6.23)$$

On the next screenshot, Figure 6.28, we see the variance of adequacy and the Fisher criterion. This statistical analysis shows that the gained model is correct and adequate and we have the regression equation in natural form that describes the employees' performance by motivation of 85%.

Performance [%] *by Motivation of* 85% = $pr(co, int, agr)$ = $-591.921937 + 3.671524^*co$

$$+ 8.791920^*int + 5.377006^*agr - 0.003125^*co^*int + 0.000694^*co^*agr$$

$$+ 0.000833^*int - 0.024559^*co^*co - 0.053047^*int^*int$$

$$- 0.037094^*agr^*agr \qquad (6.24)$$

The analysis for the response surface follows in the next part of the screenshot: if it has a center, and if so, then what the coordinates are. They are displayed in coded and natural form. Later are shown the canonical equations and the proof that the translation between the different coordinate systems is correct. This canonization gives us the information that the response surface has the form of a rotational ellipsoid and that the center point is its maximum, exactly as in the previous two experiments.

In Figure 6.29 we see the two-dimensional intersections for all the possibilities (–1, 0, 1) for each of the input factors (X_1, X_2, X_3). For every cut we have a 3D graphic in MATLAB on which we can see exactly what the response surface looks like and exactly where the maximum is.

As for the previous experiment with motivation of 75% we do not explain here the resultant graphics (see further details in Richter (2012)). The explanations and

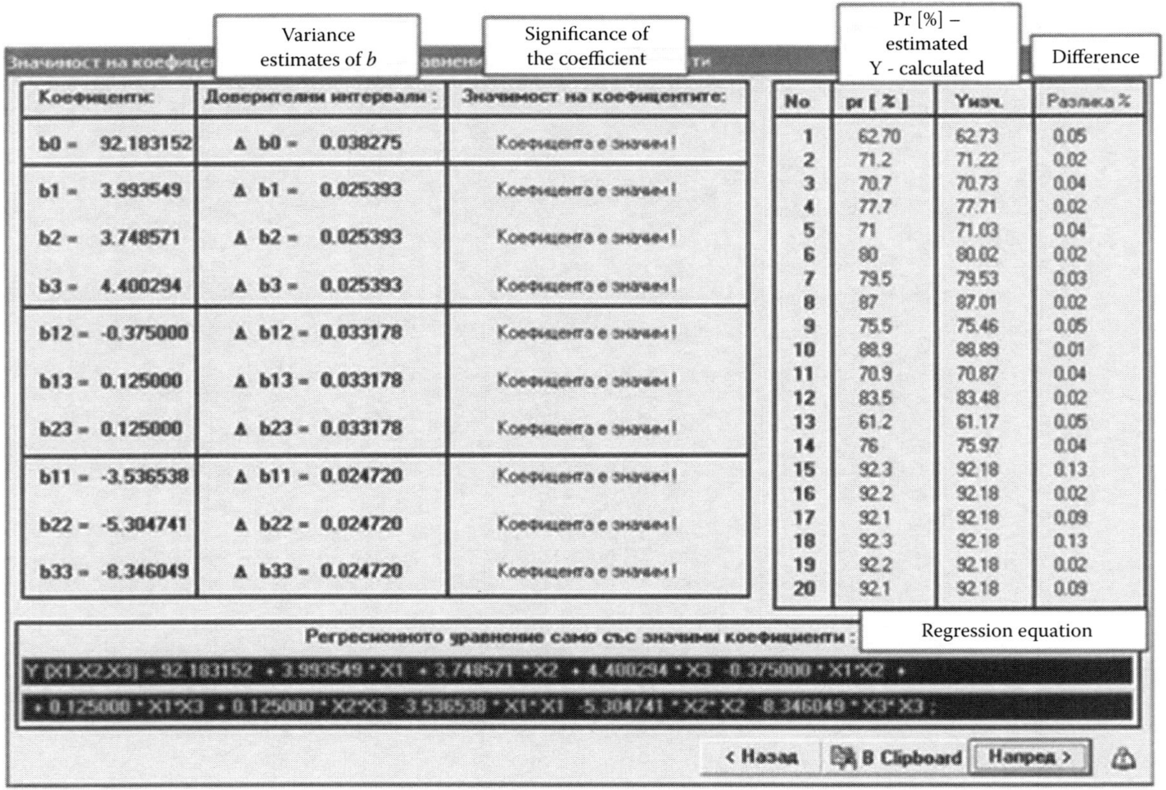

Figure 6.27 Coefficients and the regression equation in coded form.

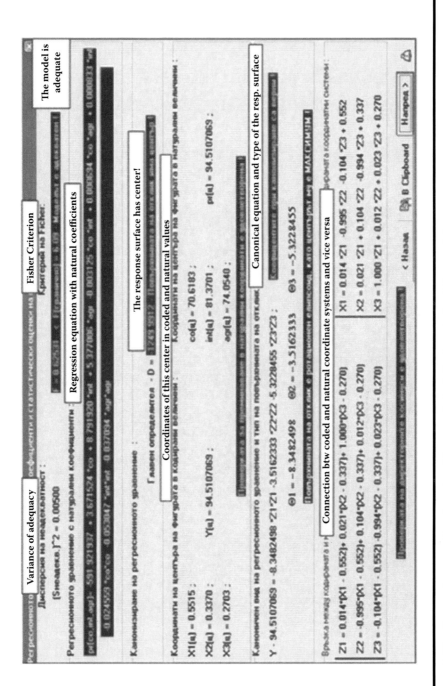

Figure 6.28 Regression equation in natural form and statistical analysis of the model.

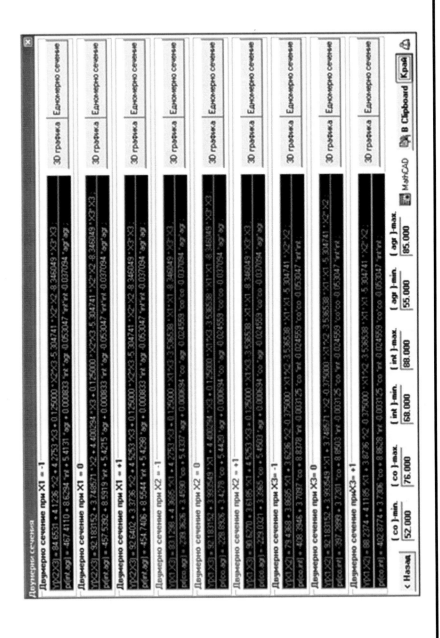

Figure 6.29 Two-dimensional intersections.

the gained data are analogous to the first experiment with motivation of 55%, only the obtained results have higher values because of the higher motivation. For better understanding we show a comparison between the resultant data from the three experiments in Table 6.6.

The comparison between the performance values with motivations of 55%, 70%, and 85% made on the outer limits/lines of the factor space represents values from Figures 6.19 through 6.21 (see other figures for the other two experiments in Richter (2012)). We can clearly see in the table that we have a significant increase in performance values with motivation of 85% in comparison with the other two experiments. Anyway the dependencies between the different characteristics and productivity stay the same as already explained. Therefore we do not give them once again but show only the differences between the maximum performance values, taken from the maximum point of the response surface (Figures 6.17, 6.24, and 6.28) for each experiment. This can be seen below:

With motivation of 55% (Figure 6.17):

Conscientiousness = 70.19% Intelligence = 81.25% Agreeableness = 74.05%	Performance = 71.35%

With motivation of 70% (Figure 6.24):

Conscientiousness = 70.47% Intelligence = 81.29% Agreeableness = 74.11%	Performance = 84.67%

With motivation of 85% (Figure 6.28):

Conscientiousness = 70.6% Intelligence = 81.4% Agreeableness = 74.05%	Performance = 94.5%

It is clear to see that the differences between the values of the psychological characteristics are imperceptible but we see a significant difference in the performance values. This can be explained by the enormous influence of the motivation over the working process. As we have seen in the very beginning the correlation value between motivation and performance is 0.968941, which is proved once again from the values above.

Table 6.6 Performance Value Comparison with Motivation of 55%, 70%, and 85%[a]

Conscientiousness [%]	Intelligence [%]	Agreeableness [%]	Motivation 55% Performance	Motivation 70% Performance	Motivation 85% Performance
52	60	40	7	8.2	16.6
		75	42	50.3	57
		80	40.7	49	55
		100	20	25	30
52	60	40	7	8.2	16.6
	80		29	33.7	40.7
	100		13.3	15.3	22.3
76	60	40	13	16	25.4
		80	49	58	65
		100	29	34.6	39.6
76	60	40	13	16	25.4
	83		34	40.4	47.7
	100		17	21.2	28.2
40	68	40	8	9	16.6
55			22	26	34
70			27	32	40
80			24.4	29.4	38.2
90			18	22	31.3
40	88	40	15.3	17.5	24.5
68			33	39	46
90			23	28.4	36

[a] Measured on factor space outlines.

6.4 Developed Model for IT Human Performance Prediction

We give a short summary of the achievements of the developed method:

- We were able to choose the most important human factors—motivation, conscientiousness, intelligence, and agreeableness—on which to build our model.
- We have conducted three experiments with three special values of the motivation factor because of the complex subjective-psychological dependence between motivation and performance. The growth of motivation up to 85% is connected with growth of the desire to give the best possible productivity at work and with higher values than 85% this desire decreases. This can be explained by the fact that people with 100% motivation find it difficult to get a perspective on development as they have already reached the maximum; this is a kind of de-motivation and results in lower performance levels. With 55%, 70%, and 85% motivation a significant change in the performance values (Figure 6.30) can be observed and because of this we design our experiments with these special values.
- For the three experiments we gained three statistically correct mathematical models as follows:

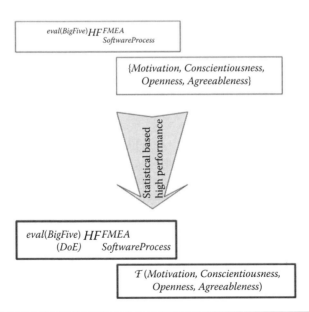

Figure 6.30 Quantified IT human factors for high performance.

Motivation of 55%:(6.25)

$$Performance\ [\%] = pr(co, int, agr) = -523.021607 + 3.139297^*co$$

$$+ 7.793311^*int + 4.525325^*agr - 0.002677^*co^*int$$

$$+ 0.001674^*co^*agr - 0.021694^*co^*co - 0.046799^*int^*int$$

$$- 0.031346^*agr^*agr$$

Motivation of 70%:

$$Performance\ [\%] = pr(co, int, agr) = -611.111026 + 3.619927^*co$$

$$+ 9.066844^*int + 5.388229^*agr - 0.001979^*co^*int$$

$$+ 0.001319^*co^*agr - 0.025236^*co^*co - 0.054906^*int^*int$$

$$- 0.036977^*agr^*agr$$

Motivation of 85%:

$$Performance\ [\%] = pr(co, int, agr) = -591.921937 + 3.671524^*co$$

$$+ 8.791920^*int + 5.377006^*agr - 0.003125^*co^*int$$

$$+ 0.000694^*co^*agr + 0.000833^*int - 0.024559^*co^*co$$

$$- 0.053047^*int^*int - 0.037094^*agr^*agr$$

■ *The connection between agreeableness and performance.* The growing values of agreeableness up to 75% correspond to growth of performance because the employee is able to communicate and cooperate with her colleagues. She is able to accept others' ideas and to follow instructions. After these values the person loses her own judgment and cannot resolve any problem alone. The software engineer agrees with everyone and is no longer able to make decisions, and this leads to low performance values. When the values are low (around 40%), she is not able to cooperate, and working with other people becomes very difficult, and this of course also means low productivity.

■ *The connection between intelligence and performance.* With the increase of intelligence after a specific point (around 80%), the observed software team members start to make very complex decisions and don't choose the optimal algorithm for resolving a problem. This leads to complications and more mistakes in the work process. The employees need more time and the solutions are not optimal; because of this it is logical to observe the decrease in performance. With low values, even with 60% we have very low productivity, which shows that we need employees with above-average intelligence in order to manage the software engineering process.

■ *The connection between conscientiousness and performance.* With growth up to 70% it shows that the software specialist is trying to do his best and to manage his work as well as possible. However this characteristic hinders the process of ignoring unimportant details in everyday work, and this leads to a decrease of performance when conscientiousness is higher than 70%. The employee loses too much time in checking details and spending time for unimportant problems which takes more time and results in lower productivity. When the values are low (up to 55%) we have very low performance and this is to be explained with the fact that such employees are not doing their job with the necessary respect and caution.

■ The results of the whole development process of the predictive model can be characterized in the following manner:

$$^{eval(BigFive)}_{DoE} HF^{FMEA}_{Software\ Process} = F\ (\textit{Motivation, Conscientiousness,}$$

$$\textit{Openness, Agreeableness}) \tag{6.26}$$

Figure 6.29 summarizes the characteristics qualification of the IT human factors for their high performance in software development teams and structures. The mathematical model developed gives the possibility of predicting the productivity of the examined person based on his or her special psychological traits. This supports the process of IT personnel recruitment and also the whole process of IT personnel development with a powerful tool for achieving better software quality.

6.5 Summary of Predictive Model Development

1. Based on the statistical analysis with which Chapter 5 ends, we have discovered the connection (correlation) between the following complex psychological characteristics and performance.
   ■ Openness
   ■ Conscientiousness
   ■ Extroversion
   ■ Agreeableness
   ■ Neuroticism
   ■ Experience
   ■ Motivation

Having the correlation analysis we were able to decide that motivation, conscientiousness, intelligence, and agreeableness are the most influencing factors that we investigate.

2. We decided to use the design of experiment method for the modeling and to build a rotatable experiment due to the following advantages (Khuri and Cornell 1996; Myers et al., 2009):

Gain maximum information from a specified number of experiments.

Study effects individually by varying all operating parameters simultaneously.

Take account of variability in experiments or processes themselves.

Characterize acceptable ranges of key and critical process parameters contributing to identification of a design space, which helps to provide an "assurance of quality."

Guarantee the invariance of the plan and of the parameter of optimization.

The model obtained by the rotatable plan describes the response surface with equal accuracy (equal variance) in all directions of the coordinate axes.

In the whole factors space, the parameter of optimization has the same variance. This ensures that the calculation accuracy of the optimization parameter is independent of the place where we are going to build the experiment.

The variance of the optimization parameter does not change by rotation and translation of its coordination system. This allows us to conduct the canonical experiment (rotation and translation of the coordination system) with the goal of finding the geometrical figure of the designed experiment.

The fact that by rotatable experiments the variance does not change ensures the correctness of the statistical analysis of the gained mathematical model.

3. The factorial space according to the values of the input factors has been determined. The input data for the experiment have been prepared. In Figures 6.13 and 6.14 can be seen the input, where the factor space is determined from the values of conscientiousness from 38% to 90%, intelligence from 58% to 98%, and agreeableness from 40% to 100%.

4. The full matrix of the planned experiment with motivation of 55% (Figure 6.15) is built and the concrete performance values have been measured. The same has also been done with motivations of 70% and 85% (Figures 6.22 and 6.26). In Figures 6.16, 6.23, and 6.27 can be seen the calculation of the coefficients of the mathematical model and after this (Figures 6.17, 6.24, and 6.28) the statistical evaluation for correctness of the models and the regression equations as the end result.

5. After obtaining the mathematical models with all important coefficients, statistical checks were made (Figures 6.17, 6.24, 6.28) to see if they are adequate. They show that all the models are adequate and this means we can

proceed with the next step, the analysis of the two-dimensional intersections (Figures 6.18, 6.25, and 6.29) of the response surface.

6. A canonical analysis has been done of all the models (Figures 6.17, 6.24, and 6.28) in order to determine the geometrical type of the response surfaces. It is in all three cases a rotational ellipsoid and the center is its maximum or we have in the center maximum performance.

7. We have built three experiments with three special values of the motivation factor, because of the complex subjective-psychological dependence between motivation and performance. The growth of motivation up to 85% is connected with growth of the desire to give the best possible productivity at work and with values higher than 85% this desire decreases. This can be explained with the fact that people with 100% motivation find it difficult to have a perspective on development as they have already reached the maximum; this is a kind of de-motivation and results in lower performance levels. With 55%, 70%, and 85% motivation a significant change in the performance values (Figure 6.4) can be observed, and because of this we design our experiments with these special values.

8. For the three experiments we have obtained three statistically correct mathematical models as follows:

Motivation of 55%:(6.25)

$$Performance\ [\%] = pr(co,\ int,\ agr) = -523.021607 + 3.139297*co + 7.793311*int$$

$$+ 4.525325*agr - 0.002677*co*int + 0.001674*co*agr$$

$$- 0.021694*co*co - 0.046799*int*int - 0.031346*agr*agr$$

Motivation of 70%:

$$Performance\ [\%] = pr(co,\ int,\ agr) = -611.111026 + 3.619927*co + 9.066844*int$$

$$+ 5.388229*agr - 0.001979*co*int + 0.001319*co*agr$$

$$- 0.025236*co*co - 0.054906*int*int - 0.036977*agr*agr$$

Motivation of 85%:

$$Performance\ [\%] = pr(co,\ int,\ agr) = -591.921937 + 3.671524*co + 8.791920*int$$

$$+ 5.377006*agr - 0.003125*co*int + 0.000694*co*agr$$

$$+ 0.000833*int - 0.024559*co*co - 0.053047*int*int$$

$$- 0.037094*agr*agr$$

9. Comparing the three prognostic models we see that the response surfaces (rotatable ellipsoids) and the mathematical equations are identical. The only differences are in the concrete values and we show the maximum values for each ellipsoid:

> With motivation of 55% we have maximum performance of 71.35% (Figure 6.17).
>
> With motivation of 70% we have maximum performance of 84.67% (Figure 6.24).
>
> With motivation of 85% we have maximum performance of 94.51% (Figure 6.28).

It is clear that with higher motivation we have also higher productivity.

10. The connections between the other three input factors and performance are explained in the following manner:

> The connections between agreeableness and performance is an ellipse (Figure 6.19); the growing values of agreeableness up to 75% correspond with performance growth because the employee is able to communicate and cooperate with his colleagues: he is able to accept others' ideas and to follow instructions. Beyond these values the person loses his own judgment and cannot resolve any problem alone. The software engineer agrees with everyone and is no longer able to make decisions and this leads to low performance values. When the values are low (around 40%), he is not able to cooperate, and working with other people becomes very difficult and this of course also means low productivity.
>
> The connection between intelligence and performance is also an ellipse (Figure 6.19). The observations have shown that with the increase of intelligence after a specific point (around 80%), the observed software team members start to make very complex decisions and do not choose the optimal algorithm for resolving a problem. This leads to complications and more mistakes in the work process; the employees need more time and the solutions are not optimal. Because of this it is logical to observe the decrease in performance. With low values, even with 60%, we have very low productivity which shows that we need employees with above-average intelligence in order to manage the software engineering process.
>
> The connection between conscientiousness and performance is also an ellipse (Figure 6.20). This can be explained with the specifics of this psychological characteristic: with growth up to 70% it means that the software specialist is trying to do her best and to manage her work as well as possible. On the other hand, this characteristic hinders the process of ignoring the unimportant details in everyday work, and this leads to a decrease in performance when conscientiousness is higher than 70%. The employee loses too much time in checking

details and spending time on unimportant problems that need more time and results in lower productivity. When the values are low, up to 55%, we have very low performance and this is because such employees are not doing their job with the necessary respect and caution.

11. Figures 6.18, 6.25, and 6.29 show the two-dimensional intersections used for visualization of the performance response surface. There we show performance figures with motivation of 55% (Figures 6.19 through 6.21). In this way we are able to give a geometrical interpretation of the obtained models and to find the dependencies between performance and the three specific psychological features. The additional figures for the other two experiments are shown in Richter (2012).

12. For better understanding we also have additional one-dimensional intersections, on which can be seen concrete values by different factor combinations, but this is additional information (see Richter (2012)).

13. The results of our experiment based on the *DoE* method could be characterized in the following brief manner as:

$$_{DoE}^{eval(BigFive)} HF_{Software\ Process}^{FMEA} = F\ (Motivation,\ Conscientiousness, \qquad (6.26)$$

$$Openness,\ Agreeableness)$$

References

Atkinson, A. and Donev, A. (1992). *Optimum Experimental Designs*. Oxford, UK: Oxford University Press.

Box, G. and Draper, N. (2007). *Response Surfaces, Mixtures and Ridge Analysis*. New York: John Wiley and Sons.

Box, G. and Hunter, J. (1957). Multifactor experimental design for exploring response surfaces. *Annals Mathematical Statistics*, 28: 195–242.

Brownlee, K. (1965). *Statistical Theory and Methodology in Science and Engineering*, 2nd ed. New York: John Wiley & Sons.

Cohen, J. (1988). *Statistical Power Analysis for the Behavioral Sciences,* 2nd ed. Hillsdale, NJ: Lawrence Erlbaum Associates.

Cohran, W. and Cox, G. (1957). *Experimental Designs,* 2nd ed. New York: John Wiley & Sons.

Cox, D. (1957). *Planning of Experiments*. New York: John Wiley & Sons.

Davies, O. (1967). *Statistical Methods in Research and Production*, 2nd ed. London: Hafner.

Dean, A. and Voss, D. (1999). *Design and Analysis of Experiments*. Berlin: Springer.

Fang, K.T., Li, R., and Sudjianto, A. (2006). *Design and Modeling for Computer Experiments*. Boca Raton, FL: Taylor & Francis.

Fisher, R. and Yates, F. (1973). *Statistical Tables for Biological, Agricultural and Medical Research*. Edinburgh: Oliver and Boyd.

Georgieva, K., Dumke, R., and Fiegler, A. (2011b). A mathematical model for prediction of the human performance based on the personal features. In *Proceedings of the 2011 International Conference on Software Engineering Research & Practice, WORLDCOMP 2011 (SERP 2011)*, Las Vegas: CSREA Press, pp. 459–463.

Khuri, A. and Cornell, J. (1996). *Response Surfaces: Designs and Analysis.* Boca Raton, FL: Marcel Dekker.

Mason, R.L., Gunst, R.F., and Hess, J.L. (2003). *Statistical Design and Analysis of Experiments with Applications to Engineering and Science.* New York: John Wiley & Sons.

Montgomery, D.C. (2008). *Design and Analysis of Experiments.* New York: John Wiley & Sons.

Myers, R.H. (1971). *Response Surface Methodology.* Boston: Allyn and Bacon.

Myers, R.H., Montgomery, D.C., and Cook, C. (2009). *Response Surface Methodology Process and Product Optimization Using Designed Experiments.* New York: John Wiley & Sons.

Richter, K. (2012). Modeling, evaluating, and predicting IT human resources performance. PhD thesis, University of Magdeburg, Faculty of Informatics.

Shivhare, M. and McCreath, G. 2010. Practical considerations for DoE implementation in quality by design. *BioProcess International*, 8(6): 22–30.

Chapter 7

Experimental Validation of Predictive Model for IT Human Performance

Real examples of the effectiveness of the developed mathematical model were shown in the previous chapter. We also developed a special web application that realizes the test, then transforms the obtained information into input data for our model, and ends with the predicted productivity for the person examined. The statistical information obtained shows the accuracy of the method and proves its positive use for improving the software development process in order for us to be able to choose more reliable and productive personnel.

7.1 Actual Model Application

7.1.1 Basics of Model Application

Here we prove the adequacy and effectiveness of the gained prognostic mathematical models (see Baybutt (1996), Georgieva et al. (2011c), and Khuri and Cornell (1996)). This has been done by conducting many surveys in German and Bulgarian software companies (see the principles in Figure 7.1).

As we have seen, up to now we designed a complex mathematical model that describes human productivity in the software development field based on individual personal characteristics. We show once again the three equations according to the measured motivation and after this give concrete real examples that show

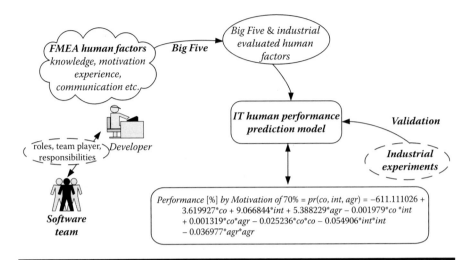

Figure 7.1   Validation of the performance prediction model.

the correctness of the model (see Georgieva et al. (2009b, 2010b), Vose (2008), and Wang (2008)).

Motivation of 55%

$$Performance\ [\%] = pr(co,\ int,\ agr) = -523.021607 + 3.139297^*co + 7.793311^*int$$

$$+ 4.525325^*agr - 0.002677^*co^*int + 0.001674^*co^*agr - 0.021694^*co^*co$$

$$- 0.046799^*int^*int - 0.031346^*agr^*agr \tag{7.1}$$

Motivation of 70%

$$Performance\ [\%] = pr(co,\ int,\ agr) = -611.111026 + 3.619927^*co + 9.066844^*int$$

$$+ 5.388229^*agr - 0.001979^*co^*int + 0.001319^*co^*agr - 0.025236^*co^*co$$

$$- 0.054906^*int^*int - 0.036977^*agr^*agr \tag{7.2}$$

Motivation of 85%

$$Performance\ [\%] = pr(co,\ int,\ agr) = -591.921937 + 3.671524^*co + 8.791920^*int$$

$$+ 5.377006^*agr - 0.003125^*co^*int + 0.000694^*co^*agr + 0.000833^*int$$

$$- 0.024559^*co^*co - 0.053047^*int^*int - 0.037094^*agr^*agr \tag{7.3}$$

7.1.2 Examples

The following examples (as industrial cases) are a mean representative of the obtained questionnaire data. The data is summarized from 50 software employees from various companies, in the form of 12 examples (see also Khuri (1996), Georgieva (2010a), and Shivhare et al. (2010)).

Example 1:

    84% agreeableness
    92% conscientiousness
    76% intelligence
    Motivation 75%
    Estimated productivity 70%

Productivity (calculated from the model) = −611.111026 + 333.033284 + 689.080144

$$+ 452.611236 - 13.837168 + 10.193232 - 213.597504 - 317.137056$$

$$- 260.909712 = 68.32543\%$$

$$\text{Difference} = 1.68\%$$

Example 2:

    92% agreeableness
    84% conscientiousness
    70% intelligence
    Motivation 85%
    Estimated productivity 70%

Productivity (calculated from the model) = −591.921937 + 308.408016 + 615.4344

$$+ 494.684552 - 18.375 + 5.363232 + 0.05831 - 173.288304 - 259.9303$$

$$- 313.963616 = 66.469353\%$$

$$\text{Difference} = 3.53\%$$

Example 3:

    82% agreeableness
    90% conscientiousness

86% intelligence
Motivation 85%
Estimated productivity 80%

Productivity (calculated from the model) = –591.921937 + 330.43716 + 756.10512

+ 440.914492 – 24.1875 + 5.12172 + 0.071638 – 198.9279 – 392.335612

– 249.420056 = 75.857125%

Difference = 4.14%

Example 4:

90% agreeableness
58% conscientiousness
92% intelligence
Motivation 55%
Estimated productivity 58%

Productivity (calculated from the model) = –523.021607 + 182.079226 + 716.984612

+ 407.27925 – 14.284472 + 8.73828 –72.978616 – 396.106736

– 253.9026 = 54.787337%

Difference = 3.22%

Example 5:

82% agreeableness
68% conscientiousness
94% intelligence
Motivation 75%
Estimated productivity 75%

Productivity (calculated from the model) = –611.111026 + 246.155036 + 852.28336

+ 441.834778 – 12.649768 + 7.354744 – 116.691264 – 485.149416

– 248.633348 = 73.393096%

Difference = 1.61%

Example 6:

82% agreeableness
74% conscientiousness
82% intelligence
Motivation 75%
Estimated productivity 85%

Productivity (calculated from the model) = −611.111026 + 267.874598 + 743.481208

+ 441.834778 − 12.008572 + 8.003692 − 138.192336 − 369.187944

− 248.633348 = 82.06105%

Difference = 2.94%

Example 7:

94% agreeableness
90% conscientiousness
96% intelligence
Motivation 85%
Estimated productivity 55%

Productivity (calculated from the model) = −591.921937 + 330.43716 + 844.02432

+ 505.438564 − 27 + 5.87124 + 0.079968 − 198.9279 − 488.881152

− 327.762584 = 51.357679%

Difference = 3.65%

Example 8:

72% agreeableness
72% conscientiousness
78% intelligence
Motivation 85%
Estimated productivity 90%

Productivity (calculated from the model) = −591.921937 + 264.349728 + 685.76976

+ 387.144432 − 17.55 + 3.597696 + 0.064974 − 127.313856 − 322.737948

− 192.295296 = 89.107553%

Difference = 0.9%

Example 9:

  82% agreeableness
  66% conscientiousness
  96% intelligence
  Motivation 85%
  Estimated productivity 75%

Productivity (calculated from the model) = –591.921937 + 242.320584 + 844.02432

  + 440.914492 – 19.8 + 3.755982 + 0.079968 – 106.979004 – 488.881152

  – 249.420056 = 74.093197%

Difference = 0.91%

Example 10:

  96% agreeableness
  90% conscientiousness
  88% intelligence
  Motivation 55%
  Estimated productivity 50%

Productivity (calculated from the model) = –523.021607 + 282.53673 + 685.811368

  + 434.4312 – 21.20184 + 14.46336 – 175.214 – 362.411456 – 288.884736

  = 46.508915%

Difference = 3.5%

Example 11:

  90% agreeableness
  62% conscientiousness
  66% intelligence
  Motivation 85%
  Estimated productivity 70%

Productivity (calculated from the model) = –591.921937 + 227.634488 + 580.26672

  + 483.93054 – 12.7875 + 3.87252 + 0.054978 – 94.404796 – 231.072732

  – 300.4614 = 65.110881%

Difference = 4.89%

Example 12:

94% agreeableness
62% conscientiousness
94% intelligence
Motivation 70%
Estimated productivity 60%

Productivity (calculated from the model) = −611.111026 + 224.435474 + 852.28336

+ 506.493526 − 11.533612 + 7.687132 − 97.007184 − 485.149416

− 326.728772 = 59.369482%

Difference = 0.64%

We can summarize that the difference between estimated and calculated productivity is not more than 5%, which is very important proof for the accuracy of the developed model. We discuss in the next point a statistical analysis of 100 additional real examples, which shows once again the adequacy and efficiency of our prognostic mathematical model.

7.2 Software Human Factors Test Web Application

7.2.1 Description of Web Application

In order to automate the questioning process and the processing of the obtained data into actual results about a concrete person and also to show once again the effectiveness and accuracy of the developed method, we developed a web application that conducts the explained actions and supports us with the final results (Georgieva et al., 2011c; Richter, 2012).

Next we describe the test tool and present screenshots with different results. This application is of great help to us because it enables the test quiz and the evaluation of the results and their use in the already explained formulas (the mathematical model) that describe personal productivity. In this way we end with a concrete performance for every person tested and we can also observe the whole statistics of the people who have already completed the test.

Let us now start with the first screenshot (Figure 7.2) of the tool: when loading the home page the user is presented with the option to start a new test, to resume an unfinished one, or to view the results of his own completed test and also view the whole statistics for all the completed tests. If the user decides to start a new test he or she is brought to a page with the test questions in a shuffled order, which looks like that shown in Figure 7.3.

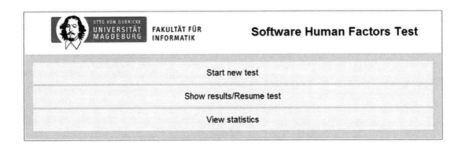

Figure 7.2   Web application home page.

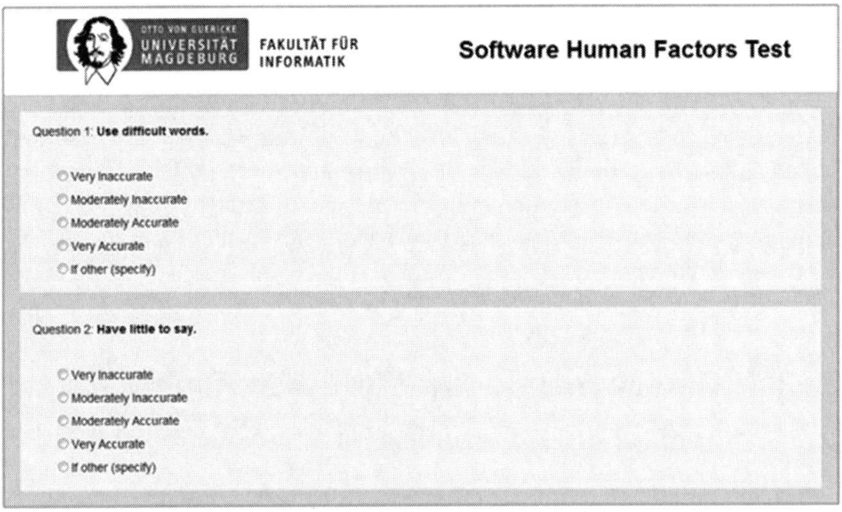

Figure 7.3   Web application quiz page.

Most of the questions have five possible answers: very accurate, accurate, inaccurate, very inaccurate, and other. When the last is selected a textbox is displayed where the user can enter a custom textual answer. Some of the questions are answered only by true or false and some need to be answered by some text. We can see these different types of questions in Figure 7.4. A more detailed explanation about the different types of questions and answers was given in Chapter 5.

At the end of the test page, the user can click Submit, which will save the answers. This can be done even if the quiz is not completed (see Figure 7.5). The user is then redirected to a page showing the ID of the taken test. From there, if the test is not completed it can be resumed, and if it is completed, the results can be viewed. The user can also go back to the home page (shown in Figure 7.6).

From the home page the user can again resume an unfinished test or view the results of a finished one by clicking the button "Show results/Resume test," using

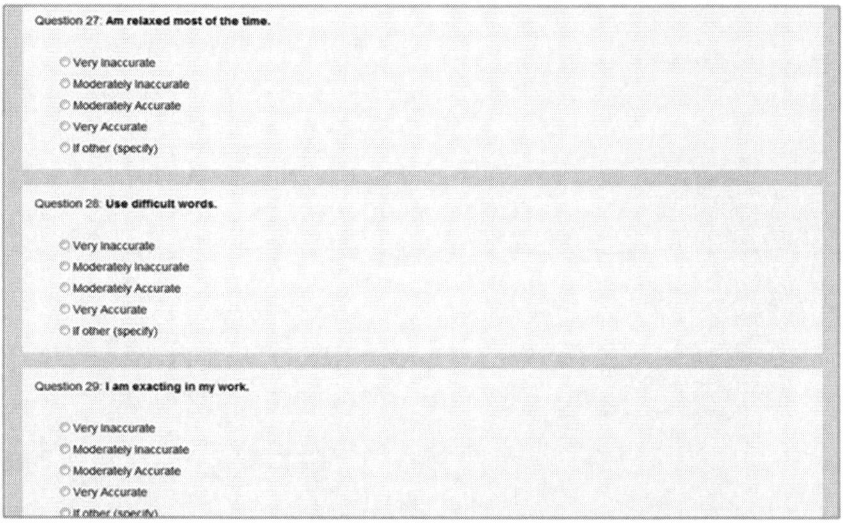

Figure 7.4   Web application question types.

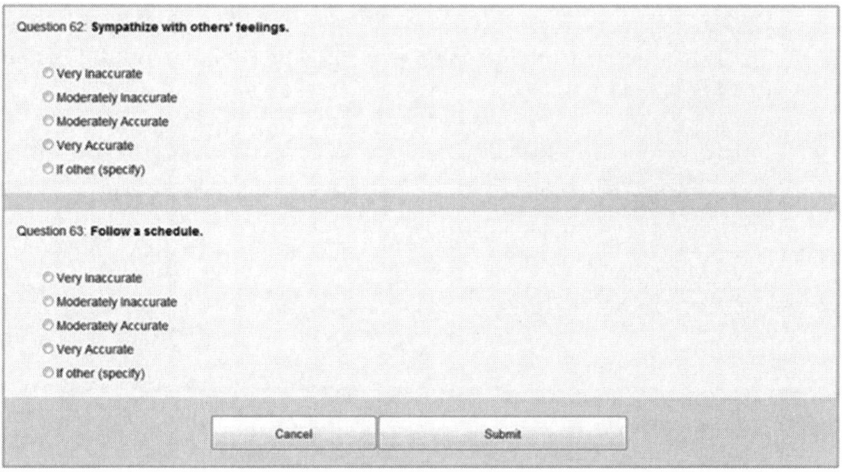

Figure 7.5   End of quiz page.

the ID of his personal test (see Figure 7.7). Clicking that button pops up a field where the user is required to enter the ID of the test she wants to resume or view the results of. If a test with the entered ID does not exist, the user is redirected to a page with a message that tells this. From there she can go back to the home page. This can be seen in Figure 7.8.

Resuming an unfinished test loads the quiz page with the questions in the order they were when the test was created. The answers are also re-created so if the user

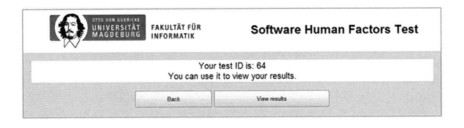

Figure 7.6 Web application quiz finished page.

Figure 7.7 Screenshot of application's pop-up when "Show results/Resume Test" button is clicked.

Figure 7.8 Window shown when the test does not exist.

wants he can change them before finishing the test. Viewing results brings the user to the page shown in Figure 7.9, showing his score for the five measured factors, the self-estimated performance and motivation, and the performance calculated by the developed mathematical model. There is also a table with statistics for all completed tests. The columns in the table represent each factor, and the rows, a range of scores. The cells in the table show how many people have scored a value in the respective range for the corresponding factor. The text in gray shows between which values the current test result is.

On the result page the values for extroversion and emotional stability can also be observed. Although they are not included in the calculation of the performance

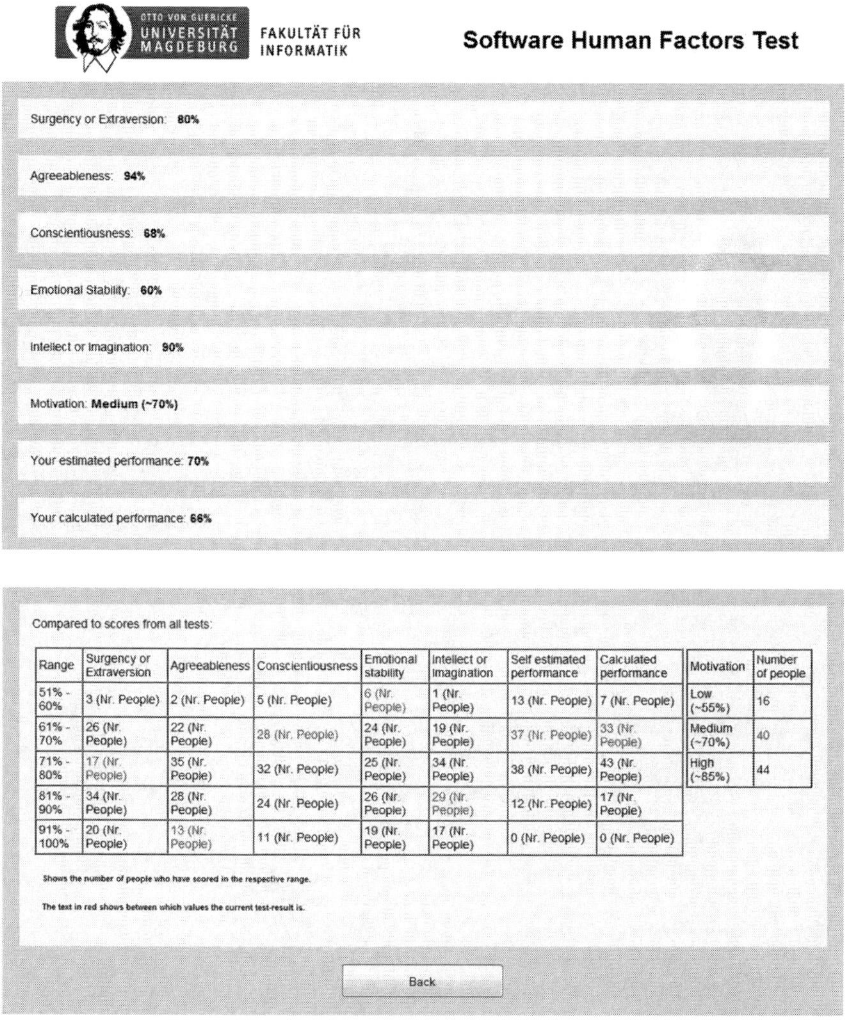

OTTO VON GUERICKE
UNIVERSITÄT
MAGDEBURG

FAKULTÄT FÜR
INFORMATIK

Software Human Factors Test

Surgency or Extraversion: **80%**

Agreeableness: **94%**

Conscientiousness: **68%**

Emotional Stability: **60%**

Intellect or Imagination: **90%**

Motivation: **Medium (~70%)**

Your estimated performance: **70%**

Your calculated performance: **66%**

Compared to scores from all tests:

Range	Surgency or Extraversion	Agreeableness	Conscientiousness	Emotional stability	Intellect or imagination	Self estimated performance	Calculated performance	Motivation	Number of people
51% - 60%	3 (Nr. People)	2 (Nr. People)	5 (Nr. People)	6 (Nr. People)	1 (Nr. People)	13 (Nr. People)	7 (Nr. People)	Low (~55%)	16
61% - 70%	26 (Nr. People)	22 (Nr. People)	28 (Nr. People)	24 (Nr. People)	19 (Nr. People)	37 (Nr. People)	33 (Nr. People)	Medium (~70%)	40
71% - 80%	17 (Nr. People)	35 (Nr. People)	32 (Nr. People)	25 (Nr. People)	34 (Nr. People)	38 (Nr. People)	43 (Nr. People)	High (~85%)	44
81% - 90%	34 (Nr. People)	28 (Nr. People)	24 (Nr. People)	26 (Nr. People)	29 (Nr. People)	12 (Nr. People)	17 (Nr. People)		
91% - 100%	20 (Nr. People)	13 (Nr. People)	11 (Nr. People)	19 (Nr. People)	17 (Nr. People)	0 (Nr. People)	0 (Nr. People)		

Shows the number of people who have scored in the respective range.

The text in red shows between which values the current test-result is.

Back

Figure 7.9 Test results page for a real person.

values, they are displayed for additional information of the test-taker and for completeness of the questionnaire.

Going back to the home page, the user can see all the statistics (Figure 7.10) of all the tests already taken. They are shown on a separate page in a shuffled manner and without the test IDs, so that no one can connect a particular ID with the shown statistics. We can also see a table similar to the one in the results page, but because the statistics is global, it is not matched to any specific test. We can see the percentage range of each psychological feature and the number of people who belong to it.

OTTO VON GUERICKE UNIVERSITÄT MAGDEBURG — FAKULTÄT FÜR INFORMATIK — **Software Human Factors Test**

Surgency or Extraversion	Agreeableness	Conscientiousness	Emotional Stability	Intellect or Imagination	Motivation	Self estimated performance	Calculated Performance	Difference
92%	72%	72%	76%	98%	Medium (~70%)	70%	69%	1%
94%	78%	74%	92%	64%	High (~85%)	76%	74%	2%
94%	66%	72%	74%	94%	High (~85%)	76%	78%	2%
84%	78%	64%	88%	74%	High (~85%)	82%	85%	3%
80%	68%	66%	88%	70%	Low (~55%)	68%	64%	4%
62%	88%	70%	76%	74%	Low (~55%)	65%	63%	2%
78%	72%	78%	84%	82%	Low (~55%)	72%	70%	2%
90%	74%	70%	60%	62%	High (~85%)	75%	71%	4%
90%	80%	68%	94%	96%	High (~85%)	76%	76%	0%
72%	78%	96%	64%	72%	High (~85%)	66%	70%	4%
66%	84%	78%	60%	84%	Medium (~70%)	75%	79%	4%
66%	66%	82%	64%	84%	Medium (~70%)	80%	78%	2%
84%	80%	70%	64%	72%	Medium (~70%)	75%	79%	4%
90%	88%	76%	80%	86%	Low (~55%)	62%	64%	2%
72%	86%	96%	86%	72%	Medium (~70%)	60%	59%	1%
100%	94%	86%	84%	78%	High (~85%)	72%	68%	4%

Range	Surgency or Extraversion	Agreeableness	Conscientiousness	Emotional stability	Intellect or Imagination	Self estimated performance	Calculated performance	Motivation	Number of people
51% - 60%	3 (Nr. People)	2 (Nr. People)	5 (Nr. People)	6 (Nr. People)	1 (Nr. People)	13 (Nr. People)	7 (Nr. People)	Low (~55%)	16
61% - 70%	26 (Nr. People)	22 (Nr. People)	28 (Nr. People)	24 (Nr. People)	19 (Nr. People)	37 (Nr. People)	33 (Nr. People)	Medium (~70%)	40
71% - 80%	17 (Nr. People)	35 (Nr. People)	32 (Nr. People)	25 (Nr. People)	34 (Nr. People)	38 (Nr. People)	43 (Nr. People)	High (~85%)	44
81% - 90%	34 (Nr. People)	28 (Nr. People)	24 (Nr. People)	26 (Nr. People)	29 (Nr. People)	12 (Nr. People)	17 (Nr. People)		
91% - 100%	20 (Nr. People)	13 (Nr. People)	11 (Nr. People)	19 (Nr. People)	17 (Nr. People)	0 (Nr. People)	0 (Nr. People)		

Shows the number of people who have scored in the respective range.

Back

Figure 7.10 Software human factors test statistics page.

7.2.2 Analysis of Gained Information

The developed web application "Software Human Factors Test" was given to a number of software companies in order to gain real results and to observe the accuracy of the developed prognostic method. We have gained exactly 100 useful test results, a part of which can be seen in Figure 7.10 and Table 7.1. The complete list can be seen in Richter (2012).

Table 7.1 Part of Received Employee Information

Agreeableness (%)	Conscientiousness (%)	Intellect (Openness; %)	Motivation (%)	Estimated Performance (%)	Calculated Performance (%)	Difference (%)
88	82	70	High (~85)	78	73	5
68	74	86	High (~85)	86	87	1
82	86	66	High (~85)	72	70	2
82	62	92	High (~85)	75	78	3
92	88	76	High (~85)	65	68	3
92	64	80	High (~85)	78	75	3
72	94	68	High (~85)	64	68	4
80	60	68	Low (~55)	60	59	1
76	86	72	Low (~55)	60	62	2
70	60	78	Medium (~70)	85	81	4
90	64	74	Medium (~70)	70	71	1
92	62	92	Medium (~70)	62	65	3
88	70	74	Low (~55)	65	63	2
86	74	60	Medium (~70)	56	54	2
82	84	94	Low (~55)	60	57	3
74	94	74	Low (~55)	60	57	3
76	82	76	Medium (~70)	82	80	2

The data that we have collected show that the mathematical model developed really predicts human performance very accurately: the differences between the estimated and calculated performance are not bigger than 5%, which is the confidence interval, and this means that the method works very accurately and can be applied in the praxis without any doubts.

Analysis of the information from Table 7.1 shows that the developed prognostic model about the influence of motivation, agreeableness, conscientiousness, and intelligence on performance is adequate. The experimental testing of the method in a real environment shows minimal mistakes or a difference of 5%, which allows us to claim that it works correctly and can be used in the real process of employee evaluation.

The "Software Human Factors Test" is a reliable tool for productivity assessment in the software engineering field, which can be used by individuals and companies. Our research showed that it is an adequate source for performance assessment and at the same time provides users with good insight on the factors affecting their performance so they know what they need to work on. The test can be used in addition to an interview for a job or as an addition to a set of some proven methods for improving productivity such as personal and team software process and capability maturity model integration.

7.3 Summary of Experimental Model Validation

1. Automated questioning was conducted in different companies in order to build first ideas about the validation and effectiveness of the developed method for performance evaluation. These examples showed that the difference between estimated and calculated productivity is not more than 5%, which is a very important proof for the correctness of the developed model.

2. In order to automate the questioning process and the processing of the obtained data into actual results about a concrete person and also to show once again the effectiveness and correctness of the developed method, we devised a web application that conducts the explained actions and supports us with the final results.

3. The developed web application "Software Human Factors Test" was given to a number of software companies in order to gain real results and to observe the correctness of the developed prognostic method. We have 100 useful test results, a part of which can be seen in Figure 7.10, in Table 7.1, and the complete list can be seen in Richter (2012).

4. Observation of the collected data shows that the mathematical model really predicts human performance very accurately; the differences between the estimated and the calculated performance are not bigger than 5%, which means that the method works very accurately and can be applied in the praxis without any doubts.

5. The "Software Human Factors Test" is a reliable tool for productivity assessment in the software engineering field, which can be used by individuals and companies. Our research showed that it is an adequate source for performance assessment and at the same time provides the users with information about their personal factors affecting performance. In this way they can also use the tool for self-evaluation and to further their own development. The test can be used in addition to an interview for a job or as an addition to a set of some proven methods for improving productivity such as PSP, TSP, and CMMI (definitions in List of Acronyms).

6. The validated results *of* high-performance IT human factors could be characterized as follows:

$$\substack{\text{eval(BigFive)} \\ \text{eval(DoE)}} HF^{FMEA}_{Software\ Process} = PERF\ (Motivation,\ Conscientiousness,$$

$$Openness,\ Agreeableness) \tag{7.4}$$

References

Baybutt, P. (1996). Human factors in process safety and risk management: Needs for models, tools and techniques. In *International Workshop on Human Factors in Offshore Operations, US Mineral Mangement Service*, New Orleans, December, pp. 412–433.

Georgieva, K., Farooq, A. Dumke R.R. (2009b). Analysis of the risk assessment methods—A survey. In *Software Process and Product Measurement. International Conferences IWSM 2009 and Mensura 2009*. Berlin: Springer, pp. 76–86,

Georgieva, K., Neumann, R., and Dumke, R. (2010b). The influence of personal features on the project success. In *5. Hochschul-Roundtable der CECMG/DASMA, Industrielle und gesellschaftliche Herausforderungen beim flexiblen Sourcing von IT-Projekten/Dienstleistungen*. Aachen: Shaker, pp. 61–72,

Georgieva, K., Neumann, R., Fiegler, A., and Dumke, R. (2011c). Validation of the model for prediction of the human performance. In *Proceedings of the Joint Conference of the 21st International Workshop on Software Measurement and the 6th International Conference on Software Process and Product Measurement (IWSM-MENSURA 2011)*. Los Alamitos, CA: IEEE Computer Society Press, pp. 245–250.

Khuri, A. and Cornell, J. (1996). *Response Surfaces: Designs and Analysis*. Boca Raton, FL: Marcel Dekker.

Richter, K. (2012). Modeling, evaluating, and predicting IT human resources performance. PhD thesis, University of Magdeburg, Faculty of Informatics.

Shivhare, M. and McCreath, G. (2010). Practical considerations for DoE implementation in quality by design. *BioProcess International*, 8(6): 22–30.

Vose, D. (2008). *Risk Analysis: A Quantitative Guide*, 3rd ed. New York: John Wiley & Sons.

Wang, Y. (2008). On cognitive properties of human factors and error models in engineering and socialization. *Journal of Cognitive Informatics and Natural Intelligence*, 2(4): 70–84.

Chapter 8

Conclusions and Future Directions

This book starts with a large analysis of the existing methods for risk assessment with a special focus on their human factors. The literature review conducted showed that the existing methods don't consider the human being as a factor responsible for different risks in the software engineering process and in this way influencing the end performance.

The second point in the research was to look from the other side. We looked for psychological methods that measure and evaluate the influence of personality over the software engineering process. We discovered that such methods, at least in software development, do not exist but the overview conducted on human factors in the software process has shown different perspectives:

- Slips and mistakes occurring in everyday human work including their base
- Malfunctions and their relation to the behavioral model of the human being with regard to performing a certain task
- Clearly recognized connection between emotions and risk behavior and different stressors influencing people
- Different levels of failures and factors that influence human actions
- Frameworks and taxonomies listing personal characteristics that influence the working process

This observation was the major motivation for us to decide that there is an urgent need to develop such a method based on specific psychological characteristics that would be able to prognosticate/evaluate IT productivity for a specific person.

The following analysis of the basic IT roles gave us the description of the roles' most important competencies, which we used in further research.

$$HF_{ProjectManager} = \{communicative, managerial\ skills, disciplined,$$

$$respects\ the\ others, resolves\ conflicts, open\ minded,$$

$$willing\ to\ develop\ himself, well\text{-}organized, goal\text{-}oriented, seeks\ improvement\}$$

$$HF_{TeamLeader} = \{plan\ and\ prioritize\ the\ work, reviews\ team\ progress,$$

$$flexible\ and\ adaptable, communicative, an\ effective\ advocate$$

$$for\ the\ team, ability\ to\ lead\ and\ to\ impress\}$$

$$HF_{BusinessAnalyst} = \{communicative, conceptual\ thinking, creativity,$$

$$strategic\ and\ business\ thinking, problem\ solving,$$

$$negotiation\ and\ decision\ making, customer\ oriented, team\ player\}$$

$$HF_{SoftwareArchitect} = \{good\ decision\ maker, team\ player, performance\ oriented,$$

$$technical\ understanding\ that\ supports\ the\ team,$$

$$optimizing\ abilities, seeks\ new\ knowledge\}$$

$$HF_{SoftwareDeveloper} = \{creativity, team\ player, tolerant, always\ in\ a\ learning\ mode,$$

$$able\ to\ articulate\ own\ thoughts, respects\ others'\ ideas, structured\ thinking\}$$

$$HF_{SoftwareTester} = \{creativity, flexibility, communicative, open\text{-}minded, respects\ others\}$$

$$HF_{QualityEngineer} = \{flexible, team\ oriented, positive\ attitude, systematic\ and\ organized,$$

$$respects\ others, seeks\ knowledge, persuasive,$$

$$ability\ to\ interact\ with\ managers\ and\ customers\}$$

Having the personal competencies we made an effective analysis of the corresponding responsibilities and found the factors that most influence individuals. We adopted the FMEA (failure mode and effect analysis) method for this goal as it gives the possibility of breaking each process into small pieces and looking inside for possible failure modes and their causes. The analysis of the software team roles involved in a typical software engineering process ended with the discovery of the human factors that influence the different potential failure modes, which can be seen in Table 8.1.

Table 8.1   Human Factors Influencing Failure Modes

1. Coordination	2. Fear
3. Self-management	4. Management skills
5. Mental overload = stress	6. Intelligence
7. Competence	8. Analysis skills
9. Knowledge	10. Openness
11. Effectiveness	12. Creativity
13. Concentration	14. Emotional stability
15. Communication	16. Judgment
17. Self-development	18. Problem-solving ability
19. Liberalism	20. Perception
21. Control delegation	22. Professionalism
23. Selfish = egoism	24. Persistence
25. Over–self-confident	26. Dutifulness
27. Self-organization	28. Motivation
29. Hardworking	30. Achievement
31. Attention	32. Responsibility
33. Conscientiousness	34. Talkativeness
35. Leader skills	36. Personal attitude
37. Experience	38. Technical understanding
39. Personal growth	40. Imagination
41. Understanding ability	42. Patience
43. Planning skills	44. Friendliness
45. Observing ability	46. Cooperation
47. Appreciation	

Having all the critical human factors for the software process, we were faced with a new problem. How can we measure these traits and how can we examine a person to understand which features he possesses and to what extent so that we can find out how they influence his work performance?

For this purpose we adopted a well-accepted method in personality evaluation: the Big Five theory. Of course we had to change it so that it could be applied in the software engineering field and then we defined seven psychological characteristics that are complex enough to be matched with the human factors and be used for the description of personality features and software productivity. They are as follows:

1. Openness
2. Conscientiousness
3. Extroversion
4. Agreeableness
5. Neuroticism (Emotional Stability)
6. Experience
7. Motivation

Analyzing the characteristics and the type of connection between them and human performance in IT, we decided to design the whole process as an experiment and to analyze it in order to model the desired dependence.

We conducted three experiments with three special values of the motivation factor, because of the complex subjective psychological dependence between motivation and performance. For these three experiments we obtained three statistically correct mathematical models that describe the connection between the psychological characteristics (motivation, conscientiousness, openness, and agreeableness) and performance in software engineering. They are as follows:

$$\textit{Performance by Motivation of } 55\% = pr(co, int, agr) = -523.021607 + 3.139297^*co$$

$$+ 7.793311^*int + 4.525325^*agr - 0.002677^*co^*int + 0.001674^*co^*agr$$

$$- 0.021694^*co^*co - 0.046799^*int^*int - 0.031346^*agr^*agr$$

$$\textit{Performance by Motivation of } 70\% = pr(co, int, agr) = -611.111026 + 3.619927^*co$$

$$+ 9.066844^*int + 5.388229^*agr - 0.001979^*co^*int + 0.001319^*co^*agr$$

$$- 0.025236^*co^*co - 0.054906^*int^*int - 0.036977^*agr^*agr$$

$$\textit{Performance by Motivation of } 85\% = pr(co, int, agr) = -591.921937 + 3.671524^*co$$

$$+ 8.791920^*int + 5.377006^*agr - 0.003125^*co^*int + 0.000694^*co^*agr$$

$$+ 0.000833^*int - 0.024559^*co^*co - 0.053047^*int^*int - 0.037094^*agr^*agr$$

The decision to make three experiments came from the observation that with 55%, 70%, and 85% of motivation a significant change in performance values can be seen. The growth of motivation up to 85% is connected with growth of the desire to give the best possible productivity at work, and with higher values than 85% this desire decreases. This is because people with 100% motivation find it difficult to keep a perspective on development as they have already reached the maximum; this is a kind of de-motivation and results in lower performance levels.

The most important result from the models is the dependencies between the three examined features and human performance:

- *The connection between agreeableness and performance:* The g   g values of agreeableness up to 75% correspond with performance gro   ecause the employee is able to communicate and cooperate with his colle   s, he is able to accept others' ideas and to follow instructions; after these va   the person loses his own judgment and cannot resolve any problem alone. The software engineer agrees with everyone and is no longer able to make decisions, and this leads to low performance values. When the values are low, around 40%, he is not able to cooperate and working with other people becomes very difficult; this of course also means low productivity.
- *The connection between intelligence and performance:* With an increase of intelligence after a specific point (around 80%), the observed software team members start to make very complex decisions and don't choose the optimal algorithm for resolving a problem. This leads to complications and more mistakes in the work process; employees need more time and the solutions are not optimal. Because of this it is logical to observe the decrease in performance. With low values, even with 60%, we have very low productivity, which shows that we need employees with above-average intelligence in order to manage the software engineering process.
- *The connection between conscientiousness and performance:* With growth up to 70% it shows that the software specialist is trying to do her best and to manage her work as well as possible. On the other hand this characteristic hinders the process of ignoring the unimportant details in everyday work, and this leads to a decrease in performance when conscientiousness is higher than 70%. The employee loses too much time in checking details and spending time on unimportant problems that need more time and results in lower productivity. When the values are low, up to 55%, we have very low performance because such employees are not doing their job with the necessary respect and caution.

The results of the whole development process of the predictive model can be characterized in the following manner:

$$eval(BigFive)\atop DoE}\; HF\; {FMEA\atop Software\; Process} = F\; (Motivation,\; Conscientiousness,\; Openness,\; Agreeableness)$$

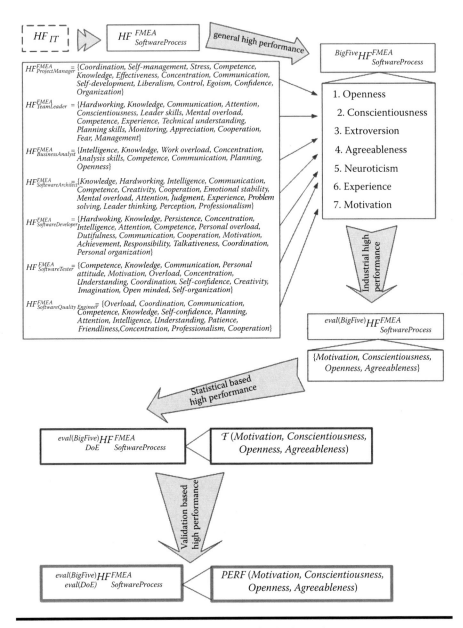

Figure 8.1 The IT human factors approach for high performance.

This IT human factors evaluation approach could be summarized in a simplified manner as given in Figure 8.1. The developed models were shown to be correct and adequate using special statistical formulas and further on with the development of special software. The web application aims to show once again the models' correctness and effectiveness. The developed website represents a test with the special questions needed for personnel evaluation and then uses these data as input for the developed model. In this way the model can be very easily used in the process of recruitment for selecting the best employees for a specific company. Everything that we have said up to now shows that:

- The problem described in the beginning of the research work: the connection between the personality and the individuals' performance in the software engineering is found!
- A method that models human performance in IT based on the specific psychological traits has been developed.
- We gained three different models with the special values of motivation that calculate the expected performance.
- The developed model was tested and validated in real conditions and proved its correctness and usefulness for software development.
- The model is an absolutely new scientific contribution that is extremely important for the process of improving the IT recruitment process.
- The developed method can also be used for prognosis of the productivity of the whole software company based on the performance of the individuals.
- A modeling of the critical psychological features, which take part in the model, is another idea that can be applied and in this way the expected performance can be increased.

The scientific work in this book makes the following main contributions to research within the field of software engineering:

1. An up-to-date review of software risk assessment methods with special focus on their incompleteness
2. An up-to-date review of the methods for employee evaluation and research on their existence and application in the software engineering
3. Detailed research of the concepts in the software field and on the software team members with their specific capabilities and responsibilities
4. Development of a new scientific method "Software Human Factor FMEA" for the extraction of critical human factors
5. Development of a new scientific method for the evaluation of human psychological features in IT (with the adoption of the Big Five theory in software engineering)
6. Development of a unique mathematical model for the prediction of the individual's performance in IT based on his or her personal characteristics
7. Development of a web-based application realizing the mathematical model and supporting the software engineering research with a concrete tool for employee evaluation and personnel selection

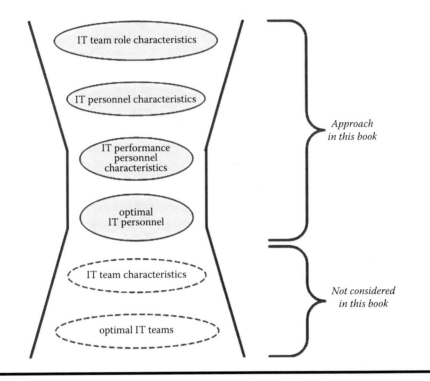

Figure 8.2   The personal optimization approach in this book.

The considered approach in this book can be summarized in Figure 8.2. Future work considering our approach in order to improve human factor involvement in the IT area will be as follows:

■ *Further application areas*: The specification of the method for each role in the software development process for different software process approaches (e.g., agile development, V&V teams, PSP, and collaborative software evolution).

■ *Methodology improvements*: The actual application of this new approach considers a special kind of systems and software processes and should be extended by experienced repositories such as SLIM, ISBSG, and QSM.

■ *Team-oriented model extensions*: The current new approach supports the evaluation process of IT personnel and should be extended by further involvement of team characteristics (e.g., pair programming, test teams, and egoless approaches).

■ *Human characteristics modeling*: The development model can be extended with additional methods for influencing the individual's psychological traits. In this way productivity will be increased by stimulating motivation, for example.

■ *Whole evaluation:* A whole assessment of the software company can be built based on the performance of each individual.

We can summarize once again with the following. The developed mathematical model gives the possibility of predicting the productivity of the examined person based on his or her special psychological traits. This supports the process of IT personnel recruitment and also the whole process of IT personnel development with a powerful tool for achieving better software quality. The right people chosen in the right manner and also their motivation are the most important software resources, crucial for the achievement of better results in the IT field.

Index

Note: Page numbers ending in "f" refer to figures. Page numbers ending in "t" refer to tables.